AFROCUBA

AFROCUBA

AN ANTHOLOGY OF CUBAN WRITING ON RACE, POLITICS AND CULTURE

EDITED BY
PEDRO PEREZ SARDUY AND
JEAN STUBBS

LATIN AMERICA BUREAU

Published in association with the Center for Cuban Studies (New York)

For our son Ilmi and our daughter Sahnet

Ocean Press ISBN 1-875284-41-9
Latin America Bureau ISBN 0-906156-75-0

Cover design by Robert Williamson and David Spratt
Cover serigraph by Manuel Mendive

First edition, 1993

Printed in Australia

Published by Ocean Press,
GPO Box 3279, Melbourne, Victoria 3001, Australia

Distributed in the USA by The Talman Company,
131 Spring Street, New York NY 10012, USA
Distributed in Australia by Astam Books,
162-8 Parramatta Road, Stanmore, NSW 2048, Australia

Distributed in Britain and Europe by the Latin America Bureau
1 Amwell Street, London EC1R 1UL

Contents

Acknowledgements and note on terminology 1
Introduction: The rite of social communion *by Pedro Pérez Sarduy and Jean Stubbs* 3
For a Cuban integration of whites and blacks *by Fernando Ortiz* 27

Part 1: The die is cast
The 19th century black fear *by Rafael Duharte Jiménez* 37
Mariana and Maceo *by José Luciano Franco* 47
People without a history *by Pedro Deschamps Chapeaux* 55
Drum ballad *by Jesús Cos Causse* 60
Claudio José Domingo Brindis de Salas *by Odilio Urfé* 64
Back to Africa *by Rodolfo Sarracino* 67
Solutions to the black problem *by Pedro Serviat* 77
Times I walk with my father *by Domingo Alfonso* 91
The 20th century black question *by Tomás Fernández Robaina* 92

Part 2: Myth and reality
Imaginary dialogue on folklore *by Rogelio Martínez Furé* 109
An initiation ceremony in Regla de Palo *by Gladys González Bueno* 117
The principle of multiple representation *by Joel James* 121
Abakuá signs *by Argeliers León* 125
Sara, one way or another *by Tomás González* 128
The Orishas in Cuba *by Natalia Bolívar* 137
The strokes of magical realism in Manuel Mendive *by Gerardo Mosquera* 146
Bembesiana *by Marcelino Arozarena* 154
Asere *by Eloy Machado* 157
Ifa says *by Tato Quiñones* 159
Ofumelli *by Excilia Saldaña* 163
María Antonia *by Eugenio Hernández* 169
Adire and broken time *by Manuel Granados* 180

Part 3: Redrawing the line

Birth of a national culture *by Walterio Carbonell* **195**
A white problem: Reinterpreting Cecilia Valdés *by Reynaldo González* **204**
The black and white in the narrative of Alejo Carpentier *by Salvador Bueno* **214**
Runaway story *by Miguel Barnet* **222**
Race and nation *by Nancy Morejón* **227**
Rethinking the plantation *by Alberto Pedro* **238**
Matilda *by Pablo Armando Fernández* **243**
The maids *by Pedro Pérez Sarduy* **250**
Questions only she can answer *by Georgina Herrera* **262**
The true door *by Soleida Ríos* **263**
Images and icons *by Sergio Giral* **264**
Rey Spencer's swing *by Marta Rojas* **273**

Notes on contributors **287**
Glossary **297**
Bibliographical note **303**
Index **306**

Notes on the editors

Pedro Pérez Sarduy (b. Santa Clara, 1943) is a black Cuban writer and journalist. He studied classics at the Central University of Las Villas, and then English, American and French literature and language at the University of Havana. He has been a radio journalist in Cuba since 1965 and with the BBC Latin American Service since 1981. He was 1989-1990 writer-in-residence at the Center for Cuban Studies and Center for American Culture Studies, Columbia University, and on the CUNY-Caribbean Exchange at Hunter College, New York. His first major work was *Surrealidad* (1968). Recent English-language publications include "The Ibelles and the Lost Paths" in Faustin Charles/(ed), *Under the Storyteller's Spell* (1989) and a bilingual anthology *Cumbite and Other Poems* (1990). He is completing two new books: *Journal in Babylon*, set in Britain's black community, and *The Maids*, based on his mother's life stories about pre-revolutionary Havana.

Jean Stubbs (b. Marple, 1946) is a white British social historian who lived and worked for almost 20 years in Cuba. She studied politics at the University of Essex, before going on to do her PhD on Cuban labour history for the University of London. She has combined translation and journalistic work with academic teaching and research. She was 1989-90 Visiting Associate Professor on the Latin American and Caribbean Program at Hunter College, CUNY. She is currently Senior Lecturer in Caribbean Studies and Latin American History at the University of North London and also coordinates the Caribbean Studies Programme of the University of London Institutes of Commonwealth Studies and Latin American Studies. She is the author of *Tobacco on the Periphery: A Case Study in Labour History, 1860-1958* (1985) and *Cuba: The Test of Time* (1989), and co-editor with Sandor Halebsky and John Kirk et al of *Cuba in Transition* (1992).

Center for Cuban Studies

The Center for Cuban Studies is a non-profit, tax-exempt educational institution which publishes a quarterly magazine *Cuba Update,* as well as a number of Cuban documents and creative work in translation. Its library of resource material on Cuba is open to the public. Information on membership and activities may be obtained by writing to the Center for Cuban Studies, 124 West 23rd St., New York NY 10011, USA.

The Executive Director of the Center for Cuban Studies is Sandra Levinson.

The Center for Cuban Studies has copublished with Ocean Press *The Cuban Revolution and the United States: A chronological history* (by Jane Franklin), *Island in the Storm: The 4th Congress of the Cuban Communist Party* (by Gail Reed) and *Images of Cuba* (edited by David Deutschmann).

Acknowledgements and note on terminology

Many people have helped bring this book to fruition but five should have special mention. Sandra Levinson, director of the Center for Cuban Studies in New York, has for over 20 years now been close to us and our work, and the Center became a friendly second home as this book initially took shape. David Deutschmann, head of Ocean Press, responded enthusiastically to the project and was a distant gentle pressure as deadlines were not met. Reynaldo Peñalver, retired journalist, was our frontman in Havana, troubleshooting on our every request. Finally, two colleagues were key to ensuring the quality of translation and edition: Olivia Macdonald, who went over the whole Spanish and English texts with a fine eye; and James Ferguson, who applied his editing skills to the overall product.

There is reference to many terms and names, with a profusion of language usage, terminology and spelling which is in itself the product of a process of creolisation. We respected each author's usage, leaving the Spanish, African or Afro-Cuban words in italics, explaining where appropriate in the text, endnotes or end-glossary. There is only one word in Spanish — *negro/a* — which translates as both Negro and black. We opted for using Negro when it was a text or quote from the past, and black when it was more contemporary. We have left it in Spanish when it had particular connotations, as in *negrona, mi negra* and *negra rica*. On the whole, we used the term mulatto, which is the direct English translation of the Spanish *mulato/a,* but it can be found interchangeably with brown, which is broadly used in the anglophone Caribbean. We preferred to leave in Spanish the multitude of variants such as *mulato indio, mulatillo, mulato blanconazo, mulatero.* For *cimarrón,* we used the more Caribbean term maroon in preference to the North American usage of runaway slave. Several of the literary pieces are written in colloquial fashion. Should we use a West Indian creole, or the language of Harlem or the U.S. South, black Britain or the Australian outback? We chose to use a "standard" English and leave the slang element to the imagination of readers in any of those places.

PEDRO PÉREZ SARDUY AND JEAN STUBBS

Introduction: The rite of social communion

The 4th Congress of the Cuban Communist Party, held in October 1991, was an event rich in historical, geographical and racial symbolism. The choice of locale was the eastern city of Santiago de Cuba, home to a much larger black population than the capital, Havana, and cradle not only of the 19th-century wars of independence but also of the insurrection against Batista which was to lead to the Cuban Revolution of 1959. The Congress was opened by the black Party Provincial Secretary for Santiago, Esteban Lazo, on 10 October — the anniversary of the outbreak of the first war of independence against Spain. On that date in 1868 Carlos Manuel de Céspedes, owner of La Demajagua sugar mill, freed his slaves and invited them to fight with him to liberate Cuba. The Congress was closed by the white Party General Secretary and President of Cuba, Fidel Castro, in the square named after the mulatto hero of Cuban independence, General Antonio Maceo. In 1878, in the small eastern town of Baraguá, General Maceo refused to sign a peace treaty with Spain. His act of defiance, although unsuccessful at the time, led eventually to the end of Spanish colonial rule. "Cuba is a Baraguá", said Castro.

The symbolism was obvious. With the demise of communism in eastern Europe, and in the face of hardening US hostility, the Party and Cuban government were returning to the indigenous roots of their own brand of nationalism and socialism. This was the context in which the Afro-Cuban heritage was being catapulted to the forefront of national politics. The breakdown of Cuba's integration into the eastern European bloc and the tightening of the 30-year-old US blockade put the island under siege in such a way that black Cubans likened Cuba to a modern-day *palenque* — maroon or runaway slave settlement. Many blacks' response to the government-declared "special period" of austerity in the new situation was that blacks were used to it; theirs had always been a "special period", and now the special period was for all.

Religious symbolism also played a part. A lead article in the Cuban press weeks before the Congress announced "The Nation is an *Nganga*"; *nganga* is the receptacle containing and representing the spirits in the Afro-Cuban belief system of *regla de palo*. *Regla de ocha* or *santería* believers said that their *babalaos*, or spiritual priests, were standing by Fidel. On 4 December, the saint's day for *Santa Barbara* or *Changó*, the 13th Latin American Film Festival uncharacteristically opened with a ceremonial *toque de santo*.

The political ramifications were equally clear. In December 1991, then Party Politburo member Carlos Aldana gave a hard-hitting end-of-year speech to the National Assembly of People's Power, calling for tough measures against lumpen elements in Cuban society and against "fifth-columnist", "counter-revolutionary" grouplets playing into Miami hands. In doing so, he alluded to race politics on two counts: first, it would be racist to equate lumpen with blacks in "marginal" neighbourhoods, and second, there should be no mistaking that the grouplets harbored known racists of the Miami-ilk (elsewhere compared to Afrikaaners in their designs).

In April 1992, the 6th Congress of the Communist Youth openly debated many problems affecting the country and society, including prejudice against young people and their life styles. One striking aspect of the Congress was the composition of the young people taking part: many were black and many were women. It was a moving moment when a young black musician with dreadlocks took the microphone and asked that he and those like him be judged not on appearance but on their support for the Revolution, and then went over to embrace Fidel who was attending the Congress. Significantly, two hit songs of the moment were "Beautiful Faces of My Black People" and the rap-salsa "What

D'Ya Want From Them?" (invoking African Gods) by the popular Cuban group, Adalberto y su *son*.

Reference to Baraguá in the present moment of crisis is double-edged. The nationalists lost the 1868-78 first war of independence: Spain was not about to give up easily its "pearl of the Antilles", largest and most prosperous of the Caribbean islands, and the independence forces were weakened and divided, not least over the question of slavery. However, Cuba would never be the same again. Blacks, mulattoes and whites had fought the war together, albeit on unequal terms; and Maceo was one of many who kept alive principles involving not only an end to colonial rule but also the abolition of slavery. Slavery was abolished on paper in 1880, in reality by 1886.

The second war of independence (1895-8) liberated the colony from Spain, but led to US intervention in the war and subsequent military occupation. The occupation, accompanied by massive foreign investment, had implications not only for sovereignty but also race, as there was an attempt to introduce into Cuba a segregation system not unlike that of the US South. At the same time, a massive seasonal flow of black migrant labor was brought in for the sugar harvest from neighboring Caribbean islands. A plentiful source of cheap labor, the presence of the migrants fuelled new racial tensions, especially in eastern Cuba, with its huge US-owned sugar mills and plantations.

The 1959 Revolution marked an abrupt break with the United States and a hemispheric isolation for Cuba that was only offset by its closer integration into the eastern European bloc. With the collapse of that bloc, Cuba was again isolated. White Cubans now talk about the "Haitianization" of Cuba. Internationally, Cuba and Haiti are often dubbed the pariahs of the Caribbean. Again, there are obvious historical parallels. After the 1791-1804 Revolution in Saint-Domingue, "jewel in the French crown", richest of the overseas colonies of France, there was a mass exodus, a significant part of which went to Cuba; and white Cuba shared with the rest of Caribbean planter society the great fear of the specter of black slave uprising. Reprisals were taken by both European colonial powers and their colonial governments and militia, against the newly declared, independent, black nation state of

Haiti, the first of its kind in the Caribbean. Internally, the country was pitted against itself. For its sins, Haiti was ground down and is, today, the poorest of the region's countries. Fears are that Cuba could, 200 years later, be driven along a similar road.

'The blood of Africa'

With isolation and defiance, the Afro-Cuban heritage appears to have asserted its central place in a new definition of national politics and culture. Yet, how important has the question of race been within the revolutionary experience of the last three decades? There can be no doubting that the Revolution moved rapidly to dismantle institutionalized racism. On 22 March 1959 Fidel Castro announced what has come to be known as the Proclamation against Discrimination: "We shouldn't have to pass a law to establish a right that should belong to every human being and member of society... Nobody can consider themselves to be of pure race, much less superior race. Virtue, personal merit, heroism, generosity, should be the measure of men, not skin color", Castro then declared. He denounced racial discrimination and racial prejudice as "anti-nation": "What the eternal enemies of Cuba and the enemies of this Revolution want is for us to be divided into a thousand pieces, thereby to be able to destroy us."

The "race question" is one that has surfaced at key points in revolutionary politics, for both domestic and foreign policy reasons. Many black Cubans certainly stood to benefit from programs of the revolutionary government aimed at the poor and at promoting cultural revival. They were proud of Cuba's involvement in Africa in the early 1960s (Congo) and in the mid-1970s (Angola), when Castro defined Cubans as not only a Latin-American but also a Latin-African people. "Many of our forebears came to this land from Africa as slaves. And slaves put up strong resistance and fought hard in the Liberation Army. We are brothers of the Africans and ready to fight for the Africans," he said then. "The blood of Africa runs deep in our veins." This sentiment was strengthened when Cuba became chair of the Movement of Non-Aligned Countries, embarked on its own bilateral programs with, and received visiting dignatories from, several African countries. The visit of Nelson Mandela in July

1991 was but one of the more recent. In the southern African context, the negative drain of Cuba's war effort and solidarity with Africa has to be offset by the positive conviction that Cubans ultimately helped to disarm the forces of apartheid.

Cuba's growing contact with and knowledge of Africa was paralleled closer to home in the Caribbean and through links with radical black movements in the US. In the 1970s and 1980s Cuba promoted bilateral programs with Jamaica, Suriname, Guyana and Grenada. Maurice Bishop was an immensely popular figure in Cuba; his leadership of the Grenadian Revolution of 1979-83 was likened to Fidel's leadership of the Cuban Revolution. The two leaders obviously liked and respected each other enormously, and were perceived to be two of a kind. Bishop's death and the US invasion of Grenada in October 1983 provoked mass mourning in Cuba, and his legacy has been marked in recent commemorative conferences in Cuba, as have those of Marcus Garvey and Bob Marley (Jamaica) and Martin Luther King and Malcolm X (USA).

But what does this tell us about the wider society and change within it? How deep does race run? It is our contention that few countries can boast the advances made in Cuba since the Cuban Revolution in breaking down institutionalized racism. It would, however, be shortsighted to think that racism has been eliminated.

Historians have long had to come to grips with contradictory concepts of Cuban nationhood and national Cuban institutions in a society of huge divides. The most obvious in the context of 19th-century sugar plantation society was race, and this was carried over in new forms into the 20th century. Equally evident were cleavages along regional, class, gender, cultural and religious lines, which both reinforced, and cut across, race boundaries. The abolition of slavery and independence from Spain, the 1930s labor uprising, the 1950s insurrection and 1960s revolutionary euphoria were key moments in contemporary Cuban history when levels of unity and social cohesion were achieved that could bridge the divides. The return to a more routine social order almost inevitably entailed their resurfacing, in newly defined forms.

There has been a rich history of many diverging views on the race question among Cuban blacks, mulattoes and whites. And, if many black and mulatto Cubans developed a sense of dignity based less on the separateness of their race and more on their sense of a rightful belonging to the Cuban nation, this grew out of a history of national resistance in Cuba that transcended racial cleavage. Cuba, like the rest of the Hispanic Caribbean, differed markedly from the English, and in lesser degree the French and Dutch Caribbean, in ultimately building up colonial settler societies that produced a more even balance between the races. White Cuban planter society was possibly at its most racist in the 19th century, precisely because its sugar boom rested on a rapidly growing black slave population. This generated a Haiti-style "black fear", complete with the infamous massacres of Aponte in 1812 and La Escalera in 1844, in which not only slaves but also the growing free black and colored, largely city-based, professional, petit bourgeoisie and artisan class were victims. The independence struggle could not but incorporate the struggle for abolition, and envision a people, as the white independence leader José Martí proclaimed, that was "more than white, more than black, Cuban."

The growing US presence emboldened the 20th-century white elite to again impose more rigid forms of racial segregation into certain sectors of society. Cuba's only black separatist party was short-lived as the country was plunged into the 1912 "race war", in which the black and brown bourgeoisie was again targetted and the Rural Guard massacred thousands of black peasants in eastern Cuba. Subsequently, race politics in Cuba meshed with class and national politics. Whole segments of the labor movement and labor leadership were black, heavily involved in the 1933 and 1959 uprisings, and sensitive to class and national issues as much as, if not more than, race. It should not be forgotten that the two important communist trade union leaders who lost their lives in the Cold War assault on organized labor, sugar leader Jesús Menéndez and dock workers' leader Aracelio Iglesias, were black. A third, tobacco union leader Lazaro Peña, escaped with his life but was forced underground. At the Congress of the resurrected trade union movement in 1973, it was Peña who was elected general secretary. Black construction workers Armando Mestre and Juan Almeida were among those with Fidel Castro in the abortive 1953 attack on the Moncada garrison in Santiago de Cuba, in prison on the then Isle of Pines, in exile in Mexico, and on the journey back to Cuba aboard the *Granma* to start the insurrection. Mestre lost his life but Almeida went on to be a key figure in the revolutionary government.

While 20th-century pre-revolutionary Cuba did not evolve into a US South or South Africa, it was considered to be the most racist of the Hispanic Caribbean territories. At the same time, its race dimension was comparable to Brazil's, in that the color spectrum ran from black through varying shades of brown to white. The "whitening factor" continued to give those of mixed race greater social mobility than blacks within the broader society, and shaped socio-psychological aspirations.

After 1959, the race question was almost entirely subsumed under a broadly redemptive nationalist, and subsequently socialist, umbrella. Significantly, the slogan "neither Black nor Red" formed part of a white backlash against major redistributive measures in the early revolutionary years. Even before socialism had been proclaimed, racism and anti-communism were being equated. Similarly, there was a growing voice within the Revolution arguing that access to public facilities was no substitute for ethnic democratization of Cuba's new cultural and socio-economic structures.

Official discomfort with all religions since the 1960s only abated in the 1980s with growing Church-state rapprochement informed by liberation theology. In the case of syncretic Afro-Cuban religions, anti-religious sentiment was fuelled by accusations of obscurantism and the seemingly widespread belief among the political leadership that popular religions and cult ceremonies would die away with a more educated and scientific approach to life. The three main religious currents in Cuba, Catholicism, Syncretism and Protestantism, can each be traced to periods and facets of the island's historical development: Spanish colonialism, African slavery and US domination. While Catholicism was the official religion up until the Revolution, the Church as such was identified with the more conservative, Hispanic oligarchy. It never established itself much in institutional terms outside the urban middle and upper classes.

This left a gap that could be filled by the Protestant denominations coming in with US settlers in the first two decades of the 20th century. However, the mass of the poorer, largely non-Church-going, urban and rural people developed a fusion of quasi-religious, quasi-mystical beliefs that colored daily life in the form of syncretic spiritualism, *santería, Abakuá, palo monte...* Officialdom's failure to recognize the historical socio-cultural legitimacy of those religions in terms of survival and rebellion was already being acknowledged when, in 1987, two major traditional African leaders visited Cuba. The first was the Asantehene of Ghana, king of the Ashanti, and the second, the Ooni of Ife, sacred capital of the Yoruba. Both, but especially the Yoruba, are peoples from whom many Afro-Cubans are descended. In 1991 the Communist Party Congress took the landmark decision to open the Party to religious believers, in tacit recognition that their numbers were on the increase, not least among Afro-Cubans.

The 1980s closed in what was a critical moment for the revolution in Cuba, for domestic as well as external reasons, with the inevitable questioning of communist theory and practice arising out of the eastern European experience. The crisis in Cuba reverberated beyond policy makers and planners into every corner of life, on the streets and in homes throughout the island. Again, race was one of the dimensions of the crisis. For, if Cuba could boast of broad trends towards equality, it could also be argued that complacency was hardly appropriate.

Demographically and socio-culturally, Cuba is far less white after three decades of revolution than it was in 1959. The initial exodus of the 1960s was predominantly Hispanic and monied. That of 1980 and since has been more mixed, but out of a population that many believe is far more mulatto than census figures suggest. Statistics in 1981 suggested that one-third of the overall population is non-white, though the figure is two-thirds in eastern Cuba, and there are pockets of Cuba where the population is overwhelmingly white, and others where it is overwhelmingly black.

The country can today boast of great achievements among

blacks, but they tend to be concentrated in sports, music, medicine and the armed forces, probably in that order. But why, despite the mass housing programs, do blacks continue to predominate in older, poor neighborhoods? Why, in the context of generalized petty crime and corruption, are there more blacks in the country's jails? Why are blacks prominent in 'folklore for the tourists' and tourist hustling? Why do blacks continue to be marginalized in the sphere of personal, social and cultural relations, as the butt of racist comments and jokes? Why, despite the evident interracial mix of the country, are black skin and black-white relationships considered socially undesirable?

The paradox is not that such questions should have to be asked after 30 years of revolution. Thirty years is a relatively short period of time for deep-seated attitudes and values to change. It is rather that they cannot be adequately answered, and largely because of revolutionary policy. Within revolutionary structures and ideology, betterment has been linked to merit, through work and education; to the individual and the collectivity being able to rise above circumstance. In striving for the unity of a people in revolution, no race-specific, affirmative action policy was implemented, with the exception of the mid-1980s, when the Party stipulated that its leadership should reflect proportionally the rank-and-file membership of blacks and women. No studies have been published in Cuba whose express intent was to assess contemporary racial composition or attitudes. At the same time, there has been an implicit, underlying language of racial (and other) codes, signs and meanings. One Cuban-American scholar has written provocatively of the tensions personified in the contrast between the female, mythical, hedonistic, Yoruba deity *Oshun*, celebrating life and pleasure, and the male, pragmatic, hard-working revolutionary symbolized by Che, sacrificing present for future.

There are two sides to every crisis: one bodes extreme difficulty, while the other holds the promise of new possibilities. This is as true in the realm of theory as it is in daily life. The vision of Marxism-Leninism has been bound by 19th- and 20th-century Eurocentrism, with assumptions of a lineal progression from barbarism to civilization that has had much in common with mainstream, western, modernization development thinking. The two combined in 20th-century revolutionary experience to create serious obstacles to analysis of theoretical categories beyond nation and class, such as race and wider value systems within the socialist experiment. Contemporary Cuban political thinking, on the one hand, is still heavily constrained by Marxist orthodoxy when it comes to race, and, on the other, is itself imbued with racist and counter-racist thinking, the latter always with its undercurrents of challenge and resistance.

In the 1960s, pronouncements on race took their cue from Martí: man should be judged according to merit, not race, and above all, the enemy should not divide and thereby rule. Thirty years on, as Cuba entered the 1990s, the maxim was unchanged. In December 1991 the National Assembly of People's Power voted to drop Marxism-Leninism from the Constitution as the official state thinking, and return to the thinking of Martí. Whatever the shifts in official ideology, blacks are arguably one of the groupings in Cuban society with the fewest illusions about any switch to western-style market democracy or Eastern-style perestroika. The contemporary resurgence of racism in both of those camps has not gone unnoticed in Cuba. The problem, as seen by many, is to make functional an existing system that, for all its contradictions, has provided non-white Cuba with the basis for an alternative agenda.

The contributions to this book are in their entirety by Cuban scholars, writers and artists, whose skin color is in the main varying shades of black or brown. The few who are color-coded "white Cuban" would be quick to remind us of nebulous sanguinary boundaries and points of crossover, and we have left it to the reader to realize how hard it is to "box" the writer in terms of racial origin on the strength of his or her writing. With the exception of two pieces — one by the late Fernando Ortiz, Cuba's eminent ethnographer who from the turn of the century did much to legitimize the study of black Cuba, and the other by the late musicologist, Odilio Urfé — all the contributions have been written since 1959. The pieces of writing, like most of their authors, are little known outside Cuba. This was a major criterion for inclusion in the book. In the case of the better-known contributors who have been more widely published abroad, we have endeavoured to include their lesser-known work: thus, we have taken excerpts from essays by Nancy Morejón and Miguel Barnet, known best for poetry and testimonial novel. There are some glaring omissions. An obvious one is Cuba's National Poet, the late Nicolás Guillén, for the sole reason that his poetry has been extensively published and written about, in English and other translations outside Cuba. All of their work should be read in conjunction with this anthology, as should volumes that exist in English of the writings and speeches of Maceo, Martí and Castro.

Much has inevitably had to be left out. Among the work of the now deceased historian Emilio Roig Leuschenring, there are invaluable pieces on black Cuban history. Historians Manuel Moreno Fraginals, Jorge Ibarra, Fe Iglesias and Olga Cabrera have all written extensively on aspects of economic, political and social history directly relevant to race. The year 1986 was the centenary of the abolition of slavery in Cuba and was marked by the publication of many articles and books, of which those by Carmen Barcia and by Eduardo Torres and Eusebio Reyes are but two. Isaac Barreal and Rafael López Valdés have contributed important research in the field of anthropology; Samuel Feijóo, Roberto Fernández Retamar, Emilio Jorge Rodríguez and Ileana Rodríguez in the field of literature. From Casa del Caribe, Bernardo García has worked on Garveyism in Cuba and, with Rafael Brea and José Millet, on popular festivals. Millet has also studied Haitian religious belief systems in the eastern part of the island.

A hard decision to take was the exclusive focus on AFRO-CUBA, and an even harder decision the title. A comprehensive book on race would need to look at the various strands of Hispanic and white Cuba, the once considerable Chinese population which resulted from 19th-century indentureship (on which there is the invaluable scholarship of the late demographer Juan Pérez de la Riva) and the smaller groupings of Syrians, Jews, and so forth. We both share the conviction that the creolization process has affected all groupings to such a degree that it is difficult to talk of any form of racial purity, whether in physiological or socio-cultural terms. Nonetheless, we also feel that the "melting pot" approach begs the question of strong racial differences, which must be recognized and respected as such, if "assimilation to white" assumptions are to be challenged. Since there are many ways in which black continues to be sedimented at the bottom of the melting pot, our primary aim was to look at black Cuba, but in the context of black-brown-white relations.

The book opens with an introspective address from the 1940s by Fernando Ortiz on the experience of race and integration in the Cuban context. Ortiz influenced much contemporary Cuban thinking; since in his time he was an internationally recognized anthropologist, and yet one hardly translated, it seemed fitting to start in this way. Ortiz explains his use of the term Afro-Cuban and outlines five phases of what he calls "reciprocal transculturation of the races" — hostility, compromise, adaptation, vindication and integration. He places the Cuba of the 1940s on the threshold of the fifth and last phase, and describes those at the forefront as being bound in "the rite of social communion." Taking his concept as our title to this introduction seemed equally fitting as a statement on the book, although we do not wholly subscribe to his ideas. It is interesting that Ortiz should have been so optimistic 50 years ago. His optimism in fact led him to deny the very concept of race, again a current of thought that fed into the revolutionary experience.

The rest of the book is divided into three broad sections, in which key interpretative essays are interspersed with poetry and prose. Part I, "The Die is Cast", attempts a primarily historical overview of race and the race question. Part II, "Myth and Reality", explores Afro-Cuban folklore and religion through ethnography, drama, film, art and literature to explain the everyday here and now. Part III, "Redrawing the Line", retraces key concepts of national culture, employing historico-cultural forms. There is only a tenuous chronological concept to the book. Rather, it moves backward and forward in time, blending past and present markers for the future.

Part I opens with the historian Rafael Duharte reappraising the two great fears of 19th-century Cuba — the fear of the black, which he traces back to the Haitian Revolution, and the fear of the caudillos, from the experience of the newly independent Latin American Republics — and how the two fears crystallized in the form of the mulatto generals, Antonio and José Maceo. The late José Luciano Franco was exceptional among the old school of historians; he was largely self-taught and devoted much of his writing to documenting the African diaspora in the Caribbean, from major events such as the slave trade and slavery to key Afro-Cuban figures. Here he regales us with both eulogy and obituary to the stoic Mariana Grajales, "glorious mother of Maceo," and the epic Antonio Maceo, whose death reverberated internationally, who in life was a "sword for Cuba when Cuba needed a sword." The now retired Pedro Deschamps Chapeaux is of the same school, of similar interests and background: the contribution included here, on 19th-century urban runaways, tribal markings and colored midwives, testifies to his life's work which painstakingly documents the anonymous "unsung" heroes of black Cuban history.

Poet Jesús Cos Causse offers the archetypes of rebellion: the maroon, the drum and the *güije*. The drum is, of course, but one instrument among many that have evolved from Cuba's Hispanic-African roots, to give Cuba a vibrant musical heritage, from the *danzón, son, guaguancó* and *columbia,* to the *mambo, cha-cha-cha* and *rumba*. Odilio Urfé, musicologist, composer and musician, appeals to a lesser known turn-of-the-century "classical" music tradition through Cuba's "black Paganini," the violinist Brindis de Salas.

Rodolfo Sarracino rounds off this earlier period, writing on the return to Africa movement, which raises interesting questions with implications for the historical roots of Cuba's contemporary involvement in Africa. The contribution is constructed from interviews, correspondence and other documentary evidence provided by present-day family members living in Lagos, Nigeria, and Matanzas, Cuba. From the 1840s and slavery to the 1980s and the Angola War, Sarracino reconstructs a moving personal account of two sides of a family, each of which only know what the other looks like through photographs, substantiated with letters "full of simple, everyday, intimate details that people tend to write in letters all over the world." As Sarracino says, "it's easy to forget" that theirs is a family divided by events of epic proportions.

By far the clearest exposition of the thinking that informed revolutionary policy, and how it relates to other currents of 20th-century thinking on race, can be found in the piece by the late Pedro Serviat, and he is unique in attempting such a panoramic view. He identifies proponents of more integrationist ideas in the early 1900s, like Juan Gualberto Gómez, in contrast to the separatist, independent colored movement of Pedro Ivonet and Evaristo Estenoz and black nationalism of Rafael Serra. He analyzes the different racist positions taken vis-a-vis Caribbean migrant labour, mobilization in the 1930s and 1940s around Communist Party politics and the civil rights movement, and the black cooperative capitalism of the 1940s and 1950s. Serviat's own background as a militant communist worker led him to see the Revolution as destroying the economic basis of racial discrimination and therefore as providing the definitive solution to the black problem. The black worker movement was not without its own cultural history, and we have included a short poem by Domingo Alfonso. Construction worker, architect and poet, Alfonso is a modern-day Regino Pedroso, the 1930s working-class poet and contemporary of Nicolás Guillén.

The final and most recent piece in this section, by Tomás Robaina, documents much of the same period as Serviat, through the press of the time. Read together, Serviat and Robaina open a Pandora's box of conflicting viewpoints and interpretations. Robaina depicts blacks Cubans as among those most uneasy about the pro-US governments of the 1900s and Juan Gualberto Gómez, the black leader, as most outspoken against the Platt Amendment; he sees Ivonet and Estenoz, with their Independent Party of Color, as legitimate defectors from the Liberal Party which was obstructing both blacks and mulattoes; he scrutinizes the 1930s Kuban Ku Klux Klan and Communist Party policy of black self-determination for the Oriente "black strip"; he quotes Fidel Castro on how both poor and rich can be racially prejudiced, and subscribes to unity in revolution working to make real Martí's dictum.

'Drum Magic'

Part II opens with Rogelio Martínez Furé, and his early self-questioning on folklore, which he defines as the cultural habits and customs of, and for, the people — the very opposite of "official" and "bookish." Recognizing the pejorative connotations of the term, he attacks bourgeois notions of folklore as a tourist or museum curiosity, and outlines concepts of negative and positive folklore, the former of which he sees as superstitions, taboos, supernatural beliefs, and the latter as traditions of solidarity, struggle, folk medicine and art forms with a new revolutionary social function. The excerpt concludes defending the concept of a Caribbean civilization born of the incessant clash of cultures, of reciprocal influences: a folk culture of music, dance, food and beliefs.

What Martínez Furé has done for the National Folklore Group in Havana since the 1960s, Gladys González and Joel James have done likewise for Casa del Caribe in Santiago de Cuba over the last decade, helping to build up cultural institutions grounded on solid research. All three go to prove that there is but a fine line between researcher, performer, practitioner. In her contribution here, Gladys González gives a detailed practical description of a contemporary initiation ceremony in *regla de palo*. Joel James develops a theoretical exposition of the philosophical formulations contained in Cuban magical-religious systems. In the case of *regla de ocha, regla conga, vodú* and *cordón,* he singles out elements within a given plurality that shape a system of multiple representation in one or another form out of necessity or convenience, which he sees as the basis of all human praxis. They are followed by the now deceased ethnologist Argeliers León explaining the nature of *Abakuá* "treatises," wherein each *gandó* or sign, rather than telling a story that is intelligible and discursive, is interpreted by the initiate, who acts much like an agent of transmission, according to the accepted code of knowledge of a given *Abakuá* fraternity.

Playwright Tomás González is also a singer, actor, painter and scriptwriter of two classics of contemporary Cuban cinema: **The Last Supper** (Dir: Tomás Gutiérrez Alea) and **One Way or Another** (Dir: Sara Gómez). González wrote this personal tribute to Sara Gómez 15 years after her tragically premature death. In her lifetime Cuba's only black filmmaker, Sara left a gap that only now looks as though it may be filled with young directors like

Gloria Rolando. Here, González bares intimate feelings and details of his own love story with "Sarita", just as Sara on film "bared all the family had wanted to cast into deep oblivion." He describes her rejection of petit-bourgeois family prejudice and tells the story of how they worked together on Gómez' first and last feature film about *Abakuá barrio* culture.

For many years, the work of folklorists had been painstaking, laborious and backstage. In 1990 this changed when museum director Natalia Bolívar was thrust into the limelight and her "handbook" of the *orishas* in Cuba became a best-seller. The excerpt included here is in two parts. The first gives a brief history of the Yoruba religion in Cuba and its fusion with Catholicism, giving rise to *santería*. It concludes that, while there is existential uncertainty on the path to conquering real knowledge and control, "hundreds of thousands of years of drum magic will be in our blood." The second explains *Elegguá*, the major *orisha* who holds the keys to destiny, and must open the way for all other *orishas*.

Elegguá personified might be Manuel Mendive, considered the most important artist in Cuba today, acclaimed as much for his performance art as his still painting. Here, art critic Gerardo Mosquera places Mendive in the tradition of the earlier Wifredo Lam and traces Mendive's eclectic naif art forms to their origins in a mulatto worker family of believers in *regla de ocha*. This is also the thread to the descriptions in this piece by Nancy Morejón of the painting *Eri Wolé*; by Rogelio Martínez Furé of the Mendive family home in Havana's worker neighborhood of Luyanó; and by Pedro Pérez Sarduy of Mendive's present home in the village of Santa María del Rosario where the artist has recreated his mythical world. For, as Sarduy says, "a culture without myth would be a tree without leaves."

Mendive's artistic world of *santería* finds its poetic equivalent in the work of Marcelino Arozarena. A contemporary of Nicolás Guillén, Arozarena has a similar style. The poetry is essentially musical in its rhythm, to be read aloud or performed, and in this it predated dub and rap. **Bembesiana** is an unpublished last poem Arozarena read in public in March 1992 on his 80th birthday. Eloy Machado (*El Ambia* — 'The Brother'), in **I'm all**

that and **Asere I say**, also plays with musical and religious elements, and with creole language. Machado masterminded a Sunday 'jam session' or 'yard' in Havana's downtown Cayo Hueso for street musicians, painters and poets. Cayo Hueso, it should be added, was the home of Cuban conga player Chano Pozo, who revolutionized jazz percussion by infusing Cuban rhythm into Dizzy Gillespie's 1940s big band "Cubop". In early 1992 the police closed down Machado's yard on marijuana-related charges. Three months later, Machado won his case against the police and the 'yard' was functioning again.

Tato Quiñones, Excilia Saldaña and Eugenio Hernández weave their prose, poetry and drama around religious mythology. In two short stories, Quiñones tells about *Ifá* and his own birth, and about a plump cockerel that assuaged the family's hunger. Saldaña recreates the myth whereby *Oyá* wills death to enter her foreign lover's mind: it is symbolic death, too much love, too much fear, too much solitude. Eugenio Hernández took Havana by storm in the mid-1960s with his play about María Antonia, a black woman of the streets and of *Oshún,* and her lover Julián. The play ran to packed audiences identifying with street heroes whose values, according to political orthodoxy, should not be celebrated but left to die. The play — though not the writer — was put into cold storage until the 1980s, when it again became a box-office hit and signalled a wider theatrical revival. Hernández himself continued to be prolific in theater, film and television.

Also writing in the 1960s, Manuel Granados was the novelist equivalent of Eugenio Hernández, producing prose that celebrated marginal culture as it interfaced with both religion and politics. We follow characters like Julián from the *toque* to the Sierra Maestra, through encounters which include one with a disorientated, black, repatriated Cuban who is ready to go back to Little Rock or pimping in New York where he can identify the enemy!

'Rescuing Africa from oblivion'

Walterio Carbonell was a key figure among the intellectuals of the 1960s who called for a black reappraisal of Cuban history and culture. He, along with several of the contributors to this book, was responsible for a position paper drafted at the time of the 1968 Cultural Congress. Subsequently, Carbonell and others found themselves ostracized internally in varying forms and degrees, and labelled by some outside Cuba as the so-called "Black Manifesto Group." In the excerpts of his work that open Part III, Carbonell calls for "rescuing Africa from oblivion," decrying the revolutionary "cultural idealism" that reduced national culture to patrician figureheads. He argues that the 20th-century bourgeois republic had tried to obliterate the once considerable knowledge of Africa on the part of planters as well as slaves. In contrast, he describes a process whereby amidst the contradictions of neocolonialism "Spain was Africanized." Attacking the shortcomings of the Marxist dictum that religion is the opium of the people, he attributes a progressive role to African religions which functioned also as political organizations. His main message is: "one of the tasks of the revolutionary writer today is to clarify our historical past... While confusion reigns over our ideological past, we will suffer... not only the ills of the present, but also those of the past."

Reinaldo González moves from myths of religion to myths of sensuality, with his rereading of Cirilo Villaverde's 19th-century Cecilia Valdés as the archetypal creole Cuban "femme fatale." For better or worse, he claims, the "little bronze virgin," living symbol of the fusion of two races, the beautiful mulatto woman almost passing for white, has come to epitomize a cultural version of feminine essence and presence. Salvador Bueno then shifts the discussion to the black *criollista* techniques of *negrismo* in the work of the 1920s and 1930s by the late Cuban writer Alejo Carpentier, whereby blacks came to signify autochtony and the essence of nationhood under siege from deforming forces. Magical realism, he concludes, was not an intellectual concept Carpentier learned from Europe, but rather emerged from the mix of cultures, beliefs and superstitions from Africa within reach of his own home.

Miguel Barnet explains formative elements of his writing, from the epic, adventure and historical novel to ethnographic research, leading him to the "ethnographic story" or "testimonial novel" form. He reflects on two of his prime characters, the runaway slave Esteban Montejo and the cabaret dancer and singer Rachel. Nancy Morejón returns us explicitly to Fernando Ortiz and the concept of transculturation as a "heiroglyphic of races and cultures" out of which would come "a new race, a new culture." She rejects assimilation and asserts the great creativity in producing a mixed people, inheriting and embodying both Spain and Africa (but no longer either Spain or Africa), and examines this through two poems by Nicolás Guillén.

Alberto Pedro takes apart the "plantation" as a political institution, accepting it more as a socio-cultural institution, which, he proposes, could produce anomalous permissive white masters and black Uncle Toms. The plantation, he argues, existed within the confines of a given society and according to time and place. In a 20th-century context, he points out the contradictions within Cuban plantation society, among other things, over Caribbean migrant labor. North American companies favored English-speaking blacks to their Cuban counterparts, and were least disposed to creole-speaking Haitians. There were similar tensions between the various black communities and, while there were strict restrictions on staying in the country after the harvest period, pockets of "West Indian" communities formed. The migratory wave was at its height in the second and third decades of the century and after the 1959 Revolution came to a virtual halt, but communities of the descendants of especially Jamaicans and Haitians, can still be found today. Significantly, it is eastern Cuba, which has a markedly more "Caribbean" flavor, that has produced a body of Caribbean research, writing and cultural festivals.

The theme of Caribbean migrant labor is taken up in literary genre in the excerpt from Pablo Armando Fernández's novel set in the eastern sugar mill town of Delicias. Through Matilda's flashbacks to her pre-revolutionary childhood of Caribbean migrant life in the plantation yards, she recollects hunger, desperation and promiscuity through feelings that verge on the hallucinatory. Pedro Pérez Sarduy takes us to a less stark but no less poignant reality. This departure from surreal poetry comprises two chapters of what is in some ways a surreal novel of black maids, set in 1940s Cuba. The first is the story of the maids dressed in their finery for the acceptably sedate *son* and *danzón* of Santa Clara colored society's ballroom at the annual spring Floral Dance. The second finds the maid caught up in the saga of the white family Havana home. What comes through strongly is the strength and dignity of his own mother's storytelling. This is then followed by the quieter, more introspective women's poems by Georgina Herrera and Soleida Ríos.

The scope of analysis broadens as Sergio Giral reflects on his visual rereading of history, taking three of his films based on literary deconstruction of three characters: Francisco, the slave in the 19th-century novel of the same name; and characters from two plays, the mid-19th-century poet Plácido and the mid-20th-century street woman María Antonia (in his version mulatto not black). Through all three, he attempts to lend contemporary meaning and universality to characters and events from specific historic contexts.

The book ends with an attempt to synchronize many short fragments from Marta Rojas' epic historical novel, interweaving the love story of Juliana and her "high brown", Andrés, with that of his black Jamaican migrant mother Clara Spencer and mulatto Santiago (but Haitian descended) father Arturo Cassemajour. It is a story full of symbolism and one whose unexpected final twists concern the year 1992 in several senses.

Taking the book as a whole, our aim was to achieve the fluidity of a discerning lens, probing fact and fiction. Many of the individual contributions stem from personal experience, and in many cases that experience has had its personal costs. Without wishing to single out names, or to suggest that race was the single or even foremost issue of concern, there are contributors who have found themselves at such odds with the cultural establishment that for extended periods they were unable to publish, lost their jobs and in some cases even their sanity. Others served spells in agricultural work camps. Some are now outside the country. What distinguishes them all, however, is that they firmly believed in the liberating potential of revolution.

Over the years we have been close to many of the contributors, sharing their concerns, though not always seeing eye to eye. As for the two of us, for over 20 years now, we have both striven to respect and learn from each other's culture. Marriage is never an easy institution, and is perhaps most taxed when it challenges established boundaries of race, class, nation and gender. An invaluable ingredient over bumpy patches has been, without a doubt, our open-ended approach to life, which is what we hope is reflected in our approach to this book.

It is a book that has grown with us. We were convinced of the need in Cuba to put together a volume on race and color that would open up the debate on contemporary race politics. Moreover, in our own journalistic, creative and academic work, exposed as we have been to a broad range of people outside Cuba, and able as we are to move in and out of languages, we have long experienced the frustrations of those who cannot read Spanish and therefore cannot gain access to a whole range of material on a key subject such as this. Then, while in New York in 1989-90, we found ourselves at the heart of a new controversy over the publication of a book by the Cuban-born Carlos Moore, **Castro, the Blacks and Africa** (University of California Press, 1989). Moore's study skirted around crucial areas of black Cuban history, yet did so with an alarming blend of truths and untruths, lacking in historical context and overly narrow in its race analysis. When combined with his avowed anti-communism and anti-Castroism, this led Moore to downgrade any organizations and movements in which race had not been the sole defining issue, ultimately denigrating black Cubans supposedly "duped" by Castro who used race as a tool in his "Afrocentric" foreign policy while practising "negrophobic", "Afrophobic", integrationist domestic policies. Put crudely, his main thesis was that Castro had tricked blacks into supporting his own national and international self-aggrandizement, not least through his policy in Africa during the 1970s.

The controversy was such that in a space of three months Moore himself did a complete volte-face, from the initial launch of the book when he painted Cuba as the world's "last militarized regime... threatening a holocaust for Black Cubans worse than Romania" to acknowledging in the mainstream US press that "under Mr Castro Blacks have materially benefitted and slowly climbed the social ladder." Moore also later observed that Cuba's blacks "would rally around Mr Castro, or a successor regime, if it appeared that the financially powerful, predominantly white Cubans of Miami were a serious threat to their social position."

In late 1992, Moore himself was appealing to the nationalism of black Cubans on both sides of the water to join forces against the newly signed U.S. Torricelli-Graham Act, on the grounds that it would strengthen a white Miami business elite's return to Cuba. Among other things, the Act aimed to tighten the U.S. policy of attrition against Cuba, extending the trade embargo to subsidiaries of U.S. companies in third countries. The Act was endorsed by both Republican and Democratic parties. Signed by U.S. President George Bush shortly before his ousting in the November 1992 elections, it was proposed by Democratic senators and first backed by Bill Clinton in his Democratic presidential campaign. Although widely opposed by governments throughout the Americas and Europe as an infringement of their sovereignty, it continues on the statute books of the current Clinton administration. Interestingly, Clinton named black Cuban American Mario Baeza, a moderate who had headed a U.S. business delegation to the 1992 Euromoney Conference in Mexico and Cuba, to the State Department Latin American Desk. The furor of the Miami Cuban lobby caused Clinton to back down, and place Baeza in the Department of Commerce. This was something that would hardly escape Moore's attention.

Moore's greatest weakness was perhaps to be trapped in his childhood and young adulthood memories of Camagüey — a particularly virulent centre of sugar and racism, and also the only heartland of black nationalism in mid-20th-century Cuba. His experience of race there, and his early, fleeting first-hand acquaintance with revolutionary Cuba (1962-4 were the only years he returned to live and work in Cuba), are clearly what fuelled his extrapolation of race suppression ever since in Cuba. He sought support for his claim in this respect from Cuban American Jorge Domínguez, a would-be ethnic enemy, who, in his preface to the Moore book, referred to the race factor as a "classic 'non-topic' in Cuban history."

Anybody reading this volume can hardly fail to doubt the validity of that claim. While it is true that it has been more comfortable to deal with race historically or culturally, it is equally the case that such treatments of the theme have cast significant light on Cuban political realities. A reformulation of the 19th-century independence struggles as not the patrimony of the patricians but a popular history of resistance, whose protagonists were slaves, freed blacks and coloreds and peasants, workers (men, women and children), has obvious parallels for the insurrection of the 1950s and beyond. Race, class, gender and religion have all become such interlocking categories of analysis for contemporary civil society and polity that they cannot be reduced to the fields of black separatist or black middle-class politics.

Rather than dismiss the current icon of Baraguá as yet another manipulation, we would rather ask what has made it acceptable — in the thinking of white and black Cubans — for Maceo (and not Martí) to be the current national personification of non-capitulation. Similarly, as Cuba enters the 1990s, affirmative action programs for blacks, women and religious believers (Catholics, Protestants, *Santeros, Paleros*) have to be seen as indicative of new social and political forces in an ongoing struggle.

While we could not include everything and everybody, we tried to include a sufficiently broad range as to indicate the richness and diversity of Cuban writing on race. Our concern was primarily socio-historic and cultural, looking at the way in which the internal race dynamic affected people in their everyday lives. Whole areas such as foreign policy we have not touched on at all. One regret is the gender-bias in the collection, in terms of the contributors and to a lesser extent subject matter. With certain notable exceptions, Cuba has yet to see a flourishing black woman writer's movement and a rethinking of her story and culture. The "*mulata* femme fatale" says it all: the black Cuban woman has yet to come into her own. From 19th-century *mambisas* Carlota, Rosa "La Bayamesa", Mariana Grajales, María Cabrales, Dominga Moncada and Paulina Pedroso, through 20th-century militant woman tobacco stemmer Inocencia Valdés, to the myriad anonymous women strategizing resistance and survival, we would do well to remember the strengths of Afro-Cuban women in work, struggle, family, community and religion. There is, moreover, an erotic imagery that begs for a new, unchaperoned discourse that is beyond the scope of this book.

Our hope is that this collection of writing will serve to contribute to the ongoing re-assessment of race, gender, class and nation, one that might help inform meaningful policies and a change in society's values. One can arguably expect racist manifestations to surface more in the crisis 1990s, and it will be crucial to monitor the unfolding of events in this respect.

The pervasiveness of racism should not be underestimated. The problems facing blacks in revolutionary Cuba cannot be ignored, pretending that they will go away. Neither should blacks' own revolutionary history be underestimated; blacks have in the past taken history into their own hands. Today Cuba has a blacker population than it had in 1959, a more educated black population, and one with a growing sense of pride in being black as well as being Cuban. No matter what happens in Cuba, no matter what sort of government comes to power, black Cubans are a force to be reckoned with and will not easily tolerate their own perceived gains from the Revolution being taken away. Rather, they will want to see those gains extended.

Maceo might have lost at Baraguá but his legacy remained. And so did Mariana's.

Pedro Pérez Sarduy
Jean Stubbs
London, March 1993

FERNANDO ORTIZ

For a Cuban integration of whites and blacks

Excerpt from a retrospective — and introspective — address of the 1940s, published in Salvador Bueno **Los mejores ensayistas cubanos** (Best Cuban Essayists), Imprenta Torres Aguirre, Lima, reprinted in Havana in 1960, and in **Orbita de Fernando Ortiz** (Orbit of Fernando Ortiz), UNEAC, Havana, 1973, pp.181-188.

For 40 years I have been exploring, classifying and analyzing the most intricate fronds of black culture in Cuba, and from time to time I have brought something to light as a frail example and attempt at all that can be done, and is yet to be done in that virtually unexplored field of inquiry.

In 1906, I published my first book, a short piece of basic research on the retention of magical and religious elements of African cultures in Cuba, as they were in reality and not what they were thought to be, i.e. an extravagant variation of white witchcraft. That age-old pact with demons or evil spirits, with the horrible practices of European witches who sucked the blood of children and flew on broomsticks to celebrate their Sabbath and indulge in the most repugnant orgies with the Satanic he-goat, in whose entrails monstruous beings were spawned, half-human, half-demon. Thus it is affirmed in the edicts of the Holy Inquisition and the works of wise theologians, such as the Jesuit P. Martín del Río, with as much knowledge of structure as barbarity of thought. It was fortunate that in the early research on the mysteries of witchcraft in Cuba, we were able to affirm that there were no such diabolic aeronautical flights and that so-called witchcraft in Cuba was above all a complex combination of

African religion and magic with ritual, hagiographic legend and Catholic superstition, and with vestiges of pre-Christian paganism.

In that book I introduced the term Afro-Cuban, to avoid the risks of using terms prejudiced in meaning and to express precisely the duality giving rise to the social phenomenon we set out to study. That term had been used in Cuba once in 1847, by Antonio de Veitia, a fact I learned due to the courtesy and great erudition of Francisco González del Valle; but it had not become established in general language as it is today. My first book, though written with calm objectivity and from a positivist point of view, and despite the honorable prologue by César Lombroso, was on the whole received by white people with benevolence, but always with that complacent and at times disdainful smile with which they would listen to stories of Bertold, village idiot tales or silly jokes; and among people of color the book was met with a distasteful silence, broken only by some writings of manifest, albeit refrained, hostility. For whites, that book on black religions was not a descriptive study but colorful reading, at times amusing and even open to ridicule at times. To blacks, it seemed a work professly against them, since it unearthed well-hidden secrets, sacred things that were revered by them, and customs that could be taken out of context to be shameful and could foster collective contempt. I felt that hostility at close range but was undaunted.

The years passed and I went on working, writing and publishing on analogous themes. As there was no derogatory attitude in my analysis and comments but rather observation of things, explanation of their ethnic origin and sociological human meaning, and moreover comparison with identical or analogous phenomena in cultures typical of whites in other times and countries, the hostility with which people of color prejudged me gave way to cautious silence and indecision and respectful courtesy, a mixture of apologetic timidity and requests for refrain. My publishing on those subjects displeased them, but they did not concretely oppose me. "What is that little white up to?" is what I heard more than once behind my back. On several occasions I was asked directly: "Why are you into Negro things? What is your reason or what pleasure do you get from it? Wouldn't it be better to leave things alone?" Then I had the misfortune of going into politics, and during those ten or twelve years, when I was already well-known and with a certain popularity, each time I went through Marianao, Regla, Guanabacoa and certain other Havana neighborhoods on exploratory visits to *cabildos, santerías,* initiations, *claves, toques,* carnival masquerades, dances and other gatherings which carry over ancestral traditions of the Negro world, I would hear some curious new interpretation of my persistent inquiry. A liberal said: "This Doctor's a sharp one, wanting to cajole Negroes into giving him their vote!" A conservative, a mulatto of various distinguishing features, added: "This liberal is doing a great disservice to Cuba, reviving things from slavery!" And there was also some high and mighty lady saying that I was drawn to the *bembés* more by the daughters of the Virgin of Regla than the beliefs of the Mother of Water. I gave up politics, having neither gained nor lost through my writings. Among people of color the distrust began to abate; there were moments when some came to me, as a practising lawyer, for protection against those who were abusing them. At the very least, I was looked on as a tourist from home, a friend amused by things exotic, something of the same kind as those fair Northerners passing through Cuba who pay for the rumba to be danced to their obscene taste. But among the blacks and the whites, my work was no more than historical entertainment and picturesque writing on local customs and manners. There were some cases when a colored informant in good faith felt obliged to highlight his reporting of things African with the most pejorative comments, in the belief that by absurdly denigrating his forbears his person grew in my esteem.

Allow me to say in passing, as the moment is so appropriate, that the sad phenomenon of self-denigration is perfectly understandable and forgivable, knowing the enormous pressure with which the dominant forces have for centuries put down subjugated human groups and the tremendous singular social hostility directed against those who have had the misfortune of that subjugation being aggravated by their ostensible, ineffaceable, skin pigmentation. This is why that attitude of denial of personality has been more frequent and more lasting among blacks. It was already documented in the Middle Ages, when the Americas had still not felt Africa's embrace.

> Negro woman reviles herself
> to be considered white

Thus observed the famous Archpriest of Hita, Juan Ruiz, in his **Libro de Buen Amor** (Book of Good Love) over six centuries ago. And it has to be recognized that among the less fortunate colored groups that submissive, denigratory inferiority complex still abounds. But that negativist phenomenon, in reality psychiatric and of collective pathology, is not exclusive to blacks. We constantly see it in individuals and peoples of the most diverse races; and it is, without a doubt, the gravest obstacle to the dignification and social ascent of races dependent on higher levels of non-discrimination.

In 1928 I went to Europe and in Madrid, speaking before a gathering of the Spanish intelligentsia, I protested against a policy of rapprochement with the Americas invoking religion and race. Against the misuse of religion, because there is no one Spanish religion, though there are fanatics who behave as if they believed there were, and would impose an Inquisitorial Catholicism, as interpreted by themselves in Toledo, on the whole of Latin America. I fought the propaganda on race because neither is there a Spanish race as such, seeing how Spain, from whose civilization we are honorably descended, is made up of one of the most miscegenized peoples on earth; and because, even were such a Hispanic race to exist, racism is an anachronistic concept of barbarism, incompatible with the contemporary demands of culture, and an enemy to the Cuban nation. By then some understood, whites and coloreds, that my ethnographic work was no mere hobby or distraction, like taking up hunting or fishing; it was rather a basis on which to better lay the foundations for solid criteria on greater national integration.

Today, there is growing confidence in ethnographic research, and there is in Cuba a conscious, capable, select minority with a clear vision of the future (you yourselves are the vanguard of that minority), who understand that the only path of liberation from all prejudice is through the knowledge of realities, devoid of passion and apprehension, based on scientific research and on the positive appreciation of fact and circumstance.

Recently, in my two short courses on Ethnic Factors in Cuba for the University of Havana Summer School — which were well-received, with great interest, by studious elements of all races — I became aware that Cuba has embarked on that culminating phase of interracial understanding; and the fact that the Rector of the University was thanked by the Atenas Club for the initiative of organizing those courses and asked for them to be made permanent, shows how decisive and clear a position the more educated coloreds are taking now as regards approaching ethnic problems on a realistic scientific basis, divorced from emotional propaganda in the form of diatribe or apologetics.

This gradation of attitudes towards my intellectual endeavor over 40 years is exactly the same as that with which the impact of two races and cultures through all the phases of their reciprocal transculturation is expressed. First phase: hostility. The white attacks the black to uproot him from his land and enslave him by force. The black rebels as he can; he makes war, creates runaway slave settlements, and even commits mass suicide. It is preached that the black is of an accursed race; he was cursed by Noah, say the theologians. Everything about him is subhuman and bestial. Man of color is finally conquered but not resigned. Thus it was until the 19th century.

Then comes the second phase, which tends to occur in the first generation of creoles: compromise. The white, with or without slavery, exploits the black who finds himself impotent against force but cleverly defends himself, and adopts distrusting subterfuges of accommodation. Sensual love intertwines the races through miscegenation. The white gives ground to his mulatto offspring; and the black who has lost homeland, family and consciousness of his historical past, readjusts to the new life and the new land, feeling love for his new country. The black can dance and the white take enjoyment with him. The "good Negro" and the "good mistress" types are exalted; but the dominant and the dominated each distrust the other. The one draws out his days, the other awaits his; both take advantage of what is coming to pass. There is a truce; there is a Zanjón. That was up until recently.

And so little by little the third phase arrives: adaptation. The individual of color of the second generation of creoles, tries to better himself imitating the white, at times blindly, for better and for worse. It is perhaps the most difficult phase. Man of color on desperate occasions goes so far as denial of self. The mulatto becomes white by law, by money or by lineage; but his life is a constant frustration, aggravated by constant pretence. The words "black" and "mulatto" still carry with them a sense of opprobrium; they have to be substituted by others as a euphemism in everyday language. The grandmother or mother spend their unhappy lives hidden away, in fear of their dark presence publicly damaging their descendants, in turn exhausted by their constant inhibition. The dominant white tolerates conventional whitening, accepts certain advantageous cooperation, even marriages of convenience, and comes into closer contact with the dominated one of color, but always with the latter "in his place." Thus it was until yesterday, and is still so today where life continues in the pattern of the past.

Then comes the fourth phase: vindication. Man of color regains his dignity, control and value of self. He no longer reneges on his race or his skin shade, nor is he ashamed of his traditions, or surviving values of his ancestral culture. "Negro" and "mulatto" are no longer taboo words. There is growing mutual respect and cooperation between whites and blacks; but the habits of age-old prejudice and the discriminatory weight of economic factors still come between them. We are now on the path of comprehension in Cuba, but with an onerous burden of unliquidated prejudice, heightened even by predatory foreign policies, whose present spokesman is Hitler with his brutalitarian racism. This is the phase of today.

These phases of inter-race relations are not exclusively Cuban; sociologists can observe them on all continents. Nor are they peculiar to relations among all races and in all epochs and all latitudes, where such impacts are produced. Neither are these phases that all persons, given their relative social positions, have to go through in the coexistence of different and opposing ethnic groups: for circumstance and the genius of individuals can hasten or elude one phase or another; but the further the analysis goes, social anthropology can observe these schematic phases in the process of transculturation. As they have been clearly experienced by myself in social contact with my compatriots of color during the 40 years that have elapsed since my first Afro-Cuban studies: from hostility and distrust to compromise, and finally cooperation.

But a fifth phase still has to be reached: integration. In that phase only a small minority can be found. Those of us who are gathered here are part of it. It is the phase of tomorrow, of the tomorrow that is dawning. It is the last, where cultures have fused, and conflict has ceased, giving way to a tertium quid, a third identity and culture, a new and culturally integrated community, where mere racial factors have lost their disassociative ill-intent. For this reason, the present act of a group of Cubans of different races coming together for a rite of social communion, consecrating the need for mutual understanding on an objective grounding of truth to move toward achieving the definitive integrity of the nation, is a new moment charged with deep, transcendental meaning in the history of our country, and it should be interpreted as such.

PART 1

The die is cast

RAFAEL DUHARTE JIMÉNEZ

The 19th century black fear

Excerpts from "Dos viejos temores de nuestro pasado colonial" (Two Old Fears of Our Colonial Past) in the author's **Seis ensayos de interpretación histórica** (Six Essays in Historical Interpretation), Editorial Oriente, Santiago de Cuba, 1983, pp.83-100. Editors' title and subtitles.

There were two great fears in colonial society: "fear of the black" and "fear of the caudillos." Each was shaped by a blend of falsehood and truth that allowed for the existence of their fanatics and detractors. For decades, they acted as a brake on the forces for independence, which were obstructed, divided and debilitated, until finally these two forces disappeared from our political universe, one through a barbaric act of genocide, the other transformed into bitter reality.

In Cuba, these two fears took shape from the historical experience of the Caribbean and South America. The "fear of the black" goes back to the late 18th century and the time of the Haitian Revolution, and the "fear of the caudillos", to the first half of last century, with the fatal cycle of anarchy and dictatorship in which the South American republics were submerged after their revolutions for independence.

Revolution in Haiti

The Haitian slave revolution had an extraordinary impact on Cuban society of the time. It was on the one hand a unique economic opening in the island's colonial history as Haiti was wiped off the map of Caribbean production, a heyday for Cuban sugar and coffee. It was on the other, the start of the "black fear", a specter which politically froze the creole planter class for a whole half century...

The black revolution in Haiti also brought to Cuba a wave of French settlers fleeing from the insurgent slaves. These refugees arriving in Santiago and other cities of Cuba told exaggerated, distorted stories, weaving a black legend around the Haitian Revolution — an uprising born of the violence and hatred of centuries of slavery in that French island colony and truly the first of the independence struggles of Our America.[a] As told by demographer and historian Juan Pérez de la Riva:

> ...in November 1803 the last settlers and troops fled. Saint Domingue, pride of the gentlefolk of Nantes and Bordeaux, had gone forever... The flotsam of this sad tide came in such numbers to Santiago de Cuba that the sleepy city saw its population increase by alarming proportions... It wasn't clear how to go about feeding and clothing this torrent of starving refugees, most of whom possessed only the clothes they had on them... The once flourishing colony was reduced to ashes and dust... This would be the image held not only by the refugees; the Cuban bourgeoisie was not to forget the disaster, and right up to La Demajagua the specter of Haiti was to spread the most negative attitudes throughout Cuba.[1]

Francisco Arango y Parreño, a leading exponent of the planter class of the time, provided a clear economic analysis of the slow progress of the island's economy and the means for taking good advantage of the great economic conjuncture afforded to Cuba by the slave uprising in Guarico. However, he also warned of the danger that the events of the neighboring island be repeated in Cuba:

> ...the insurrection of the blacks of Guarico has broadened the horizon of my ideas... I have seen that all my work was built on air; that I had not worked to give it substance... that the good fortunes of my compatriots were held together by one thread: the subordination and patience of a mass of barbarous men. This disagreeable foreboding is not what alarms me most today... My greatest concern is for the future, when the

island has grown in wealth and harbors five thousand or six thousand Africans. I speak now, for the time to come, that we take precautions as of today. [2]

Creole fear of the black

There can be no doubting this birth of the black fear. Before the black revolution in Haiti, there was no fear of the slaves in Cuba — despite the already considerable record of runaways — largely because there were many more whites than blacks on the island. This can be seen from the 1787 population count, and between the 1774 and 1791 censuses the proportion of slaves to the overall population actually declined... From 1791 on, the black fear would grow with each new shipload of African slaves. It was the black fear, together with the economic bonanza, which explains why creoles did not take advantage of the tremendous political opportunity afforded by the Napoleonic invasion of the Iberian peninsula to cast off the Spanish colonial yoke. While in 1808 the independence revolution erupted in volcanic proportions over the whole continent, Cuba did not break its political inertia and remained the "ever faithful Isle". Moreover, it served for many years as a key base of operations for the Spanish metropolis in its efforts to regain a lost colonial empire.

The historical responsibility for our country playing that sad role during the independence wars of the continent falls on the only social class that at the time had all the conditions to lead a revolution in Cuba: the creole bourgeoisie. The main reason for the political immobility of a class that shouldered years of accumulated grievances against colonial rule... was its fear of the blacks. [José Antonio] Saco, perhaps its leading ideologue, wrote in 1848: "There is no country on earth where a revolutionary movement is more dangerous than Cuba... Under present circumstances, political revolution is necessarily accompanied by social revolution; and social revolution is the complete ruin of the Cuban race." [3]

With the outbreak of revolution in 1868, it was the eastern sector of the landowning class that broke the inertia, and the whole creole bourgeoisie was faced with a fait accompli. Carlos Manuel de Céspedes' act of freeing his slaves at La Demajagua dealt the first blow to a paralyzing myth, as the freed slaves joined the revolutionary troops and the crucible of Cuban nationhood was forged, incorporating the black as an active political element. But it was not a death blow. Our wars of independence were pitted with this old fear. This was astutely exploited by Spain whose ideological attacks were systematically directed at fostering reservations regarding black officers, especially the Maceos. And the colonial press cleverly unleashed an intense campaign presenting the "Little War" as a race uprising. Playing on the fact that the main pillars of revolution in Oriente province — Antonio and José Maceo, Quintín Banderas, Guillermón Moncada and Mariano Torres — were black, the Spanish press began talk of an alleged black republic. Antonio Maceo, as a black and a caudillo from the east, was accused of having designs on the presidency of that republic. The campaign succeeded in sowing confusion among the ranks of the *Mambí* Army and undermined the support of certain sympathetic sectors of the bourgeoisie. The agrarian bourgeoisie echoed the watchword: "Cuba, better Spanish than African," as did the oligarchic Autonomist Party...

Fear of the black Caudillo

Throughout the wars of independence there was a patently sordid fight between civil and military power, underlying which was a terrible fear of the caudillo... Two examples suffice to show the negative effect of this fear...

One is the deposition of [Carlos Manuel de] Céspedes by the House of Representatives, a political act which deprived the Revolution of its most capable leader and, without a doubt, marked the start of the collapse of 1878.

[José] Martí, whose civic values and regard for democratic principles are beyond question, wrote in reponse to *civilista* fears about Céspedes:

> ... He thought that authority should not be divided; that unity of command was the salvation of the revolution; that several leaders, rather than accelerate, hindered movements. He had a single, rapid end in mind: the independence of the country. The House had another, what the country would be after

> independence. The two were right; but in times of struggle, the House took second place...[4]

A second example was in 1896, when the military successes of the revolution were growing and the invasion of the western part of the island was a reality through the heroism of [Máximo] Gómez and Maceo, the *civilista* members of the Government Council stepped up their actions against the military; they even went so far as to annul the military rank of the main leaders of the revolution. The balance Martí put forward had not been achieved; the old conflicts of the Great War between civil and military authority resurged stronger than ever.

The myth of the fear of the caudillo reached its zenith in the latter part of the 1895-98 Second War of Independence. The Government of the Republic in Arms blocked a relief column of 500 men to the Lieutenant General, caught up in the final throes of the invasion of the west... and decided to use them instead in the battle of Zanja. The decision went beyond political or military considerations, broke the agreement between Gómez and Maceo in El Galeón, and put in question the authority of military commanders whose powers had increased extraordinarily as a result of the invasion.

This action was condemned strongly by Gómez... and in a tone more measured, though no less firm, by Maceo... as the bitter reproach of one who had devoted his life to the independence of his country and could find no explanation for the action of that Government Council in Jimaguayú. For Maceo, this action only confirmed his reservations about civilian government. In a letter to Mayía Rodríguez of July 27, 1896, he wrote:

> Had it not been for the valor, abnegation and skill shown by all the men in this Department's forces,[b] the Revolution would have failed here, while the gentlemen of the government watched from the sides, with impassive indifference, the sacrifice of this army, unaided, of its own accord, to save itself from the constant threat of going under... Is this how a government, patriots and military fulfill their obligations?[5]

The fear of the black and the fear of the caudillo merged on the Maceos, as black military commanders. At the centre of the opposition to the Maceos was the Marquis of Santa Lucía, whose war correspondence could not be more explicit... In a letter to [Tomás] Estrada Palma of August 22, 1895, he wrote: "I believe Maceo will have sent **El Cubano Libre**, which is being published over there. We have read the second issue, and been shocked by it being called the official organ of the insurrectional forces of Oriente. I don't know what this means, and I fear the ant wants to grow many wings. Such wanton ambition means we have our work cut out." In a letter of July 4, 1896, also to Estrada Palma, he commented: "... Here also we have had our black points. José Maceo thought that he should be in command in Oriente and his brother in Occidente..." And on May 16, 1896, in a letter to Miguel Betancourt, he added: "He [José Maceo] was thinking of resigning. That came as most welcome to us because José Maceo is not trusted by us. He is not fitting for the post... We have designated Mayía as Department Chief to contain the ambitions of José Maceo."[6]

Twenty years earlier, José Maceo himself had written a letter to the then President of the Republic in Arms, Cisneros Betancourt, in which he referred to attacks on his person by certain racist elements:

> Bariguá [sic] Camp, May 16, 1876
> ...for a long time now I have been putting up with ways and conversations that I truly relegated because I took them to come from the enemy, who is notorious for brandishing any class of weapon to divide and thereby defeat us; but later, seeing that there was a growing class question taking on new form, I tried to find out where it was coming from, and was convinced in the end that it wasn't from the enemy, but sadly enough, from individuals who are brothers of ours who, forgetting the republican principles they should observe, were more concerned with serving a particular political outlook... The writer, Citizen President, was told some time ago now, by a person of good repute, that a small circle exists who, he disclosed, had manifested to the Government that they did

> not wish to serve under the orders of the speaker, for belonging to the class, and later through a different channel I learned that that they have not wanted to serve because they are opposed to, and have set their sights on men of color above white men...[7]

[The two letters] encapsulate 20 years of ruinous black fear in action in our history...

Martí and the black as Cuban

The weight given to the black problem in Martí's writings is a measure of how important the black fear still was as the century drew to a close. Fernando Ortíz wrote:

> The Ten Years War was hardly over when Martí was hounded by racism, that of the white against the black and vice-versa. The problem of the "fear of the black," which synthesized the conflict of all forms of racism in Cuba, was singularly controversial. For many whites the fear of a rebellion of the subjugated was real; for others it was another pretext for subjugation; for some blacks it was a sign of their own power, which was feared as a true threat; for others, a new taunt to keep them shackled in their servitude. For all, whites and blacks, it was of grievous concern, a wall blocking liberty and progress, an inhibiting complex that for centuries had been embedded in the sinews of our history.[8]

The ideology of '68 had placed the black in the insurrectional ranks; Martí restored the dignity of the black as a Cuban in the struggle for nationhood. Martí approached the black problem first and foremost conceptually. He denied the existence of races: "There can be no race hatred, because there are no races. Shallow thinkers, lamplight thinkers bookishly weave and reheat ideas of race, while the just traveller and cordial observer seek in vain in the justice of nature, where in triumphant love and turbulent desire, the universal identity of man is to be found."[9]

Martí depicted the independence struggle as the crucible of freedom and irrefutable proof that the black fear was unfounded:

> What, then, is there to fear?... Shall we fear he who has suffered most in Cuba from the privation of freedom, in the country where the blood he shed for her has made her too dear to be threatened? Shall we fear the black, the noble black, the black brother, who, in the Cubans who died for him, has forgiven the Cubans who still maltreat him?
>
> The revolution, which has brought together all Cubans, regardless of their color, whether they come from the continent where the skin burns, or from peoples of a gentler light, will be for all Cubans. [10]

Before embarking with Gómez on taking the war to Cuba, Martí wrote at Montecristi:

> Another fear would perhaps take hold, under pretext of caution and cowardice: the senseless and never justifiable fear of the black race in Cuba. The revolution, with its toll of martyrs and warriors, and its subordinate, noble warriors, bears indignant lie to the taint of threat from the black race, as does the long trial of migration, and the truce on the Island... There are Cubans in Cuba of one and another color, forgetting forever — with the liberation war and work which brings them together — the hatred in which slavery kept them divided. [11]

Death of a myth

Martí studied carefully the fears engendered concerning the black and the military caudillos, explaining them sociologically and offering solutions as regards any basis they might have in reality... And yet, in the new republic born under the frustrating sign of U.S. intervention, the old 19th-century fears gained new vigor and continued to erode the nation.

The black uprising of 1912 seemed to materialize the fear that had chilled the creole planters ever since 1791, and to negate Martí's visions of a solution. And yet, the *Independientes de Color* (Independent Colored Movement), far from being a racist movement, was, sociologically speaking, a reply to the deep-seated racism enshrined in the republic. Blacks who since 1868 had won the right to be a founding part of the republic saw to their amazement that the republic they had helped create turned its back on them; their response was to organize to reclaim the place Martí had recognized as rightfully theirs and to which their heroism had entitled them.

The 1912 black uprising in Oriente provided the historical moment for the death of the black fear. The death of this fear that had taken shape in the late 18th century around the blacks, was a physical death. The black fear vanished from our political mythology along with the over 3,000 blacks brutally massacred in the Oriente countryside by the republican army. General Monteagudo, in his report to President Gómez on the military operations against the insurgents, said: "It is impossible to tell the number of dead, because it has degenerated into widespread butchery in the hills."[12] The latent fear of the creole bourgeoisie for over a century had created a fierce explosion. Having become the dominant class through the independence revolution, the bourgeoisie felt sure of itself, and in 1912 decided to eliminate the specter that for so many years had disturbed its peace. After the genocide carried out by the Liberals, the bourgeoisie as a class would be free of any vestige of fear of the black who faced a suffering existence of humiliation and discrimination throughout the pseudo-republic.

Endnotes

1. Juan Pérez de la Riva (1975) **El barracón y otros ensayos**, Editorial de Ciencias Sociales, Havana, pp.370-371.
2. Francisco Arango y Parreño (1952) **Obras**, 2 vols, Dirección de Cultura, Havana, pp.149-150.
3. José Antonio Saco (1974) **Contra la anexión**, Editorial Ciencias Sociales, Havana, p.101.
4. José Martí (1973) **Obras completas**, Vol. IV, p.358.
5. José Antonio Portuondo **El pensamiento vivo de Maceo**, p.96.
6. Benigno Souza (1972) **Máximo Gómez, el Generalísimo**, ICL, Havana, pp.188-193.
7. Hortensia Pichardo (1969) **Documentos para la historia de Cuba**, Editorial de Ciencias Sociales, Havana, Vol I, pp.394-396.
8. Fernando Ortiz (1953) **Martí y las razas**, Havana, 1953, p.26.
9. ibid.

10. José Martí (1973) **Obras completas**, Editorial Nacional de Cuba, Havana, Vol IV, p. 276.
11. **Historia de Cuba** (1963), Dirección Política de las FAR, Havana, pp.309-310.
12. Pichardo, op cit, Vol II, p.364.

Editors' notes

a. The concept of Our America is that of Martí, developed in an essay of the same title, referring to the Americas south of the Río Grande, that is, excluding North America, seen by Martí as the giant poised to devour the south.
b. Colonial Cuba was divided into two Departments: East and West.

JOSÉ LUCIANO FRANCO

Mariana and Maceo

The following two pieces stand as eulogy and obituary to two great names as they have gone down in Afro-Cuban history: Mariana and Maceo. The first is "Mariana Grajales, madre y revolucionaria" (Mariana Grajales, mother and revolutionary), **Revolución y Cultura**, No. 27, November 1974, pp.72-74. The second is taken from **Antonio Maceo: apuntes para una historia de su vida** (Antonio Maceo: Notes for the Story of His Life), 3 vols, Ciencias Sociales, Havana, 1975, Vol III, pp.369-372.

Mariana Grajales

The active presence of women in the struggle against slavery, and for national liberation and the conquest of the most basic human rights, is of singular importance in the history of Cuba, reaching new heights from the early 19th century on.

In 1812, María de la Luz Sánchez was held prisoner for over six months for being a propagandist in the revolutionary movements of 1810 and 1812 in the region of Peñas Altas sugar mill. Fermina, *Lucumí* leader of the Acana revolt of 1843, was sentenced to death by a summary War Council, and María Rita Armand was sent to prison as one of the leaders of the revolutionary movement of El Cobre in 1867.

Mariana Grajales Coello, "glorious mother of the Maceos", was a symbol and compendium of the protests and rebellions of 50 years of constant battle against the hated colonial regime. Born in Santiago de Cuba on June 26, 1808, of Dominican parents, she was united in life to Venezuelan-born Marcos Maceo.

Marcos Maceo and Mariana Grajales lived with their entire family in the refuge of La Delicia, in Majaguabo, San Luis, sheltered from the tragedy surrounding the Caribbean waters. Their family grew. After the first-born Antonio, came María Baldomera,

José, Rafael, Miguel, Julio, Dominga, Tomás and Marcos. "When she had nine children by Marcos", wrote Raúl Aparicio, "she had to be prepared for the exhausting task of any home with many offspring. She made this battalion of children an example of respect. She gained experience bringing them up and knew how to impose discipline. Moreover, everything about her inclined to keeping an orderly clean home, maintaining personal cleanliness and dressing as decently as possible. These were habits which she was to observe always, until her death."

Mariana, helped by Marcos, with singular good sense, guided the morals of family life. With great humility she prepared the children for great feats in life. A uniform, regular life, free from sterile hypocrisy, nurtured from joyous daily contact with exuberant tropical nature, created, in the clean and honest Maceo home, the calm that came of unequalled happiness. Not unsurprisingly, a noble sentiment of solidarity bound together that incomparable family...

Two days after Carlos Manuel de Céspedes started the revolutionary struggle in La Demajagua, Captain Rondón arrived at the Maceo farm with a group of rebels to invite Mariana and Marcos and their offspring to join the liberation forces: "and old Mariana", wrote María Cabrales in her letter to Francisco de Paula Coronado, "bursting with joy, went into her room, picked up a crucifix she had, and said: 'on your knees everyone, parents and children, before Christ, who was the first liberal man to come to earth, let us take oath to liberate or die for our country'."

The heroic tribe, as Lino D'ou called the Maceo family, all joined the revolution. Antonio Maceo was wounded in May 1869 in the attack on Armonía sugar mill, and was transferred to the improvised bush hospital in the mountain settlement which Mariana ran. The death of loved ones had filled Mariana Grajales with sorrow. After the death of her son Justo, she lost her life companion; her affliction could only have been that much greater when they brought Antonio wounded. But, "the magnitude of her misfortune only pressed her to continue the work of destroying the chains shackling Cuba"; and Mariana Grajales, living effigy of Cuban patriotism, shouted to the younger of her children, a boy still: "You, go now, it is time now to fight for your country."

As the Ten Years War came to an end, General Máximo Gómez, just before he left the island, met for a last time with General Antonio Maceo on February 18, 1878, but he wished to bid his farewell to Mariana Grajales and noted in the Campaign Diary: "The 19th, wishing to see the General's family, set off for the settlement. The General sent his brother José to accompany us and we spent the night there. Being among those patriotic women, our comrades in the hills during that terrible ten-year struggle, in which we had all suffered so much, was one of the saddest nights for me."

After the Baraguá Protest, in April 1878 Colonel Lacret arranged that the seriously wounded, the invalid and sick, along with their families, should leave the *mambí* camps. Among the first was Tomás Maceo, who left for Kingston, Jamaica, with Mariana Grajales and her daughters.

"Doña Mariana was a superior being," wrote Leonardo Griñán Peralta, referring to the description Martí gives of her in his article on Maceo, when he says: "He is his mother's son, more than his father's, and it is a great misfortune to owe one's body to one who is weak or useless, to whom one cannot owe one's soul; but Maceo was fortunate, because he was born of a lion and lioness. He is losing his mother, the glorious old lady is dying in indifferent foreign parts, and yet still has a girl's hands to caress one who speaks to her of her country. Her eyes are off round the world, as if looking for another, still sparkling, as when the Spaniard came, to hear of a good move on the part of her sons. She lifts her wrinkled head, wearing her headscarf like a crown. And, knowingly, she kisses the hand. At the bedside of her sick grandson, a slip of a man, the old lady speaks ardently of her sons' battles, the terror and the joy, of what he will again be. Huddled in a hole in the ground, she spent mortal hours while saber and machete crossed pommel. She saw her son, covered in blood, and with only ten men, disband 200. And she serves with her own hands and accompanies to the door all those who in Cuba's name go to see her."

In late November, Mariana Grajales, glorious mother of the Maceos, died in Kingston. In the 12 December 1893 edition of **Patria**, Martí paid a last tribute to her memory: "With her old lady's scarf about her head, with eyes of a loving mother for the unknown Cuban, with a fire that was not to be extinguished, with the homeland on her face and in her look, when speaking of the glories of yesterday and the hopes of today, a woman of 85 years whom an entire people, rich and poor, arrogant and humble, sons of master and serf, follow to the tomb in foreign lands: in Jamaica, on November 27, Mariana Maceo has died."

The Bronze Titan

The masses of the people were racked with anguish and grief over the tragic news of the death of the *Bronze Titan* in San Pedro. And the most authentically representative voices of democratic endeavor in that period of history were raised in unanimous clamor the world over with the message of rebellion. The extraordinary feats of the soldier, the clear, progressive, firm line of the exemplary revolutionary, the shining beacon of an unparalleled life wholly devoted to fighting colonial tyranny and social injustice, all meant that, in the most distant, remote corners of the earth, the fortunes of the glorious epic the Cuban leader of popular democracy was to write with his own blood were followed with devote admiration. The name of Antonio Maceo was a symbol and banner in the universal struggle for the liberation of the oppressed. And his death, which appeared then to be veiled in mystery, and was presumed to be a vile and cowardly assassination by the hidden hand of a reactionary plot, unleashed an impassioned debate around the historic figure of one who was the 19th century's last Great Captain. There was wild rejoicing in the Spanish colony in Cuba echoed by pleased reactionaries of all persuasions, and also the muffled confession of traitors to the Revolution who whispered to each other, faintheartedly, in their coteries and cliques, that it was high time Maceo died. That his disappearance swept away the obstacle blocking the path of turncoats of every ilk conspiring even within the ranks of the Revolution, against the absolute independence of the Cuban people.

Volunteers, guerrillas, newspapers and journalists at the service of tyranny, the official colonial apparatus and Weyler's puppets, drank and partied in bacchanalia over the death of the

Great Hero of Freedom. The bells of the Catholic churches and thousands of fireworks deafened the cities and towns of the enslaved island. Rough and ready soldiers insulted Cubans with the most indecent phrases in their obscene barracks repertoire. In the Spanish Casino in Cárdenas, the Presbyterian priest Antonio Pascin, setting an example of ignobility, hitched up his cassock and danced on a table, to celebrate the death of the champion of democracy... News of Maceo's death reached Spain and was cause for celebrations throughout the Peninsula. Likewise in Lisbon, where the Opera was stopped to play the Spanish anthem."[1]

But the attitude of democrats and intellectuals in the rest of the world to the unexpected death of the immortal leader was different. In the Indian Parliament, the radical member Imbriani spoke in memory of General Maceo, killed in the struggle for his country's liberation. "Rebellion", declared Imbriani, "is not only a right, it is a duty of the oppressed, and glory is for those who die fighting for a cause."[2] University students in Rome rallied in fraternity, to pay tribute to the memory of Maceo and protest against Spanish despotism. Later, a great wake was organized by the Antonio Maceo Circle in Rome's Esquilino Theater, at which progressive deputies, university professors and students, and trade union delegates gathered; and a bust of General Maceo was unveiled, to a vibrant speech given by the illustrious Italian sage Giovanni Bovio.[3]

In the United States, Representative Woodman, of Illinois, responded to popular clamor and put forward a motion to Congress recommending that the president of the Republic officially make known to the government of Spain its strong censure of the methods used by its forces in Cuba and especially the means employed in the assassination of General Antonio Maceo. The **New York Journal** lead "Maceo is dead!" caused consternation among North American friends of Cuba. But there were also the racist insinuations in certain circles of nascent Yankee imperialism closely linked to colonial sugar interests in Cuba. An extensive article in **Harper's Weekly** of January 30, 1897 assured that the death of Maceo was favorable to the revolution because it averted the danger of a race war...[4]

Professor Joseph E. Wisan, of City College, New York, in a

highly interesting book which studies the Cuban crisis through the U.S. press, wrote about how rumors of growing tension in Hispanic-American relations were invariably accompanied by a drop in the price of shares on Wall Street and by financial editorials clamoring for peace, and cited the example of the price drop caused by the intense commotion over the news of Maceo's assassination.[5]

The great Puerto Rican writer and revolutionary Eugenio María de Hostos wrote unforgettably of the sentiment gripping all the Americas over the tragic loss of Maceo:

> While he was neither the first nor alone, he was second to none in patriotism or fortitude or abnegation or heroism, and, in the eyes of the contemporary world, which has seen him fighting day after day in the most visibly dangerous position, he will always be the most genuine representative of Cuba at arms. He will be a symbol for posterity...[6]

Henri Rochefort, the militant pamphleteer of **L'Intransigeant** of Paris, who had won the Cubans' gratitude for his articles against "the reactionary clerical government oppressing the Spanish people", wrote a strong manifesto that was also signed by outstanding figures in the French literary world such as Lucien Descaves, Paul Adam and Henri Cauer:

> Despite the laws of war and of humankind, Maceo has fallen victim to insidious treason, to the most cowardly assassination. The Spanish government, overwhelmed by that son of the people that none of the Spanish generals could defeat, had to turn to treason to rid itself of him...[7]

"I never saw such spontaneous, intense and visible grief as that shown in the Dominican capital over the death of Maceo," wrote D. Manuel de Jésus Troncoso de la Concha.

> For days, there wasn't a piano, a phonograph, or any music to be heard; there was expression of nothing but grief. And since it has been said that it is but a step from sorrow to anger,

> there were incidents between those who mourned the death of Maceo and those who could not hide the satisfaction this caused them. The night of the terrible day on which the news of his death was confirmed, a group of Dominicans and Cubans and another of Spaniards, were on the verge of a fist-fight in Columbus Park, with who knows what grave consequences, because the former thought the latter had uttered irreverent words sullying the memory of the hero...[8]

A quarter of a century later, the Spanish writer Marcelino Domingo commented on the fall of the Titan:

> In an everyday military manouver, Maceo, who was always at the front, lost his life. His valor was no longer necessary, as the word of Martí was no longer necessary when he died at Dos Ríos: the Revolution had triumphed. The Revolution was not only in the minds of all those who had fought for it, but was also favorably viewed around the world. Proof of this lay in the words pronounced in the Italian Parliament in honor of Maceo; the show of solidarity with Cuba which took place throughout the Americas over the news of the death of the caudillo; the protests of grief in England and France. Maceo was a sword for Cuba when Cuba needed a soldier...[9]

Endnotes

1. Gaspar Carbonell Rivero **Enrique J. Conill, Soldado de la Patria**.
2. **Patria**, New York, December 16, 1896.
3. In a letter of condolence Ramón L. Betances wrote to María Cabrales de Maceo, Paris, March 5, 1897, "He is exalted: and — if this might be consolation — let us recall that on February 28, 1897, the former Queen of the world, Rome the Great, has celebrated the apotheosis of Maceo."
4. Hermino Portell Vilá **Breve biografía de Antonio Maceo.**
5. I am grateful to my friend and colleague Rafael Soto Paz, a tireless researcher, for a series of very important bibliographical references on Antonio Maceo, not only for the commotion through the world over his tragic death at Punta Brava but also the favorable comments of writers and journalists on the life and work of the great soldier and revolutionary leader. Among them, the piece published in

Prensa Libre, Havana, Friday November 6, 1947, December 7 1950, and the book by Joseph E. Wisan **The Cuban Crisis as Reflected in the New York Press (1895-1898)**, University of Columbia, 1934.

6. Emilio Rodríguez Demorizi **Maceo en Santo Domingo.**
7. Documents provided by Norberto López Barceló.
8. Rodríguez Demorizi, op.cit.
9. Marcelino Domingo "Maceo, la espada de la independencia" in **La isla encadenada.**

PEDRO DESCHAMPS CHAPEAUX

People without a history

Excerpts from "Cimarrones urbanos" (Urban Runaways) and "Las comadronas o parteras" (Midwives) in Deschamps Chapeaux and Juan Pérez de la Riva **Contribución a la historia de la gente sin historia** (Contribution to the History of People Without a History), Ciencias Sociales, Havana, 1974, pp.29, 37-9, 43-6, 67-69.

Urban runaways

Flight was the slaves' first step to liberation. First individually, then collectively, it represented permanent protest against the regime of servitude to which they were subjected. Runaway, uprising and maroon settlement were synonymous with struggle throughout the long, three hundred years of slavery in Cuba.

Writers and historians like Cirilo Villaverde, Rufino Pérez Landa, José Luciano Franco, Miguel Barnet and others have described the slave flight, the runaway condition and finally settlement as a symbol of collective rebellion. Sigua, Limones, El Frijol, Moa, Bumba, Maluana... exemplify the rural maroon's armed resistance. But there were not only maroons from sugar and coffee plantations; there were also the urban runaways, domestic slaves seeking freedom in their flight...

Inconformity with the slave system was manifested among the vast population of African origin in different ways. One of the most common was to hide the fugitive, thus encouraging urban runaways. In countless press advertisements for fugitive slaves, there was often reference to the help they received from free blacks, principally those living in hamlets outside the city walls...

Diario de la Habana of July 7, 1831 announced:

> Fugitive from the house of his master a black Congo named Joaquín, known to be missing the big toe and part of the third toe of one foot, thought to be living outside the city walls with other free blacks of his nation: whosoever turns him over to 28 Damas Street will be rewarded for his capture and whosoever harbors him shall be held liable for the damages.

Slavery failed to break tribal solidarity, as was evidenced in the cooperation and help between people, despite the legal liability this entailed, as slave owners were wont to remind people in their escape notices... Female as well as male urban domestic slaves took flight...

> For a month now the master does not know the whereabouts of the mulatto woman Francisca Angulo who is tall, stout, with a birth mark on the upper lip, and with no upper teeth: she is hired out as a cook and never sleeps where she has been sent: the person handing her in will be recompensed by her master who lives on the corner of Campo de Marte...

Tribal markings

With the physical description of the runaway slave, the master added the characteristic markings of each tribe, which were differentiated even within the same nation. It was common to see in a description "face with the line markings of a *Lucumí*" or "teeth filed like a *Carabalí*", yet each *Lucumí* group had its own markings and the *Carabalí* not only filed their teeth but also had facial markings. These markings were used to help identify African slaves, though the creole-born did not as a rule adopt tribal markings beyond those habits such as filing the teeth or making a wound on the hair line. [This can be seen from the following inserts in **Diario de la Habana**:]

Lucumís

...a black named Francisco, of the *Lucumí* nation, about 40 years old, average height, a little on the heavy side, reddish, scarred face, wears an earring (February 8, 1826) ...a pure black named Mónico, of the *Lucumí* nation, *elló*, normal build, with three lines on the cheeks (April 20, 1826) ...a black of the *Lucumí* nation, *aguzá*...two long lines on each side of the face (January 1, 1834) ...a black *Lucumí* named César, a cook, with three lines on each jowl and ears pierced (January 2, 1834)

Mandingas

...a black, of the *Mandinga* nation, *osusu,* named María Dolores, of small build, slim, with two lines on the forehead in a half-oval (May 23, 1812)

Minas

...a pure black, of the *Mina* nation, named Tiburcia...with a scar on the right temple and three more lines on each like the *Carabalí* (October 26, 1831) ...Pedro Antonio, of the *Mina* nation...three lines on each temple characteristic of the nation (September 28, 1815)

Gangás

...a black named Joaquín, of the *Gangá* nation...back and belly with the markings of the nation (January 1, 1826) ...one named Alejandro, with the following markings, lines on the face, both ears pierced and in one a metal ring... Miguel, reddish eyes, *Carabalí* teeth (July 13, 1831)

Congos

...a pure black *Congo muriaca,* who can't speak and only responds to Lorenzo, with a star on the forehead, one on each temple (May 21, 1831) ...a black *Congo loango,* about 12 years old, thin, long face, scar on each temple, the marking of the nation (July 2, 1831) ...age 10 or 11, *Congo real,* lines on the forehead (January 1, 1834) ...a pure black responding to the name of Lázaro, short, plump, the two front teeth cut in half-moon shape, *Congo real* (January 1, 1834)

Carabalís

> ...age about 28 or 30, *Ladino*, of the *brican* nation, metalsmith, with a scar on the head over the left temple, left ear pierced (September 21, 1815) ...a *Carabalí* black named José Manuel... upper teeth cut back, circle-shaped lines on each temple (January 18, 1826) ...a black named Francisco, *Carabalí viví*, normal height, slim, reddish with lines on the temple (July 1, 1831) ...a black *Carabalí* named Pedro, about 20, handsome round face, with two or three black lines on the temples (September 2, 1831) ...a black who went out to sell water from a barrel, *Carabalí*, named Nicolás... who has round markings the size of a coin from the wrist to the shoulder on both arms some two inches apart (September 3, 1831)...

Creoles

Save in rare exceptions, creoles did not adopt the tribal markings of their forbears and could more easily escape their persecutors. Even so:

> ...runaway from his house since the beginning of November, the black Bernardo, creole, normal height, slim, long face, with a pronounced scar on the forehead toward the left side on the hairline (January 3, 1834) ...runaway from her master's house, the black Jacoba, creole, around 36, fairly tall and slim, bright eyes, thick lips and hair, uneven teeth and with the upper teeth filed (March 4, 1845)

Midwives

In Havana during the period 1820-1845, midwifery was in the main carried out by women of color, principally those classified as free *pardas* (mulatto women). This fact of the social division of labor on the island under slavery was cause for comment in **Diario de La Habana**, February 6, 1828, in an article entitled "The Public Good":

> It is a very sad fact that in all parts of the civilized world the art of midwifery is considered among the honorable professions, and that only on the island of Cuba, through deep-

> seated tradition, perhaps originating in the scarcity of white persons in the nascent population, should it be degraded and left wholly to the most wretched and destitute women of color in the city.

A few days earlier, the paper had informed readers that the Academy of Midwifery in the Women's Hospital of San Francisco de Paula was about to open and exhorted enrolment in the institution. While the Academy did not set limitations on color, it did practise the separatist policy of primary schools and allocated different days for white students and students of color...

The increase in the Havana population and growing number of women practising midwifery without adequate knowledge motivated publication of the **Examen y cartilla de parteras teórica y práctica** (Manual on Theory and Practice for Midwives) in 1824 by Dr Domingo Rosaín, whose prologue emphasizes the need to bring white women into the profession of widwife...

According to the manual, midwives should observe three points, related to the morality of slave society and religion.

> First: How they should conduct themselves during clandestine births, with women who give birth in the secrecy of their homes.
>
> Second: The care they must take in having them take the last rites given the risks entailed.
>
> Third: The great attention to having infants baptized when they have little chance of survival. If these requirements were not met, they would not be fulfilling their obligation and would have to answer to God.

In addition to the requisite of being a good Christian, clean, charitable, careful and pleasant, the midwife, in whose discretion lies the honor of "women who give birth in the secrecy of their homes", must be respectful of her patients, "observing the utmost silence in cases where this is necessary, endeavoring to forget even their names; because very often such a lack of precaution exposes one of good repute..."

JESÚS COS CAUSSE

Drum ballad

Poems taken from **Balada de un tambor y otros poemas** (Drum Ballad and Other Poems), Unión, Havana, 1987, pp 22, 67-68 and **Como una serenata** (Like a Serenade), Letras Cubanas, Havana, 1988, pp 85-86, 78-80.

Maroon settlement

Silence

The Maroons are gathered together
fuelling the fire of cane uprisings
Cuffy hands out angry cowrie
Nanny baptizes the warriors
with the blackest waters of the Niger
Fedon kisses the land and kisses the drum
Ganga Zumba speaks of Brazil and dances
Mackandal puts out his fire and is gone

Day breaks and the settlement is deserted

Drum ballad on the map of the Caribbean (Excerpt)

A drum for the Congo and for Guinea and for Angola. A land drum for the boats and for the ashes of the conquistadors. A drum of thunder for the slave trade and for the graveyard of the ocean and for the throne and for the crown and for the king. A drum for the songs of the slaves. A drum of joy for the ceremonies of the maroons. A drum of peace and of hope for the grave of the ox. A drum for beauty and for the battle steed and for the bee calmly seeking honey. A drum for the snake and for the turtle and for the hutia. A drum for the earthenware jar. A drum for the signs of the bats and for the cross of the owl. A drum for the poinciana and for the *yagruma* and for the silk cotton and for the mahogany. A drum for the copper and for the charcoal and for the bauxite. A drum of dawn for the mist and of bearings for the storm. A drum of bamboo to weave baskets. A drum of banner and rebellion for the Caribbean. A drum with bulwark and a halberd. A drum.

The güijes

1

The *güijes* slept from Africa to Cuba
and only woke when they heard
the drums. They came through
storms and crossed the seas in the face
of Caribbean hurricanes. That's why they
are children of the rains and live in the waters. They
say a slave tired of being a slave opened
the jars and the *güijes* escaped, this the
canefield knows, the palm tree knows,
the hummingbird knows, and so does the moon
of that night the slave was seen to open
the jars and the *güijes* came out, while he sang
a freedom song.

2

Since then the *güijes* have names
like warriors and drums of battle and
songs of war and swords of stone,
to defend themselves from crabs and
snakes. They are enemies of the whip and
friends of the fire. They call on lightning
and watch over the thunder. They peep through
leaves following the lightning flashes
and at the bottom of the river have

a secret hoard of light and on the surface a map
of lost stars.

3
The *güijes*. *Güijes* dream of being like
the doves and butterflies, of flying over
the land, to steal the perfume of the
flower. *Güijes* dream of the mermaids and
are in love with the fireflies. *Güijes*
talk with the glowworms and flee from the
crickets, for glowworms light the paths and
crickets are traitors. *Güijes* are
masters of the colors of the rainbow and the
calm of dusk. *Güijes* dream of being like
the *yagruma* when it groans by night
remembering the slave hung from its trunk
and they love the beauty of the poinciana
which is a song to freedom. Dreamers
and lovers, the *güijes*.

Family legend

Grandmother took me once to see the *güijes* of the Cauto River,
but the *güijes* come to the surface at night,
when the moon is full, casting light over the earth
trembling as they come out to see if life still exists
That's why we couldn't see them.
The *guïje* is persecuted slave childhood
fleeing the body after the whip.
The *güijes* live in the rivers of Africa and the Caribbean, she said,
watching over the universe,
and they turn into a bloodstain if you catch them asleep.

Every evening grandfather sang Haitian laments and his hands
were shaking as he played the guitar of ebony notes and warbles,

he'd go off to cry under the *guásima* tree at the bottom of
the garden,
near coffee groves and canefields, a lone old man would look
out to sea.
He was happy on his travels.
Later he'd return with baskets full of birds, bellflowers
and fireflies from another island
saying he'd talked with mermaids and had thousands of
hidden corals.
My mother is an island so remote that shells are washed up
dead on her shore.
My mother is gray like Guadeloupe and sad like Martinique.
Her paths are crossed by a galloping Toussaint L'Ouverture.
Amidst her waters sails the errant crew of Marcus Garvey.

The steps of Jacques Roumain come closer seeking a door
and a woman, a foam image, recedes and I love her.

Someone beckons and it's true my blood and my island flow,
that I was born
with my fists clenched and my musical name is a tear of old.

What *güije* haunts my childhood? Who lifts the whip?
Who sings this lament and frightens this dove?
Which island sinks while a woman awaits me midst heroes
and poets?

ODILIO URFÉ

Claudio José Domingo Brindis de Salas (1852-1911)

Taken from **Pentagrama**, Year 1, No 4, July 1956, reprinted in Armando Toledo (ed) **Presencia y vigencia de Brindis de Salas** (Presence and Relevance of Brindis de Salas), Letras Cubanas, Havana, 1981, pp.135-137.

There is much need for a calmly revised, well-documented history of music and its principal exponents to be undertaken and published. While it is true that there are several works of varying length, which attempt to cover various aspects of Cuban music's historical process, we cannot single out two or three which are serious, meticulous and exhaustive in their treatment of the subject and could thus be described as "fundamental" or "major". This sad fact has meant that the great mass of people confuse or are not familiar with many outstanding Cuban musicians whose artistic and cultural merit deserves something more than the oblivion or erroneous appreciation they receive at present.

Among the great figures of Cuban music, the violinist Brindis de Salas is one of those who is perfectly well known to all Cuban people, is praised at times with exaggeration, and at others with a lack of historical realism.

It would take many more pages than those available to us here to enumerate the causes of all the phenomena currently surrounding the fascinating figure of Brindis de Salas. But it should escape no discerning eye that his ethnic, social and economic status caused serious setbacks to his artistic development.

His undeniably powerful musical faculties have been targetted by critics, who had focused on his social success in a way that derives more from his artistic qualities than from his social background.

The total lack of verifiable information of any kind about the meteoric career of the "black Paganini" has contributed to this: his record at the Paris Conservatory, concert programs, documentation of interviews, reviews and other very interesting papers such as those accrediting him with the medals and trophies referred to by almost all his panegyrists, not because this has been verified directly but because it was written in a journal or other publication — national or foreign — based on dubious sources.

These realities and comments aside, virtually no-one would deny that Brindis de Salas is one of the great among the greats of America. It has often been attempted, unwisely, to compare him with [José] White, who, along with Brindis and [Rafael] Díaz Albertini, made up the trio of most outstanding Cuban violinists of the 19th century.

White, as well as being a great figure, was a complete musician due to his technical training and solid concepts of music and culture, which have evidently come together in his compositions of a pedagogic, religious and nationalistic nature. And when, moreover, that illustrious *matancero*[a] was brilliant in the difficult field of conducting an orchestra, it is illogical to strike a comparison with Brindis.

Even as violinists, White and De Salas were opposites in a general sense, although the two came from the same school and even, I would think, mentors.[b] White was austere, albeit impassioned. His profoundly humanistic, ethical concepts of the art of music enabled him to take on the most complex works of the most sound schools, from the baroque up until his day. There are still musicians in Paris who clearly recall an already aging White interpreting Bach's Partitas and Sonatas for Violin Solo and finishing with two geniuses of the violin called Von Joachim and Pablo de Sarasate. The musicians, who are the ones who know about these things, openly expressed themselves in favor of the renditions of this modest but tremendous Cuban. He was a faithful slave to his art in general, and his instrument in particular.

Brindis de Salas was essentially a romantic in the misleading concept of romanticism of the late 19th century, stemming from virtuosity as a supreme manifestation of the instrumentalist, without taking into consideration the work, much less the composers and their schools.

He did what he wanted. He violated or altered strict basic rules, although it would seem that, thanks to his rare powers of penetration and beautiful sound, he obtained unexpectedly pleasant "effects". As a rule he always played the same composition differently; at times he was like a fourth-year student, playing out of tune and in disarray because "he was upset or apathetic" and at others he was a veritable colossus of the violin with a finesse of interpretation and abolute dominion of the technical aspects of his instrument. Broadly speaking, that was the violinist Brindis de Salas, which is not to say, I repeat, that he was any the less great.

This is why there is a fundamental need for exhaustive methodical research, to establish all that goes to make up such an impressive figure.

Today, hastily writing these lines about the famous *habanero*,[c] I do so with the impulsive aim of making a modest yet sincere contribution to bringing alive in imagination the work that musicians like Brindis de Salas, [Ignacio] Cervantes, [Manuel] Saumell, [Alejandro] García Caturla and other no less singular figures have handed down to us, showing a clearly marked way to historical greatness and dedication.

Editors' notes

a. Matanzas, a north-coast town to the east of Havana, was famed for its musical and literary tradition; *matancero/a* is a resident of Matanzas.

b. White was a pupil of J.D. Alard, while Brindis was a pupil of Sivori, Leonard and Dancla.

c. A Havana person is *habanero/a*.

RODOLFO SARRACINO

Back to Africa

Excerpts from Chapter II "Encuentros en Lagos y Matanzas" (Encounters in Lagos and Matanzas) in **Los que volvieron A AFRICA** (Those Who Returned TO AFRICA), Ciencias Sociales, Havana, 1988, pp. 47-50, 51-2, 54-62.

Contrary to what Fernando Ortiz[1] maintained, a stay in Lagos from 1980 to 1982 convinced us that there were groups of free and emancipated blacks who had sought voluntary repatriation from Cuba to Africa, and were leaving their cultural mark on the west coast, without being absorbed by other immigrant groups or by the local population.

Second and third generations have preserved a knowledge of the Spanish language, surnames, near and distant relatives in Cuba, offering irrefutable proof of a Cuban presence in Lagos, capital of the most populous African nation, as well as in other places on the African coast.

Confronting this presence with little known, unpublished documents leads us to conclude that the desire to return to Africa, for which "Cuban" free blacks went to untold sacrifice, was exploited by another colonial power. Behind the anti-slave clamor of Great Britain was the endeavor to replace the Hispanic slave system by the no less inhumane salaried exploitation on African cotton and cocoa plantations.

Our first hypothesis, based on the testimony of first- and second-generation descendants, is that, far from diminishing — as Pérez de la Riva affirmed, in the absence of documentation and oral testimony — the desire to return to the land of Nigeria took hold among a growing number of free blacks, especially Yoruba, after the 1844 Escalera Conspiracy and continued after the abolition of slavery in 1886. This is a priori convincing when we consider that, for example, in 1854 — when the social force for the 1868-1878 Great War was not yet unleashed — an emigratory wave was already apparent. Thus, there was even more reason for it to have existed after that first war of independence and after abolition was proclaimed, simply because there were far fewer obstacles, less danger in the crossing and in staying in Nigeria and on the west coast of Africa.

Beyond this general observation, in February 1981 we had the opportunity to establish relations with a group of families in Lagos, descended from repatriated ex-slaves from Cuba. This, of course, was not by chance. Before traveling to Nigeria, I had discussed the research with Professors Manuel Moreno Fraginals, Pedro Deschamps Chapeaux, Zoila Lapique Becali and Rogelio Martínez Furé, among others. In the course of my work among the citizens of Lagos, the topic of historical and cultural links between Cuba and Nigeria inevitably came up, and also the question as to the whereabouts of the 19th-century repatriated families.

In a factory in Apapa, Lagos, an old cement worker, Sam Kanokafe, now retired, talked to us at length about the "Cuban" families, and to help us locate them drew us a simple map of the place, in the center of Lagos Island, where I should be able to find Hilario Campos' family, whose descendants still live near the square and street named after him. My curiosity aroused, I paid them a visit that same day. I was received by Mr. and Mrs. Gooding. Mr. Gooding, a Yoruba from Sierra Leone, is the husband of Hilario Campos' daughter. He was 80 at that time, and Campos' daughter, 75. Our meeting, totally unexpected by them, turned out to be quite an event. We were welcomed with great jubilation, and a party was quickly organized in Yoruba tradition, with beer and palm wine. It wasn't forced, but, they told me, a natural reaction to me having been the first Cuban to set foot in the Cuban Lodge, the name of the house which, according to family history,[2] was built by Hilario Campos to house ex-slaves repatriated from Havana.

It was a single-story, stone house comprising two dwellings, each with its own entrance and mock classical facade. Above the entrance, a plaque with large lettering: Cuban Lodge. Down the side, a passage led to an inner courtyard and the entrance to four dwellings with several bedrooms, bathroom, kitchen-dining room and lounge, all small in dimension. The two main dwellings, designed for the main families and their offspring, were similarly laid out, but larger than the others. At the time of our first visit, Mr. Gooding and his wife lived in one of the interior apartments, while the main apartment was reserved for their eldest son, Okundayo, who was away studying in England, at Oxford University.

It is clear from the architectural design that an effort had been made to combine private life (apartments) and communal living (central courtyard) with the patriarchal vocation of the owner, Hilario Campos (main dwelling). The central courtyard was still used for family gatherings, children's games and various educational activities. The Cuban Lodge, painted blue-gray and white, stood out for its bright, clean paintwork and general neat appearance.

Shortly after I arrived, Mistress C.A. King, granddaughter of Campos on her mother's side, and Mistress A.M. Fakolujo, 68 years old, granddaughter of another ex-slave named Garro, came in. Both she and Campos' daughter were able to articulate and understand odd sentences in Spanish. They spoke English, but preferred to communicate in Yoruba. According to Mistress Fakolujo,[3] the two ex-slaves, Campos and Garro, returned together from Cuba and settled in Lagos. Both were carpenters by trade and with the money from their savings started up a construction business. By the start of the 20th century, Campos had made his fortune and acquired land and property on the island of Lagos.

Two small, three-storey buildings made of stone, facing the Cuban Lodge, still belonged to the family. According to Campos' daughter,[4] her father came to have considerable tracts of land on Lagos Island. In turn-of-the-century Nigerian society, Campos wielded economic power and political influence. And yet, it was difficult to find out when and where Hilario Campos was born and died. Neither the daughter, nor the grandchildren, nor close friends could tell me, produce any documents or even give me an idea of either, although family consensus inclined to think that

Hilario Campos and his friend Garro had been born near Badagry. In fact, that wasn't the case. To our surprise, on July 24, 1982, with the help of a young Nigerian Emmanuel Muñiz, to whom we will refer later, I located the white marble grave of Hilario Campos in Lagos cemetery. The inscription on the grave, because there is no register, reads:

> Hilario Campos: born in Cuba 1878. Died in Lagos, December 14, 1941, 64 years of age.

That is to say, Hilario Campos was Cuban-born after the *vientre libre* (Free Belly) Law[a] was passed, and so had probably been born free and not a slave. There is no doubt but that he was taken to Lagos by his parents as a child, because the surname existed in Lagos at the end of the 1880s. When we spoke about our findings with Zoila Lapique Becali, researcher at the José Martí National Library in Havana, she kindly drew our attention to the fact that the name of Campos appeared in a letter our noted researcher Don Fernando Ortiz had sent to the French professor Roger Bastide:

> With reference to the *babalao* Campos, whom I am told was the mayor of Lagos, I can say no more than what I have already published, which are simple personal references. For my part, I am continuing to research into this, but up until now I have found nothing new.[5]

When I took it up with them at a later date, the Campos family rejected Fernando Ortiz' version of events. Not one of the family remember Hilario having been mayor, though they did admit he had a fortune, influence and social prominence and it was possible that he had become a chief. The very hypothesis that he had been a *babaláwo* was vehemently denied by the grandson of Campos, Ekundayo... [6]

On my initial visit to the Cuban Lodge, a close relative of Filiberto Muñiz had also been present. He was a first-generation descendant of Nicolasa Muñiz, who came to Lagos at the end of the 19th century. I wasn't able to talk to Mr. Muñiz, age 68, because he was partially disabled by a stroke. Unfortunately, shortly after, his mother Nicolasa died. She had been born in Havana in 1897 and taken to Lagos at the age of two. In her memory, we were given a pamphlet of Catholic hymns in Yoruba, English and Latin, for they were all devout Catholics... This family stood out for having kept in contact with relatives in Cuba through correspondence. The Muñiz family showed me the most recent letters from their Cuban relatives and kindly gave me the address of Juana Muñiz Hérnández, old Feliberto Muñiz' cousin, in the city of Matanzas. We pursued this part of our research in Cuba.

Our meeting with the Cuban branch of the Muñiz family in March 1982 was every bit as moving. We met Juana Muñiz, her daughter Mercedes and her son Guillermo... The grandparents of Juana Muñiz were Juana Véliz and Cecilio Muñiz, both freeborn. Juana Véliz had been born in Nigeria, while Cecilio Muñiz was Cuban-born in Matanzas.[7] At the end of the 19th century, the couple decided to return to Lagos. They had a son, Andrés Muñiz, who was born in 1894 in Matanzas, and their daughter Nicolasa was born in 1897 in Havana... The family fortunes must have gone well because in 1910 they sent Andrés to study in England. It is also said that Cecilio was in the coral business.[8] In 1912, Nicolasa gave birth to Filiberto Muñiz...

Around 1919, with a bachelor's degree, Andrés Muñiz returned to Cuba as the employee of a British firm with sugar interests on the island. The fact that he spoke English and also knew Spanish through the family caused his company to send him to Cuba as an interpreter. Although his written Spanish was quite good, he always spoke with an accent, which is why his fellow workers dubbed him "the Jamaican." He went to Oriente, and was working his way through several sugar mills, getting closer to Matanzas. He was sent to work at a mill in Mariel, Pinar del Río, until a friend suggested he return to Matanzas. The decision was taken for him when the firm decided to close business in Cuba during the *Machadato*[b]. Andrés Muñiz' first concern on arriving in Matanzas was to seek out his godparents Mónica Alfonso and Bonifacio Fundora, who were still alive. He met and subsequently married Estebalina Hernández, and they had four children: Juana (53), Yolanda (51), Orlando (54) and Laudelino (48). He started work in Matanzas at Limonar sugar mill...

Since his youth in Lagos, Andrés had made a hobby of belonging to an International Postcard Club, with its base in North Wales, Britain. This enabled him to correspond with people all over the world, but especially Cuba... It is logical to think that the correspondence with Cubans helped arouse Andrés' curiosity for his country of birth... Andrés never lost this habit of letter-writing, and sending postcards and photographs. In Cuba, he would write to Estebalina Hernández, who was to be his wife, from the various mills where he was working the harvest...

It might be thought that, once he re-identified with Cuba, Andrés would have forgotten the family in Lagos. But, according to the family, because we found no letter, Andrés continued to write frequently, and punctually received letters in reply. The letters did come to an end with the deaths of Andrés and Estebalina in 1944-5. Several years went by, and then the Nigerian side of the family wrote from Lagos so insistently that the eldest duaghter Juana wrote on behalf of the Muñiz family in Matanzas. The letter, written in English by an acquaintance, and shown to us by the Muñiz family in Lagos, was dated 26 January 1950, and addressed to Filiberto Muñiz.

Juana asked the cousin she had never known to excuse her for not having replied earlier, as she was not conversant in English and therefore had to find someone who could translate the letters received from Lagos and also write back in English. In that letter Juana informed the family in Lagos that Estebalina, her mother, had died in 1944... Juana sent Filiberto the address where they were living "near some relatives on mother's side" and said that the family was receiving a pension from the company, "not much, but at least a little bit that helps." She also wrote that "Orlando is a barber, Juana looks after the house and will be getting married soon. Yolanda is studying to be a teacher, and Lino is learning a trade.

The years after Andrés died were, in all truth, a trial for his children. Relatives in Matanzas helped out, covering their most pressing needs; neither Juana nor her two brothers could study. Orlando and Laudelino both became barbers. Yolanda was able to complete her teacher training, at great sacrifice to the whole family... Yolanda wrote to Filiberto:

> You can't imagine how happy we were to hear from you, because we didn't know anything about our relatives on our father's side, and although we tried to find out, nobody told us anything about you...

In January 1980 Juana Muñiz wrote to Filiberto on the family's behalf. They were discussing the possibility of some of the Lagos Campos and Muñiz families coming to study in Cuba; from the Muñiz family it was to be "Bode", as it was his father's dream. Filiberto replied to Juana:

> Regarding my son going to see you, that will be around August this year. As for Mrs. Campos, she says it is the financial problem that is keeping her from going.[9]

That same day, "Bode" wrote on a postcard to Juana[10], would she please reply to his letters in time for him to prepare for his trip.

In March that year[11], Filiberto wrote to Juana that he had shown all the photos, including the group family photo, to the Campos family, and reiterated that his son Emmanuel would possibly be in Cuba between August 31 and September 3, 1980:

> I would like him to study about four years there for his first diploma. He would like to study 1) journalism/public relations. 2) Film production. 3) Agriculture...

In July 1980 Filiberto insists:

> Give us clearer details in your next letter, because my son must leave Nigeria at the end of August at the latest, because *I don't want him to study in Germany or the United States.*[12]

Life cut short Filiberto's plans. According to what "Bode" wrote to Juana Muñiz in October 1980, after a strong argument with his eldest son Andrés Muñiz, at the end of August, Filiberto had a stroke that paralyzed his left arm and hand. He had been hospitalized in Lagos. He had been suffering from high blood pressure. Since "Bode" was the only one available at that critical time to help his mother look after Filiberto, he couldn't travel to Cuba...

In the last letter we know of,[13] "Bode" reminds Juana that the previous letter he wrote was in March 1983 "when I was living with my sister Juana in London, before finally returning to Nigeria." In this letter, "Bode" referred to an important experience: his first visual contact with Cuba. "In London I saw a television series on the Cuban Revolution... Cuba is very beautiful..."

As usual, "Bode" brought Juana up to date on the Muñiz family:

> My mother, now as always, is a cook and calls herself Mistress María Muñiz. The first born is Michael, the second Andrés, the third Juana, the fourth Serafín. Michael got married this year. Andrés has two children, Bimbala and Peter Muñiz. Juana married and returned to London, and is now a secretary at the Home Office. She had two children, Christiana and Shala. Serafina married; has three children, Martin, Esther and Sheum; and has a business.
>
> I'm the fifth, married last year, in September, and now I am in London. My sister Agustina, the sixth, is married, with two children, Alejandra and Deiji, and is a qualified cook, and my younger brother José, the seventh, finished his studies in 1983... I'm planning to visit Cuba next summer around July and August.
>
> One of Hilario Campos' daughters, Mistress Henrieta Mambole, younger sister of Mistress Gooding, died in June 1984 at the age of 75. I was in London at the time of the burial, only my older sister Juana went back to Nigeria for the funeral...

"Bode" took his leave of the family, reiterated the family address in Lagos, and at the bottom of the letter wrote:

> Long live the Cuban Revolution! Long Live the Republic of Nigeria!

Taking a retrospective look at the Muñiz family correspondence, full of simple, everyday, intimate details that people tend to write in letters all over the world, it's easy to forget one exceptional feature: that this is a family divided by the 19th-century slave trade, whose members, some born in Cuba still under paternal tutelage, took on the incredible venture of returning to Africa and, what is even more notable, that one of the family members, born in Cuba, returned to his native country, founded a family and corresponded with the African family, a correspondence which has been kept up by the second generation, who only know what one another look like through photographs.

A singular aspect of this story is that Guillermo Lamas Muñiz, grandson of Andrés, went to Angola as an internationalist construction worker, as did Yolanda's husband, Vicente González Ramírez; and that Guillermo went to Angola with his imagination fired by returning to the land of his ancestors and wanting to visit his Nigerian relatives. Likewise, old Filiberto Muñiz, who had never been to Cuba, 69 years old and postrate, did not want to send his son to the United States or Germany to study, and insisted on him coming to Cuba, as others of the Cuban Community in Lagos also wanted to do. All of this underscores the Afro-Latin links between the lands of Nigeria and Cuba.

Endnotes

1. Fernando Ortiz **Los negros esclavos**, Havana, 1975.
2. Interview with Mr. Okundayo Gooding Campos, Lagos, 1981.
3. Interview with Mistress A.M. Fakolujo, grandson of Garro.
4. Interview with Mistress Gooding, daughter of Hilario Campos.
5. Letter from Fernando Ortíz to Professor Roger Bastide, Havana, February 3, 1954 in the Sala Cubana, José Martí National Library.
6. Interview with Ekundayo Gooding Campos.
7. Interview with Juana Muñiz, Havana.
8. Ibid
9. Postcard from Filiberto Muñiz to Juana Muñiz Hernández, Lagos, February 29, 1980.
10. Postcard from Emmanuel'"Bode" Muñiz to Juana Muñiz, Lagos, February 29, 1980.
11. Card from Filiberto Muñiz to Juana Muñiz Hernández, Lagos, March 25, 1980.

12. The author's underlining. Filiberto was particularly worried about his son's trip to Cuba because of the Mariel exodus of that time.
13. Letter from Emmanuel "Bode" Muñiz to Juana Muñiz from London, August 30, 1984.

Editors' notes

a. The Moret Law of the 1870s stipulated that those born of slaves would henceforth be free.
b. Gerardo Machado was president of Cuba from 1925-1933. His presidency was known as the *machadato*, especially as it became more and more repressive of social and political discontent as the economic depression deepened. He was ousted in the 1933 Revolution.

PEDRO SERVIAT

Solutions to the black problem

Excerpts from **El problema negro en Cuba y su solución definitiva** (The Black Problem in Cuba and its Definitive Solution), Editora Política, Havana, 1986, pp. 73-79, 98-101, 130-138, 156-164.

Black leaders and the labor movement on the race problem

From 1899 on various currents of thought were manifested regarding the solution to the black problem: the first was headed by Juan Gualberto Gómez, the independence leader and black leader with the greatest prestige after the death of the three greats: Martí, Maceo and Máximo Gómez.

Juan Gualberto Gómez believed that equality between black and white could be achieved when Afro-Cubans achieved educational levels on a par with those of the white population. His main aim in encouraging the establishment of black societies was the education of black people and this was one of his reasons for setting up the Directorate of Colored Societies at the end of the 19th century. To that end he worked tirelessly throughout the island. Juan Gualberto Gómez said to black people: "Educate yourselves, so that nobody can throw in your face that you come from a 'savage' people."

The second current was headed by Martín Morúa Delgado. Morúa, who had been pro-autonomy up until 1896 and then pro-independence, thought that exclusive groupings — even when they were founded for cultural and social betterment, or mutual aid — harmed rather than benefitted the interests of the black sector. "The Negro race, the colored classes, must on no account set themselves apart from the white race, because they thus confirm their sectorial state for life... making impossible their noble aspiration to raising their station... To group into factions would only perpetuate the race line."[1] Morúa thought that the black should be accepted into all walks of economic, political, social and cultural life.

Both believed that black people should work for their own betterment, and the most influential black people were grouped in one or the other current. The third current was what might be called the "hard" line, party to making their demands forcefully and even with violence, if necessary. Pedro Ivonet, Evaristo Estenoz and many veterans of the War of Independence subscribed to this current, considering themselves successors to Aponte, the rebel of 1812...

In response to white racism, there was what might be termed "petit bourgeois black nationalism" among blacks, that is, those who saw race as the principal means for solving the problems, not through class struggle or the struggle for democratic goals, but that of "race against race." Advocates of this current argued that unity among whites and blacks solely benefitted the former who had the power and wealth. These groups, aside from keeping up black societies as closed institutions, were in favor of setting up beaches, businesses, industries and schools for blacks only. This was the position of the leaders of some societies in the provinces of Havana, Matanzas and Camagüey. In different towns of the island, there were attempts to set up black consumer cooperatives. In some societies separate sports movements were organized solely for young blacks...

Rafael Serra, the black emigré revolutionary leader in Key West, in his book **Para blancos y negros** (For Whites and Blacks) praised the governments of the United States for their "generosity" to black people in that country. While not denying the racism in North America, Serra was taken in by illusions of Afro-North American small traders and industrialists who in fact accounted for a tiny part of U.S. capital... In his propaganda, Rafael Serra praised the thinking of the conservative black North American leader Booker T. Washington, who called on those of his race to be obedient, peaceable and orderly, and to accept white bourgeois philanthropy. According to Booker T. Washington, the Negro should be a "good" worker to win the respect of entrepreneurs, so that in the event of a strike he would be called upon to take the white worker's place. His position was reactionary and contrary to class struggle and the unity of the proletariat...

Alongside the movement of Booker T. Washington, at the turn of the century there was the Niagara Movement in the United States led by W.E.B. Dubois. This progressive protest movement found expression in the National Association for the Advancement of Colored People. A sector of the black press of the time came out strongly in defence of the interests of the Afro-American masses against the lynchings and racial discrimination. After World War I the movement led by Marcus Garvey, the Universal Negro Improvement Association, proclaimed racial purity, condemned mixing of the races and advocated the creation of a universal black empire based in Africa. This movement gained certain influence among blacks for a time but came to nothing in the end.[2]

There was also a leftist movement led by black intellectuals sympathetic to communism and influenced by the Russian Revolution. Their main task was to organize the Association for the Study of Black Culture and History. All these movements made their mark in our country, lending a more conservative or radical imprint to the black struggle...

It should be pointed out that the worker movement of the early decades, except in the case of the apprentices,[3] had no understanding of such an important social problem as that affecting the black. In Cuba, only exceptional cases of segregated guilds existed, but there were guilds discriminating against Cubans because of the color of their skin. The anarchists didn't understand this problem either, which is why guilds led by them turned their backs on the black problem... Incomprehension of the race question on the part of the labor movement was all the less explicable considering that the majority of workers, and of the more exploited, were black; if not salaried, they were of the artisan class or poor peasantry, objectively situated in terms of class and racial discrimination along with the rest of the working masses...

Immigrant Caribbean labor and the race problem

Haitian and Jamaican immigration caused a polemic around which there were three positions.

First, U.S. sugar companies in Oriente and Camagüey encouraged the immigration because it guaranteed cheap labor for the sugar harvest, especially after 1911-12 with the sugar expansion in the eastern provinces; moreover, capitalists needed a reserve army of labor as a pressure point on those employed. This reserve army could be mobilized, by force even, in the event of a strike in the mills, as under Menocal during the years 1914-21.

Second, the more recalcitrant, racist sector of the national bourgeoisie was against the immigration for fear of a "disproportionate" increase in the black population, which according to them would lend strength to this racial sector. The old colonialist legend of the "black danger" and the whitening of the island began to curry favor. To combat this, a whole propaganda campaign was built around presenting Haitians and Jamaicans as inferior, uneducated adepts of primitive religions, and the immigrants found themselves discriminated against, isolated, harassed and threatened. They subtly sowed a new version of the danger of black rebellion similar to that of 1912 in Cuba and 1790 in Haiti.

Third, worker organizations up until 1920 were against the migrant workers because they were in competition with the home work force... The General Workers League in 1899 and the Socialist Worker Party in 1911 and 1912 made their opposition manifest. After 1925, the worker movement and Communist Party demanded equal treatment for the immigrant workers and insisted on state repatriation of those who lacked their own means of sustenance and lived in subhuman conditions...

There can be no doubting the fact that, in the conditions prevailing in Cuba, being of dark skin made the situation of Caribbean immigrant labor that much worse than that of other migrant groups coming to the island from Europe. There was evident discrimination against the workers from the Caribbean. The sugar barons used them to avert the unity of Cuban workers — whites and blacks... At the Hershey mill — today Camilo Cienfuegos — in Havana province... there were five zones: the North

Americans lived in one, which could only be entered with the corresponding pass; in the second lived the trusted white employees; in the third, the white Cubans of humble origin, Chinese and some coloreds; in the fourth the Cuban blacks; and in the fifth, the Haitians, at the bottom of the pile, for whom there were limitations on entry into food stores and recreation centres. In Punta Alegre mill — today Máximo Gómez — in Camagüey province, there was a cemetery for whites and another for blacks... In the Boston mill — today Nicaragua — in Holguín province... a North American employee was paid 48 times more than a Haitian, 11 times more than a Cuban, six times more than a Spaniard, and twice that of a Jamaican... The higher relative figure for the Jamaican was due to their specialized (non-field) labor, though in absolute terms, for the same job, they were paid less than an American or British employee.[4]

It is noteworthy that... the problem of racial mixing was brought up by racist employers and some jurists, as well as elements of the Spanish bourgeoisie, by raising the old call for "whitening" the island. A May 1917 article in an anarchist paper **El Separatista** stated "that the mixing of races was damaging to the progress of peoples".

In an attempt to encourage Spanish immigration, a lawyer, Manuel Froilán, of the Agrarian Consultation Board, declared during the second U.S. occupation:

> The rebirth of our industry and public works, which we must undertake, demands a great many workers. Social considerations, moreover, demand the immigration of individuals of the white race.
>
> We must procure an increase in the white race and, through it and within it, the disappearance of the Negro race. We are not enemy to the Negro; but if, after one or two centuries, there is only one homogeneous race, though born of heterogeneous elements, nobody can deny the good that will have been done, because even in the free and most advanced countries, the United States for example, the existence of the two races leads to daily conflict.
>
> That ill, the two races, exists here also. What is the most

rational means for bringing it to an end? By increasing one of them rapidly, and it is of course the white race we must multiply. White immigration should therefore be favored by all means possible, and that of other races totally prohibited.

Spaniards, Canary Islanders, Italians, Irish, Puerto Ricans: they are the immigrants that are suitable.[5]

The repatriation of Caribbean immigrants accused by the ruling classes of becoming a public burden was a shameful, unjust, racist spectacle. Thousands were driven out of their homes and small farms by force, put on small boats and sent to their countries of origin. The worst treated were the Haitians who were beaten with sabres, rifle butts and whips.

The press of the time reflected discontent among public opinion and foreign embassies over the authorities' handling of the migrant workers. An article published in the Communist Party paper **Bandera Roja** condemned the abuse to which the workers were victim and called on people to struggle against the transportation and exploitation of Haitians; to achieve the same rights for domestic and foreign workers; and to form a united front of black and white Cuban, Polish, Jamaican and Haitian workers.[6]

The movement for civil rights

The National Federation of Black Societies — which was later named the National Federation of Cuban Societies — was founded in 1938, with the goal of achieving equality for all Cubans. From the outset it had the support of progressive and democratic forces, which enabled it to carry out important tasks aimed at regrouping certain sectors of the black population throughout the country. The Federation directed its efforts to the Constituent Assembly of 1940 adopting legislation on racial discrimination at work and in other spheres of social and cultural life. Its activities in favor of equal citizenship in the decade 1938-48, along with those of other popular sectors, helped mobilize broad sectors of the Cuban population in defence of the super-exploited black masses. It grouped together the majority of black societies.

The Federation was not numerically strong but undoubtedly

carried political weight and was held in prestige by the public during the period in question... The Federation organized several rallies in which white and black citizens took part, to pressure legislators and government to pass measures aimed at eliminating discrimination... The process of radicalization incurred the wrath of Presidents Ramón Grau San Martín (1944-48) and Carlos Prío (1948-1952), as well as the pseudo worker leader Eusebio Mujal[7] and other politicking figures who saw the Federation as a threat to their aim of keeping the black population down. On the pretext of communist infiltration, they began to gain control of the black societies through individuals on the inside who were close to the government...

During the '40s and the '50s, the Communist Party stepped up its struggle for black people's rights, inside and outside the bourgeois parliament, working with the unions and federations, through the growing activity in black societies and through the united front committees against racial discrimination, the education campaigns, the worker and communist press, and radio... As a result, the communists' prestige increased considerably among black people. This could be seen, first and foremost, in the growing number of blacks either in the party or as sympathizers: in the 1940 Constituent Assembly and general elections, a large part of the high vote came from black sectors. The party saw its ranks swell in predominantly black neighborhoods.

In the presidential elections of 1948, the communist candidate for senator, Salvador García Aguero, took 100,000 votes, one of the highest results of any of the candidates. With the support of the black and communist vote, a black mayor, Justo Salas, was elected in Santiago de Cuba... The communists' firm and principled position caused reactionary elements to start maneuvering to win over or stop the radicalization of the black masses as they became more and more aware that the solution to their problems was tied to the general fate of the nation, to profound changes in the socio-economic structure, in short, to a definitive change in society. Thus, the struggle for black rights became part of the class struggle and the struggle for our people's national and social liberation.

In the '40s and '50s, there was a process of democratization among certain student groups at the University of Havana. There was greater racial fraternization. A committee of struggle against racial discrimination was set up which involved, among others, the leaders of our revolution, Fidel and Raúl. As a result of the integration effort, the doors of some black and white societies were opened to each other. In the Atenas Club, for example, a group named Proa was set up, to which Juan Marinello belonged. The Fraternal Unión black society organized a lecture series with white and black speakers...

During that same period, through democratic voting, workers elected a large number of blacks, among whom might be mentioned Lázaro Peña, Jesús Menéndez, Aracelio Iglesias, Pablo Sandoval, Eduardo Torriente, Juan Taquechel, elected for their firmness and honesty in defence of the interests of the working class and the people as a whole. They were partial steps toward total unity, and served to demonstrate that integration was possible — above all among workers and sincere democrats — independent of race, and, when the time was ripe, this would happen in accordance with the true history of the nation.

Black nationalism

The growing radicalization of the black masses and their incorporation into the revolutionary democratic struggle of the '40s and the '50s gave rise to tendencies and groups wanting to divert it from the correct path. Some of these were the new forms of petit-bourgeois black nationalism (*negrismo*) arguing that only blacks, without whites, could solve their own problems and exaggerating the role played by black culture (negritude). With a false concept of history, these groups saw only the African contribution to Cuban culture, sowing distrust of whites.

Among the more sectarian manifestations of this trend was the propaganda put out by the black lawyer Juan René Betancourt, who set up a group called the Organización Nacional de Rehabilitación Económica (National Organization for Economic Rehabilitation, ONRE) and in his native city of Camagüey set up a black trade cooperative.

His main ideas were set out in two books: **Doctrina negra** (Black Doctrine), written in late 1950, and **El negro, ciudadano**

del futuro (The Negro, Citizen of the Future), published in 1959. These books might be considered as the highest expression of black nationalism: sectarian, and against any form of integration.

Heedless of the laws of social development, the author argued the case for the economic liberation of the black through setting up black industrial and trade cooperatives by means of shares paid for by members' work. They would accept no government handouts. The funds collected from the blacks themselves in the cooperatives would be invested in selected trades and industries. The initial capital would come from 100,000 blacks who would contribute one peso each.

Betancourt was proposing a hardly new, ahistorical form of black capitalism. He did not take into account that these utopian ideas had long ago been refuted by Marx and Engels, unmasking Proudhon's famous exchange banks and the utopian cooperatives of the disciples of Owen, Fourier and Saint Simon. Neither did he consider that the cooperative movement that grew up within the European and Cuban working class during the 19th and early 20th century had failed completely, due to the limited bourgeois nature of these bodies in a class-divided society. Moreover, among the founders of the majority of these cooperatives there was a group of opportunists awaiting their moment to make off with the money of ordinary members, who were never in contact with cooperative leaders.

But if Betancourt's economic ideas were completely ahistorical, his political and social ideas were much more alien and reactionary. He established an absurd difference between the social and the national, distinguishing between the outlook of the black as black and the black as citizen. Thus, for example, Antonio Maceo, Juan Gualberto Gómez, Brindis de Salas and communist leaders, since they were at the service of the country and their respective organizations, could not be considered black leaders. The only black leaders in Cuba were José Antonio Aponte, killed in 1812, and Evaristo Estenoz, killed in 1912. He was totally against racial integration, which he considered always favored whites. He praised the attitude of North American blacks for fending for themselves. He also denied any possibility of union with whites, even when they were revolutionary and progressive, calling them "philanthropist" rather than socially advanced in their conduct.

When he analyzed the colored independents he was not to do so on the basis of an objectively critical and historical appraisal of the facts but rather, he passionately believed that the followers of Estevenoz and Ivonet, whom he saw as martyrs of the black race, were right.

Betancourt argued that racial discrimination and prejudice was innate to all whites. If prejudice was naturally ordained in the white historical tradition, why then did thousands of whites and blacks vote freely for black political and trade union leaders? Why did thousands of whites and blacks, not all in the Communist Party, vote for the presidential ticket in 1948 which had Juan Marinello as president, Lázaro Peña as vice-president and Salvador García Aguero as senator?

According to his views, all descendants of Europeans benefitted equally from racial divisions and prejudices. At no point did Betancourt look to the labor movement in Cuba, which brought whites and blacks together. He failed to understand that the condition of exploitation was the principal factor behind unity among workers, whether white, black or mulatto, Cuban or foreign; that separation is always a temporary phenomenon until one by one they become aware that, in the last instance, their strength lies in unity and fraternity, not separation...

Revolution, the definitive solution

One of the most difficult and complex of the many problems that were the legacy of the past, was without a doubt that of racial discrimination. It was one of the questions that had been systematically sidestepped by all previous bourgeois and pseudo-revolutionary governments. Nobody familiar with the revolutionary stand taken by Fidel, from the start of the struggle, can doubt that from the outset he voiced the need to wipe out the hateful discrimination against blacks, which he saw as a blot on our country.

Revolutionaries were aware of many examples of Fidel's fraternal, humane and just nature, devoid of base prejudice... But, accustomed to the lies, the demogagy and politicking of the past — when blacks were systematically cheated and deceived —

many thoughtless or ill-disposed disbelievers did not imagine that Fidel would risk taking on such a sensitive and embarassing problem as that of the race question in Cuba.

Fidel addressed this problem in two major speeches on 22 and 29 March 1959. After pointing out that the people's mentality was conditioned by many prejudices, he said: "...the worst of all forms of racial discrimination is that of barring the Cuban black from sources of work..."[8] Fidel recalled Martí and declared that virtues, personal merits, heroism and a good nature must be the qualities by which men are judged, not the pigmentation of their skin. He denounced racial discrimination and prejudice as anti-nation, and reiterated the historical ethnic factors which make up the Cuban nation. His words were a manifestation that revolutionary power born of the people and created to serve the people, could not want to divide but rather unify the workers in the face of their enemies at home and abroad. Discriminatory practices could have no place in the new revolutionary order.

Like all humane revolutionaries, Che was sensitive to the sufferings of oppressed ethnic groups. In a speech of 7 April 1959 at the electrical workers union, he referred to this, and on 28 December 1959, on receiving an honorary doctorate from the Faculty of Las Villas, said:

> ...what do I have to say to the university as a first priority, as an essential function of its existence in this new Cuba? I have to say that it should paint itself black, it should paint itself mulatto, not only its students but also its professors; that it paint itself worker and peasant, that it paint itself people, because the university is the heritage of none, it belongs to the Cuban people...and the people that have triumphed, that have been spoiled with triumph, that know their own strength and that they can overcome, that are here today at the doors of the university, the university must be flexible and paint itself black, mulatto, worker and peasant, or it will have no doors, the people will break them down and paint the university the colors they want...[9]

In the first commemoration of the Bronze Titan — after the Revolution, in the "Year of Liberation" — Raúl Castro asked:

> ...What should we do about the men and women of black skin, for whom Maceo fought, suffering the same anguish of inequality that he suffered in his admirable body and spirit? We know what we must do. Because we take the commitment of José Martí and Antonio Maceo as our own. On this night of tribute, I wish to remember those great heroes of yesteryear, as we embark upon this new revolution, the phase which is ours to live...[10]

A National Integration Committee — which had been functioning for some ten years — reorganized in January 1959... At a meeting held by the Committee were trade union and youth leaders and prominent intellectuals such as Elías Entralgo, Salvador García Aguero, Nicolás Guillén, Juan B. Kourí, José Felipe Carneado, Lázaro Peña and others. Ernesto Che Guevara, in a closing address, spoke against racism and discrimination and in favor of national integration. Lázaro Peña, on behalf of Cuban workers, called for support for Fidel's position and asked that the unions implement measures against discrimination in employment. Employees of banks, a sector that was highly discriminatory, declared their support...

Two distinguished Cuban men of science, Doctors Fernando Ortiz and Diego González Martín, made statements supporting those of Fidel. Ortiz, as a researcher, anthropologist and ethnologist, called for an end to racism and even went so far as to question the very existence of the races, in keeping with a position he had taken years before. González Martín, a psychiatrist, delved into the socio-economic and psychological causes generating racism and racial prejudice.

The triumph of the Revolution was the clarion call for a far-reaching struggle against racial discrimination, that terrible legacy left by the imperialist colonial past. To this end, measures were taken in 1959 to implement what had thus far been dead letter...

To what extent did the Cuban Revolution achieve full racial integration, with the rights of blacks fully revindicated? Without a doubt, the main gain was to guarantee the right to work for all citizens under equal conditions. This was achieved with some concrete measures. The Revolution opened secretarial schools, with priority for former domestics, the majority black. Many of them later went on to work in banks as secretaries, clerks, etc. The opening of catering, management and foreign service schools enabled thousands of black and white citizens of humble origin to train in various fields... The beaches, sports and recreational centers were nationalized... The Revolution put culture at the service of the people; revindicated Cuban national culture; encouraged popular values in young people, irrespective of race or sex; helped to promote values previously discriminated against such as those of African origin practised by slaves, blacks and free coloreds; promoted mass study of all the popular arts; and, it goes without saying, set up a socialist education system, one for the whole island, for all citizens, male and female, blacks, whites, workers and peasants. In Cuba there is no longer any private education, which was a source of racial discrimination... Another measure taken was to permit the entry of black men and women into certain sports such as fencing, gymnastics, swimming, tennis, shooting, horse riding and rowing, previously prohibited to blacks... Today scores of young blacks and mulattoes are among the most outstanding in national sports, with international ranking... With the elimination of discrimination, housing in places once exclusive to the white aristocracy went to black and white families... The revolutionary integration of the people in mass social organizations such as the Central de Trabajadores de Cuba (Confederation of Cuban Workers, CTC), Federación de Mujeres Cubanas (Federation of Cuban Women, FMC) and the Asociación Nacional de Agricultores Pequeños (National Association of Small Farmers, ANAP) is another factor that has contributed to full racial integration... The Cubans' right to full equality, with no distinction of race, sex or national origin, is laid out in our socialist Constitution, passed by the overwhelming majority of the working people and brought into effect on 24 February 1976...

The economic, cultural and social development of the nations of the socialist community has shown that the only theory that is scientific and can offer adequate solutions to the complex social problems of any nation, is Marxism-Leninism. Because the ruling classes had a vested interest in maintaining racial discrimination as a mechanism of competition and division between the black and the white worker, and thereby profited more, it is precisely through the expropriation of these classes that the main economic factor propping up racial or sexual discrimination is eliminated...

Endnotes

1. Joel James Figarola **Cuba 1900-1908: república dividida contra si misma**, Oriente, Santiago, 1974, pp.163-4.
2. Marcus Garvey visited Cuba in 1921 to recruit followers for his movement. He was largely unsuccessful. Some members of the Atenas Club told him they were first Cuban and then black.
3. In 1902 there was a major Havana cigar makers' strike over abuses in the apprenticeship system, especially in the more exclusive trades such as cigar sorting which employed predominantly Spanish workers.
4. Ariel James Figueredo **Banes: Imperialismo y nación en una plantación azucarera**, Ciencias Sociales, Havana, 1976, p.187.
5. Manuel Froilán Cuervo (1908) **Cuestión agraria y cuestión obrera**, p.17.
6. **Bandera Roja**, Havana, 5 January 1934, p.1.
7. Eusebio Mujal came in as leader of the *oficialista* trade union movement, after a 1947-8 cold-war purge of communist-led unions.
8. Fidel Castro "Discurso en la concentración popular en el Palacio Presidencial", **Hoy**, Havana, 24 March 1959, p.6.
9. Ernesto Guevara "Discurso en el acto de investidura de Doctor Honoris Causa en la Universidad Central "Martha Abréu", **Hoy**, Havana, 1 January 1960, p.2.
10. Raúl Castro "Conmemoración del Titán de Bronce", **Revolución**, Havana, 8 December 1959, p.2.

DOMINGO ALFONSO

Times I walk with my father

Taken from **Letras Cubanas**, Havana, April-June 1987, p.51.

There are times I walk with my father among the fantastic
ironwork of the sugarmill and the old folk
who saw my mother in diapers;
or in today's storehouses where the scrub once grew,
we go among old furnaces that saw me little
or between the tracks that will see me die.

There are times the two of us walk in silence...
My father greets tired workers
returning home from their labors;
they might ask after my mother waiting
at home with our monotonous lunch,
and make some passing comment that I'm almost a man.

My father answers them with little to say,
thinking perhaps of his parents already dead.
I look quietly at his drooping head
thinking of the children I shall have one day.

TOMÁS FERNÁNDEZ ROBAINA

The 20th century black question

Excerpts from **El negro en Cuba, 1902-1958: apuntes para la historia de la lucha contra la discriminación racial** (The Black in Cuba, 1902-1958: Notes for a History of the Struggle against Racial Discrimination), Ciencias Sociales, Havana, 1990, pp.37-43, 59-63, 135-138, 144-159, 170-171, 159-162, 183-187. Editors' title and subtitles.

Juan Gualberto Gómez and the Platt Amendment

In 1901, after prolonged debate, the Constituent Assembly passed the Cuban Constitution, with the Platt Amendment. By virtue of that Amendment, the United States took upon itself the right to military intervention in the island should circumstances deem necessary such action. Moreover, the Cuban government was proscribed from entering into agreements with third countries without the consent of Washington.

Juan Gualberto Gómez and General Bartolomé Masó were the Amendment's main opponents... The elections called by the Constituent Assembly were held in December that year. The candidates were General Masó and Tomás Estrada Palma. The former did not have the US government's support. The latter had lived for many years in the United States and was overtly pro-U.S. Before the elections were held, it was clear that the Americans would not allow power to go to those who had opposed the Amendment. The coalition supporting General Masó decided to abstain from the elections, a decision occasioned also by the irregularities observed in the selection of members of the electoral commission, who were all supporters of Estrada Palma...[1]

With the victory of Estrada Palma, the already existing unease among blacks was accentuated as a consequence of his racial policy... [At a meeting of June 29, 1902, in the Albizu Theater, organized by the Committee of Veterans and Societies of the Colored Race], the first to speak was Ramiro Cuesta. He spoke of the need for that evening's meeting to show that the rumors being spread that the blacks were stirring up trouble and threatening uprising were a lie. It was sad and painful, he said, that after a long and bitter struggle for emancipation, the colored race needed to meet in such a way to claim their rights...[2]

Lino D'ou, the second speaker, condemned the prevailing social state in the name of Cubans treated unjustly in their legitimate demands. Their rights were cruelly curtailed by the delegates of Executive Power and by those who would deny to some for the color of their skin, what they would lavishly bestow on the Spanish fighter and those who had turned their backs on their country.

Silverio Sánchez Figueras... aware of the dangers involved in the Platt Amendment, added as a solution to internal problems and by way of averting its implementation: "The blacks will not be able to do anything without the whites, who in turn will not be able to do much without the blacks. Let us all come together, without reservation, or duplicity, to safeguard our nation and our existence from the threat of danger..."

The last to speak was Juan Gualberto Gómez. According to the press of the time, he gave the longest speech and the one most punctuated by applause. He gave abundant examples, some of which were important in explaining the causes of certain discriminatory measures that had met with little opposition in Cuba for fear of prolonging occupation of the island. One such example referred to organizing the Havana Police with whites only, on the initiative and express instruction of General Ludlow, the order having been given, in his own words, "...not for the Cubans, but for the Americans... and, so as colored people do not think they are being excluded by the system, they can join the police in the countryside and the cities where they have no contact with North American soldiers."[3]

Juan Gualberto Gómez declared that many of those who had

been in agreement with the policy of avoiding giving the Yankees any reason to prolong the occupation, were now raising a hue and cry, arguing that those who aimed to implement the principles of the Cuban Revolutionary Party founded by Martí were provoking the indefinite stay of U.S. troops. He emphasized that there could be no danger in the demand of the colored race that the commitments of the Revolution be met and that Article 11 of the Constitution be fully complied with. His last words were addressed to Representatives, Senators, leaders of parties and government, asking that they pay heed to the problems and demands put forward that evening, for the Committee of Veterans and Societies of the Colored Race to be dissolved when completely unnecessary... Juan Gualberto was of the opinion that Cuban whites should take up the leadership of the progressive movement, supported by blacks, given that the whites had greater possibilities for doing so. He did not see that the full materialization of his ideas could be prevented by the class contradictions within Cuban society. From the time of the Directorate, he had declared himself in favor of black and white unity. He called himself the "man of concord".

Accordingly, he declared: "If the day were to come to pass, through provocation on either side, when the black race would need to fight the white, they would have to find another man to advise or guide them. Because I represent the policy of the brotherhood of man, and should this fail, my sense of honor, my respect for the past, and the sincerity with which I uphold my convictions are such that, having failed, I would have to leave the political scene."[4]

Evaristo Estenoz and the Independent Colored Party

[There are documents] on Evaristo Estenoz' efforts in 1906 to group together the blacks in Cienfuegos. Colonel George F.C. Chase reported that the blacks were "discontented with the treatment received from the Liberal Party and had formed an independent party."

This leads us to think that Estenoz had it in mind to set up a political organization from 1905. What is certain is that during 1907 Estenoz publicized that aim. In a letter published in El

Triunfo addressed to Aguilar Tomás, he contested Aguilar Tomás' idea that a political grouping of men of color was not expedient.

Estenoz replied as follows: "...all that is said is flawed in a way that is common to these cases, making the same mistakes and the same comparisons, the express purpose being to demonstrate that there is no need to aim for our improvement because all is well with us here. Those who counter our complaints do so with the same arguments of patriotism, when we are the personification of sacrifice condemned to suffer all for the good of the Republic and democracy, the benefits of which we have not yet shared."[5]

The Independent Colored Group's constitution is indication that their work had already produced an organized political plan. A week after the Group was formed, the first issue of **Previsión**, the Independents' paper edited and circulated largely in Havana, came out. The paper is the most valuable source of documentation we have on the organization, membership, socio-political and economic program, and general activities of the Independents.

In the first issue, Estenoz laid out the reasons for the Group's formation: "The Republic's elections and the Political Parties' selection of candidates from the so-called colored race have shown many things: the first is that the colored race of Cuba can expect nothing from the procedures used to date by the POLITICAL PARTIES... We shall show that by putting forward all candidates of color, as independents, it will be apparent to all that no matter how small a minority the the results produce, it will be greater than what has so far been achieved by all the groups in the various parties.

"We shall have greater representation and greater consideration, not yet achieved nor likely to be achieved if we continue in the same way. This will not detract from the principles held by the majority of colored people, we shall continue to be liberals because we cannot in all decency, justifiably, be other than liberals with a conscience, with principles and dogmas, with democratic procedures and full rights as electors and elected in appreciable and distinguishable number, representing the Cuban people as they are. No people attains liberty on their knees before those who enslave them, no man can have rights if he does not make use of them, because it is not enough to have them and not know and defend them, and the age in which we live is such that not even ladies respond to lovers prostrate at their feet.

"Freedom is not asked or begged for, it is won; and rights are not handed out anywhere, rights are fought for and belong to all. If we go on asking for our rights, we will die waiting because we will have lost them. Faith kills the spirit when we have faith in others rather than ourselves, because it kills initiative. This is what has happened to Cuban people of color, who have lived as an immense flock and have perished in slavery because all slaves are apt for conquest, and if at times we are unjustly labelled ungovernable, we have at least not succumbed to passive servitude.

"Nobody will be able to look askance, nobody would have the right to contest the elections, deny the positions we win. Nobody can think that the peace will be disturbed when those who rule are black, when we do so with a legitimate right through suffrage as Cubans; as up until now no black sees a danger in rulers who are all white Cubans. What we blacks do see as a danger is that in the parties we become no more than mindless instruments of all political combinations and beasts of burden for all aspirations; it has been proven this time that for any desire to be considered, for any aspiration to be met, to be thought suitable for any position, it is sufficient to be white."[6]

Class struggle against racial discrimination

Our National Poet Nicolás Guillén had warned objectively in 1929 of the danger of the black problem in Cuba moving toward a Harlem-type solution.[7] This is a sign that such a tendency exists, copied from the North American black way of life. It should come as little surprise, therefore, that in October 1933 **Diario de la Marina** published a manifesto signed by the Kuban Ku Klux Klan... [referring to Cuba as a mixed race country asking]: "Must it be so?" And responding firmly in the belief of a unanimous "No!"... on the grounds that "peoples are weakened by racial mixing". On this basis, "This organization maintains that each of the races that exist in Cuba — and there should only be two —

should exist separately from the other..."[8]

The Kuban Ku Klux Klan was short-lived... the idea of a Ku Klux Klan and the slogan of self-determination for blacks, especially the so-called Oriente black strip, found little mass support, especially in such an important decade in Cuban history, when workers, peasants, and the people in general were fighting heroically against the Machado dictatorship. The black problem was set for the first time in the context of class struggle...

Fabio Grobart, then President of the Institute of History of the Communist Party and Worker Movement of Cuba, made some pertinent remarks:

> The artificial slogan of 'self-determination and even a separate state' contradicts Cuba's historical process of formation as a nation of whites and blacks, particularly since the revolution of 1868... In the so-called 'Oriente black strip', taking in municipalities like Alto Songo, Baracoa, Caney, Cobre, Guantánamo, Palma Soriano, San Luis and Santiago de Cuba, blacks and mulattos made up 58.3% of the population, according to the 1938 census, but they only comprised 22.4% of the black population throughout the country... These numbers alone indicate that, even if the slogan of self-determination were correct, that right could not have been exercised by the 77.6% of the black population not living in the Oriente black strip.[9]

He was very emphatic that the Party did not see self-determination as a central aim in the struggle against discrimination, but [as outlined in] the Resolution of the Cuban Communist Party's First National Conference, there was a very clear need:

> ...to mobilize the oppressed Negro masses who make up a third of the Cuban population, to incorporate this huge revolutionary army into the struggle for anti-imperialist agrarian revolution... if we are to prepare seriously for a decisive struggle for power. For this we need to prioritize... the struggle for the economic, political and social equality of blacks. This means concrete, systematic, every-

> day struggle against all forms of oppression and discrimination of the Negro masses.[10]

As a consequence of the experience and outcome of the struggle, the Party withdrew the slogan in practice in 1934, officially in 1935...

[In the 1940s], Cuba's political and economic situation has to be seen in the framework of world war, the closure of the European market, and increased relations with the United States, creating even greater dependence. Progressive forces in the country and people in general rejected Fifth Columnism. The working class was organized, the Confederation of Cuban Workers (CTC) had been formed in 1939...the struggle against discrimination continued backed by... legal precepts in the 1940 Constitution, although on the whole these precepts were ignored and the press continued to denounce and campaign against the continuing social abuses.

One example was an item in **Fragua de la Libertad** of 5 June 1942, accusing the mayor of Havana of taking measures against blacks.[11] A few days later the same paper printed a statement made by Dr Miguel Angel Céspedes, president of the Atenas Club, affirming that "the Cuban courts of justice are the first to discriminate against the Negro."[12]

As president of the National Executive Committee of the Unión Revolucionaria Comunista (Communist Revolutionary Union, URC), Juan Marinello replied to a survey run by **Somos** magazine:

> We see the delay in introducing a law in Cuba to make effective the equality outlined in the Constitution as malicious and reprehensible... The URC is the only Cuban party that has included a proposed law against racial discrimination for discussion at the extraordinary session of the legislature next August. We consider that certain lamentable recent events demand the immediate adoption of formulas to resolve once and for all, by legal means, this grave national problem.[13]

Despite the denunciation of concrete acts of racial discrimination, such acts continued. In 1944 a judge was criticised for having exonerated the manager of a hairdressing salon for having refused to serve a black woman...[14]

Nuevos Rumbos, the name of the society and journal, ran a first editorial: "Present times impel all of us, whatever our race, to increase our effort to create the climate of unity that can help solve the serious problems confronting Cuba in the post-war period in a satisfactory manner."[15]

An article appeared in this journal analyzing the political strength of communism, pointing to the well-founded tactic of the Socialist Party of Cuba which, "while other parties considered... the Federation (of Cuban Societies composed in their majority of elements of the colored race) as an endeavor that should be undertaken only by men and women of African origin, the Communist Party gave it every support, and what is more important, placed at the Federation's disposal those elements within its ranks with authority and support in the Federation"...[16] **Nuevos Rumbos** gave accurate coverage to the concrete campaign against discrimination on the beaches and in housing, and against disunity among Cubans, making blacks second-class citizens...

[In 1948] an article was published entitled "The PRC [Cuban Revolutionary Party] does not defend the Negro" [in response to the demagogic pose of its president in power Ramón Grau San Martín]:

> The PRC in power has not taken a single step toward solving the disgraceful problem of racial discrimination against the Cuban Negro... under the PRC government of today as under the Liberal Party of yesterday, Cuban Negroes are denied the opportunity to become industrialists or traders, they are denied access to a diplomatic career, they have to leap great hurdles to obtain a university degree and when they achieve it, if they go in for teaching, swell the ranks of those without a classroom; if they are dentists or musicians, they have to be very pushy in order to obtain some petty rural position; if they are lawyers, they are condemned to rags, because there is

> no government office, or private enterprise, or business that would give them work and the corridors of justice are closed to them.
>
> Today, like yesterday, Cuban Negroes cannot become a ministerial secretary or customs chief; they have not the slightest chance of working in the offices of any private business, nor are they taken on in shops, restaurants, cafes or stores; apartments and houses are not rented out to them, nor are they allowed in first or even second-class hotels...[17]

In 1951, Blas Roca, leader of the Popular Socialist Party (former Communist Party) argued in the Party paper, **Hoy**:

> How can those who are responsible for the assassination of Jésus Menéndez[18], Aracelio Iglesias[19] and José Oviedo[20] fight against discrimination? How can those on the CTK Executive Committee[21] who intentionally wiped out those of dark skin fight against discrimination? How can those who have excluded blacks from the leadership of unions whose members are 80% colored fight against racial discrimination?[22]

Philosophical doctrine

In this period there was also a public polemic caused by two articles published by Jorge Mañach.[23] Mañach's articles were written in response to a letter sent from a young man at Estrada Palma sugar mill... published in **Nuevos Rumbos**... claiming that what had been called black racism was simply a response to white racism, the author demanding: "That there be no racism on the part of whites and there would be no black reaction."[24]

[Mañach referred to how] "objective discrimination — which is born of social action, not ideas — would diminish as the Negro made an ever increasing effort at betterment which has already almost brought him up to the level of the white in less than three quarters of a century of freedom." He insisted that racial discrimination would cease with racial mixing in Cuba: "I think the white is and has been an incentive for the Negro's betterment. The example of Haiti would support my point. White injections into the Cuban population would undoubtedly hold back the integration process but could not frustrate it in the long run, and would compensate the more prolific black proletariat, which tends to produce an ethnic imbalance which makes intermixing more propitious. All that favors this final outcome is to be recommended... Anything that tends to deviate from what is a conscious and inevitable process is an obstacle. That is why I believe the campaign against discrimination does more harm than good.[25]

With these remarks, Mañach demonstrated not his ignorance but a deliberate omission of the true causes of the problem. His call not to fight against discrimination, because this would in time disappear, is like the Christian call to suffer humiliation, poverty and exploitation as proof of deserving paradise. His position was not far removed from that of Raimundo Menocal.

The first editorial of **Nuevos Rumbos**, in 1949, described Menocal as a man of the tropical south for having opposed the efforts of the more progressive sectors in the country, who for eight years had been demanding the education law and sanctions against racial discrimination.[26] Menocal had already been criticised when he published his book **Origen y desarrollo del pensamiento cubano** (Origin and Development of Cuban Thought) in which he put forward... racist ideas and concepts, reflecting, moreover, a tremendous ignorance of African peoples' historical development.[27]

In that same issue, Pinto made a strong case for the political failure of blacks to date being due to "the Cuban Negro having no realistic method of analysis." Pinto had already argued in 1939:

> As time passes we become more and more convinced that the capital error of the Negroes lies in not realising that they are prisoner to philosophical doctrines created by the slaveowners when slavery arose as a social system of production. They, along with the state, which is the instrument of domination designed to subjugate those who had been enslaved, created a philosophy or concept of the world and life which would serve to explain and justify their right to exploit those who had been enslaved. Unfortunately for the Negro, the philosophy continues today as

> the systematised expression of a method for acquiring truth...[28]

Race and revolution

One of the first problems the Revolution took on board was racial discrimination. In a speech of 21 March 1959, our leader Fidel Castro broached the solution in terms of education. In this respect he coincided with the idea held by many for decades, that only through education could racial discrimination and prejudice be eliminated. But this time education was put forward as a means of helping solve the problem, in the context of solid aims on the part of the Revolutionary Government to struggle against all the ills of the neocolonial republic, among which discrimination and prejudice held prominent place.

The new position was different in that previously it had been taken up without an in-depth analysis of the problem, with only philanthropic ideas, without relating the two phenomena with their economic origins and the imposition and penetration of ideological currents of the dominant class among the popular sectors... Our Commander in Chief said: "...in all fairness, I must say that it is not only the aristocracy who practise discrimination. There are very humble people who also discriminate. There are workers who hold the same prejudices as any wealthy person, and this is what is most absurd and sad... and should compel people to meditate on the problem."[29]

A few days later, he returned to the racial question in a public address, refuting opinions that blacks had been unbearable since his speech of the 21st. He responded: "There might have been an exceptional case, but is that cause for generalization? What do you want? They were kept carwashing, shoeshining and begging; they couldn't attend school and get a decent education; and now they're supposed to be finer than those who went to study in Paris..."

He spoke irrefutably of how the enemies of the Revolution tried to use the problem of racial discrimination to divide the Cuban people and achieve their ill-intentioned aim of frustrating our people's legitimate claims:

We are a small country. We have all kinds of enemies, inside and out. The international oligarchy slander us and try to present us to the world as a pack of wild wolves, to weaken us. Are we to be a small people and on top of that divided? Are we a small people who need each other, need the effort of all, and are now to be divided into white and black?... To what end if not to weaken the nation, to weaken Cuba? Are we few and yet to be divided? Are we to be weak and also divided by color?...

Why do we not tackle this problem radically and with love, not in a spirit of division and hate? Why not educate and destroy the prejudice of centuries, the prejudice handed down to us from such an odious institution as slavery? We know that in the war of independence the *integristas* came and said no revolution should take place because if we achieved independence it would be a republic ruled by blacks. Now they stir up the same fears today, fear of the black. Why? It was unfounded and false then. Why does anyone need to be alarmed and concerned when justice is sought through persuasion and reason, not force? It is a struggle we must all wage together, all Cubans, against all prejudice... I am aware that I help the Revolution when I try to unite Cubans and I can only unite Cubans on the basis of the disappearance of all injustice and signs of resentment. We have asked people to collaborate in the way which is most worthy, this is what I ask of them: that they help us find greater friendship and understanding among all Cubans, and that they help us fight against every last injustice, that they help us fight prejudice... The problem here is not a change of government but changing the essence of what colonial politics have been until today. We have to uproot the last colonial vestiges, conscious of making that phrase of Martí a reality: he said it before, we have to repeat it now, that a Cuban is more than white, more than black, and we are Cuban.[30]

Endnotes

1. "Manifesto de Masó", **Diario de la Marina**, Havana, 31 October 1901, p.1.
2. Ramiro Guerra in **La República Cubana**, Havana, 5 July 1902, p.2.
3. Juan Gualberto Gómez in **La República Cubana**, Havana, 15 July 1902, p.2 and 16 July 1902, p.2.
4. Juan Gualberto Gómez "Disquisiciones históricas" in **Juan Gualberto Gómez: su labor política y sociológica**, Rambla y Bouza, Havana, 1933, Vol. 2, pp.53-54.
5. Evaristo Estenoz "Carta abierta del general", **El Triunfo**, Havana, 20 February 1908, p.9.
6. Evaristo Estenoz "Elección y selección", **Previsión**, Havana, 30 August 1908, pp.1-3.
7. Nicolás Guillén "El camino de Harlem", **Diario de la Marina**, Havana, 21 April 1929, p.11.
8. "El Klu Klux Klan Kubano", **Diario de la Marina**, Havana, 1 November 1933, p.2.
9. **Preguntas y respuestas sobre los años 30. Fabio Grobart en la Escuela de Historia**, University of Havana, 1967.
10. ibid.
11. "El alcalde de La Habana y sus auxiliares, discriminan a los negros", **Fragua de la Libertad**, Havana, 5 June 1942, p.12.
12. "Los tribunales de justicia cubanos son los principales discriminadores del negro", **Fragua de la Libertad**, Havana, 18 June 1942, p.1.
13. Juan Marinello "Respuestas del doctor...", **Somos**, Havana, August 1943, p.4.
14. Angel C.Pinto "De los guachinangos grandes", **Somos**, Havana, November 1944, p.2.
15. "Editorial: La unidad será base de nuestro progreso", **Nuevos Rumbos**, Havana, November 1945, Year 1, No. 1, p.3.
16. Jesús Masdeu "La fuerza política del comunismo en Cuba", **Nuevos Rumbos**, Havana, November 1945, Year 1, No. 1, p.10.
17. Severo Aguirre "El PRC no defiende a los negros", **Hoy**, Havana, 5 May 1948, p.2.
18. Jesús Menéndez Larrondo (1911-1948). General secretary of the National Federation of Sugar Workers and PSP member.
19. Aracelio Iglesias (1902-1948). Leader of the Havana dockworkers, PSP member, and Abakuá.
20. José Oviedo Chacón (1902-1949). Sugar workers leader in Camagüey and PSP member.

21. The communist-led CTC was the object of officially sanctioned terrorism, and the popularly dubbed CTK (because it was funded out of Clause K) put in its place.
22. Blas Roca "El decreto sobre la discriminación racial y las masas", **Hoy,** Havana, 17 November 1951, p.1.
23. Jorge Mañach "Sobre la discriminación racial", **Bohemia,** Havana, 27 June 1948, Year 40, No. 26, pp.25 & 72-3, and "La barquilla de la Caridad del Cobre", **Bohemia,** Havana, 4 July 1948, Year 40, No. 27, pp.24 & 95-6.
24. Ariel Vera Zambrano "Acción y reacción", **Nuevos Rumbos,** August 1948, Year 3, No. 8, p.8.
25. Mañach, op.cit.
26. Raimundo Menocal **Origen y desarrollo del pensamiento en Cuba,** Lex, Havana, 1945.
27. "Respuesta a un sureño tropical", **Nuevos Rumbos,** Havana, January-March 1949, Year 4, No. 3-5, pp.3-4 & 26.
28. Angel C. Pinto **El negro, la Constituyente y la Constitución,** Democracia, Havana, 1939.
29. Fidel Castro Ruz in **Revolución,** Havana, 16 March 1959, pp.3-4.
30. Fidel Castro Ruz in **Revolución,** Havana, 26 March 1959, pp.4-5.

PART 2

Myth and reality

ROGELIO MARTÍNEZ FURÉ

Imaginary dialogue on folklore

Excerpts from **Dialogos imaginarios** (Imaginary Dialogues), Arte y Literatura, Havana, 1979, pp.257-259, 261, 253-265, 267-268, 270-275.

To my maestro Don Fernando:
Science, conscience and patience.

Here I am, sitting in the shade of the ravenalas, *the wind rustling through the green foliage of those travelers from Madagascar. You come to me — perhaps you were already here? I continue immersed in my book of anonymous Cuban protest, from colonial times to the triumph of the revolution, at the same time preoccupied by disturbing thoughts: Zionist expansionism in the Sinai, deaths every day in Santiago [Chile], unending fratricidal war in Ireland, and always South Africa, close to my heart.*

I go on organizing the book I hope will be a testimony to our people's desire for freedom, when my pen stops mid-stroke with your questions... You want to know "my" opinion on folklore. I smile. And yet, I think your question is on the mark; it is good to set areas and objectives, to clarify principles. I am happy to know you consider this science a powerful weapon in the liberation struggle, and that you see the silent labor of folklorists as useful, dedicated to recapturing the treasures created by the people. I'm ready to unravel your questions... Look here...

Rogelio, how is folklore seen in the hands of the bourgeoisie?
I see folklore as the culture a people has passed on generally through oral tradition; the habits and customs of a group of people reflecting their life experiences, tastes, aspirations, concepts

of life and death, styles of building and decorating their homes, oral prose and poetry, home remedies and cooking, popular art, beliefs and superstitions, mythology, music, dance, festivities and traditional dress... in short, what some researchers have called "popular wisdom" and others, "popular cultural tradition". Folklore is the opposite of "official", "bookish", "institutionalized". It is the product of the social and economic history of the whole community, and shows its most characteristic traits as a social entity. Folklore is of the people and for the people. It is anonymous, empirical, collective and functional.

In the hands of the bourgeoisie, folklore becomes something exotic, picturesque, a *minor form of culture* to be exhibited in festivals or spectacles for idle tourists but segregated from the great currents of contemporary civilization. It's a museum "curiosity", recreational complement, "typical" fossil belonging to an infraculture incapable of attaining so-called *universality* of great manifestations of bourgeois art. Meanwhile, the groups that keep those forms of popular cultural tradition alive are marginalized by that class society, are victims of all forms of exploitation and blocked from being a part of its technical and scientific progress.

In most countries of the Americas, folklore is used pejoratively to describe the elements of Indian, African or Oriental culture that survive among certain groups — as a form of cultural resistance and manifestation of class struggle — and the culture of peasant groups of European and mixed descent. The prevailing capitalist system has marginalized these veritable subcultures as ills that will be wiped off the ethnographic map of those countries once those minority or majority groups disappear, assimilated into the system of exploitation as manual wage labor, stripped of their culture and incapable of contributing anything of value to a modern national culture, because for the oligarchs in power this is only possible within the framework of capitalist Western culture...

Are there bourgeois tendencies in Cuban folklore..?

The most pernicious bourgeois influence persisting in our folklore is precisely in the so-called middle classes' concept of popular cultural tradition, which is seen as backward, barbaric, coarse and crude forms of expression that must be swept away. Those concepts were gaining momentum until the triumph of the revolution, which fortunately put a brake on that process of disintegration of national values. Reactionary attitudes provided the conditions for people to join the bourgeois bandwagon as aides in the exploitation of the poorer sectors, failing to see that they were also exploited in the same way. This ideology even penetrated certain popular sectors in urban and rural areas, causing them to feel ashamed of their parents' traditions, rejecting them and assuming a reprehensible posture similar in many ways to that of free blacks and coloreds of the colonial period, which prevented them from admitting the existence of any positive value in those traditions.

It is in this field that the revolution is waging one of its major battles, recapturing for the new socialist culture we are building, the valuable, positive traditions created by our people, whatever their antecedents... This will be extraordinarily enriching for our culture as our people become aware of their own heritage, whose diversity is a reflection of the many ethnic groupings that made it up and the force of our popular cultural tradition. Culture that is alive, not crystallized, because if we Cubans have preserved it up until the present, it is because it fulfills an important social function; otherwise, it would have become an historic, dead folklore.

We must also root out the last traces of bourgeois divisionist tactics employed since the 19th century. Pitting our nation's two fundamental roots against one another, they either presented them as incompatible, or only attributed Cuban-ness to cultural manifestations of Hispanic origin. Those evidencing greater African influence were considered to be little less than foreign. Both traditions, as they exist in Cuba today, in their contemporary forms, regardless of the extent of their purity, are the product of an historical process lived by our people and of socio-economic and political relations on our island over 400 years. This has been stated clearly many times by our Revolutionary Government in speeches and assemblies. Our national culture is an Afro-Hispanic Caribbean culture. The African contribution, as maestro Don Fernando Ortiz has said, did not come to be injected into a pre-existing Cuban culture, but, on the contrary, the Cuban was born out of the marriage of Spanish and African, through a long process of transculturation. This process of synthesis is as yet incomplete, but can be accelerated in revolutionary fashion.

How can folklore be stimulated?

Folklore can be stimulated in its development in an intelligent and scientific way, little by little eliminating *negative* folklore (superstitions, unsubstantiated taboos, idealistic beliefs in supernatural forces, faith-healing, xenophobia, etc) while enriching *positive* folklore (all that which helped the harmonious development of society, that helps strengthen solidarity among people, that exalts traditions of struggle against oppression, as well as ludic folklore, beneficial folk medicine, and all the flourishing art forms of popular religious beliefs whose cultural value transcends their idealist content and can be imbued with a new, revolutionary social function — music, dance, visual art, oral tradition, etc). We might recall great examples of world culture born of an era and an ideology we today consider negative but which today play a positive social role, and were in the best of cases also impregnated with elements of folklore of their time: the works of Johann Sebastian Bach, composed to be played in the churches and great cathedrals of Russia, are today appreciated by masses of working people; and yet their aesthetic appreciation does not signify conversion to Christianity... A critical and enriching approach to folklore must be based on a profound and dynamic knowledge of the laws behind these cultural phenomena and the science that is applied to them... taking care not to kill folklore in applying to popular culture erroneous criteria that are often nothing other than vestiges of petit-bourgeois mentality grounded in a Eurocentric, capitalist view of civilization.

As Mostefa Lacheraf says, tradition must be revitalized and never become prisoner of the past. Decadence and the loss of tradition should never be revived artifically in the form of *pseudo-folklore*. The regressive policy of *inventing* folklore has always ended in failure, for authentic folklore — anonymous, collective, functional, traditional and empirical — is the only one of transcendental worth...

Does Cuban folklore have elements in common with the folklore of other Caribbean countries?
Of course, there are notable degrees of coincidence, because there are many common points in our economic and social historical development. The indigenous Indian cultures on the majority of our islands came from the same geographic regions. Every indication is that Siboneys, Taínos and Caribs came from South America, emigrating in successive waves from the coasts of Venezuela. Each new emigration was superimposed on already established populations, and brought with it new techniques. Thus, the agriculture, pottery, style of dwellings and boats and work utensils are similar throughout the Caribbean islands, more evolved in some than in others, but also belonging to the same Arawak civilization.

A Western European population was added to the remains of those populations exterminated by the conquistadores and then, given the need for labor to work the mines and the plantations, captives were brought from all corners of the African continent (though we should recall that the first blacks to set foot on these lands came with the conquistadores, and were Spanish blacks, serfs rather than slaves).

Centuries later, the expansion of the sugar industry and the shortage of labor meant Chinese, Indians and Malays were brought to work in the cane fields; not forgetting the North Americans, Lebanese, Syrians, Jews and people of many other nationalities brought to our shores for different reasons. For over 400 years, all these ancestors of ours were putting down their various cultural roots in one of the most complex and violent processes of transculturation to take place in the world. Thus, scores of cultures at all levels of development fused into a new type of civilization, based originally on the sugar cane plantation economy, African forced labor and a colonial society divided into what has been called the color-caste system.

These lands were first taken by Spain, but from the end of the 16th century, and especially throughout the 17th, after countless wars, many islands and even parts of the mainland fell into English, French, Dutch and Danish hands. All these variants of Western European culture adapted to the slave system of production, creating a life style characteristic of the West Indies.

The centuries of struggle between the European powers over the Caribbean Sea and the sugar islands, helped shape our peoples: Jamaica, discovered by Columbus, was conquered by England in 1655; the western part of Saint Domingue was taken by the French in 1697; Havana was held by the English for almost a year, only returning to Spanish hands in exchange for Florida in 1763; the island of Trinidad was declared a British possession in 1802. Then, the struggles for independence, conspiracies for freedom, and victorious revolutions brought waves of immigrants from island to island, or to the coastal mainland, bringing many elements of their civilization with them.

The substratum of people of African origin, uprooted from their native lands and introduced into captivity in this New World, all have an element in common. It might have been the case that one or other African culture predominated in certain regions (Yoruba here, Dahomeyan or Fanti there), but the pre-eminence of one ethnic grouping did not exclude the secondary influence of the others. For example, in the French territories captives of *ewé-fon* origin predominated; and yet those elements were also present in former Spanish colonies such as Cuba, Venezuela or Colombia. The same goes for the Bantú, who have left their mark throughout the region, or the Fanti or Ashanti, preferred by the English, but also brought to Cuba and Haiti...

Can we talk of a Caribbean civilization?

Yes, I think so. This incessant process of the clash of civilizations, of reciprocal influences between the cultures of Western Europe and those of Africa, fused on the indigenous Indian culture — plus the contributions of certain Asiatic civilizations — conditioned by slave relations of production, a sugar-based economy, African captivity and colonial rule, created historic cultural links that find expression in music and dance tradition, popular art, oral tradition, food, religious beliefs and common superstitions, to the point that we can talk of a Caribbean civilization. It is a civilization that has its local variants — determined by the presence of the dominant culture (Hispanic, French, English, etc) — but which does not exclude the existence of such a civilization at the level of folk culture, despite the diversity of language and *official* cultural forms. And even these languages have suffered the impact of Indian and African languages, creating creole in all our islands.

The Cuban *son* is like the *calypso* of Trinidad, Jamaica and Bahamas, the *beguine* and the *lagghia* of Martinique, the *plena* of Puerto Rico, the *merengue* of Haiti and the Dominican Republic, and the *round-dance* of the Cayman Islands. The Cuban *tumba-francesa* and its rhythmic forms in our folklore (*tahona, cocuyé*) originated in Haiti, but are also present in Martinique and Guadeloupe, and even the Netherlands Antilles where one of the most popular rhythms is the *tumba*. The special form of solo-chorus structure that is undisputably African in origin, is one of the characteristic features of almost all musical genres in the Caribbean. The collective processional dances, with their polyarticulated movements, in the style of our *conga* have their equivalent in the Martinican *vidée* and the Trinidadian *camboulay*. Our colonial *caringa* of Congo origin, is the *calenda* or *calinda* of the slaves in Haiti, Martinique, Trinidad and New Orleans. The Cuban dances of Yoruba influence (from ritual dance to the modern *mozambique, pilón* and *koyudde*) are to be found in the *Shango* dances of Trinidad.

Masquerading "devils" dance in Cuba, Venezuela and Panama. The sound of the strings present in the guitar, *tres, tiple, cuatro, requinto, mejoranera* and other instruments of Hispanic origin are to be found among peasants throughout the islands and mainland shores of the Caribbean; and marímbulas, maracas, drums, bells, gourds, and scores of other instruments from Africa lend the music of this region its peculiar form, in *rumbas, cumbias, bombas, malembes, porros, sangueos, tamboritos, limbos* and *mambos*. Carnival and the parades are a most spectacular moment for our people's popular arts, showing the collective genius through masks, colorful costumes, body painting, mime, popular street theater and dub poetry. The sound of musical genres of French, British and Central European origin in fashion from the end of the 18th century have left their mark on ballroom music, generating the mulatto variants of *contradanzas, cuadrillas, lanceros., valses, rigodones, polkas* and *mazurcas*, and bringing in a whole arsenal of violins, flutes, clarinets, figles, pianos and horns, today an inseparable part of Caribbean music. The tap dance and the style of singing influenced by Semitic music came via Andalucia and can be found in the origins of the *punto guajiro* and the *zapateo* in Cuba, the *mejorana* in Panama, in the *puntillano* and the *punto cruzando* of Margarita Island and the *joropo* of Venezuela, in the *mediatuna*, the *mangulina* and the *sanjuanero* in Colombia, etc. In short, it would be impossible to enumerate all the common elements and the degrees of coincidence between our popular cultures. We share from food dishes to proverbs, stories, riddles, prejudices, historic ill-fate and above all a tradition of struggle against exploitation, symbolized in the settlements founded by Indians, continued by runaway slaves, nationalized by the *mambises* and now taken up by modern-day revolutionaries.

So, do you think that as we get to know one other better, we will become conscious of our common history and destiny?
Of course. As we come to know one another better, we will be more conscious of the cultural heritage that unites us, and can help us take on our singularity in the context of the Americas. At the same time it will act as a powerful block to imperialist penetration, and a stimulus in the struggle for definitive liberation in those lands still under colonialism or neocolonialism today. A Caribbean singularity that will not exclude, but on the contrary will strengthen other historical links, of both culture and revolutionary struggle, which unite us and make us an integral part of *Our America*.

And after this long — imaginary? — dialogue, you fade away. I go on sorting through my papers, awaiting the latest news on the Sinai war, in the shade of the blossoming ravenalas.

GLADYS GONZÁLEZ BUENO

An initiation ceremony in Regla de Palo

Published as "Una ceremonia de iniciación en *regla de palo*" (An Initiation Ceremony in *Regla de Palo*) in **Del Caribe**, No 12, Year V, 1988.

One of the most important ceremonies in *palo monte* or *regla de palo* is that of initiation, known also as *rayamiento* (marking) *en palo*. Only after initiation is the individual recognized by the religious community as part of it. Its secrets tend to be shrouded in total mystery and not many researchers have been able to observe for themselves the complex ritual involved. The present article is the product not only of direct observation but also documentation and the testimonials of almost a hundred descendants of *Congos*, mainly *casa templo* (home-shrine) priests in Santiago de Cuba.

The marking, as in any other ceremony in *regla conga*, is dominated by the presence of seven, fourteen or twenty-one piles of powdered sticks of different natural woods, scorched by fire — although in a few cases only three were observed — and they can be attended by initiates in *mayombe*, the predominant variant in Santiago de Cuba, as well as *biriyumbas* and *quirimbayas*.

As they arrive, the *tata* (father) *ngangas*, priests or *mayomberos* or initiates of other lineages, kneel before the *nganga* (pot or other receptacle), which is the center of magical-religious force of the *Congo*; crossing the other arm over their chest, they put first the right and then the left arm on the ground, while they hold in the opposite hand a gourd from which they sip cane spirit that is sprayed onto the receptacle by blowing hard from the mouth. After blowing cane spirit onto the receptacle twice, the newcomer drinks what is left in the gourd and then throws the gourd to the ground; immediately lights up a cigar, puts the lighted end in his mouth and blows the smoke over the *nganga*; and finally touches the ground with his forehead (occasionally kissing the ground instead). Meanwhile, the *tata nganga* prays and sings to the pot.

This ceremony is in greeting to the center of magical force around which all religious events takes place and is, therefore, common to all *conga* ceremonies. It is also common to all such ceremonies to prohibit any woman who is menstruating from entering the room in which the *nganga* is situated, whether she is *mayombera* or not, since it is considered that this will take away its magical force.

The initiation as such begins with the *madrina* (godmother) or *padrino* (godfather) — depending on whether a woman or a man is being initiated — bathing the initiate with seven, fourteen or twenty-one leaves from different plants and soap. The head and genitals are bathed first, and then the rest of the body. After the bathing, the godfather or godmother, accordingly, tears up the clothes and underwear, throws them on the ground with the leaves and has the godson or goddaughter trample over the whole lot, which the godfather/mother afterwards drags to one side with their foot, until after the ceremony, when it is then taken away.

After the bathing, the godson/daughter is dressed in trousers rolled up to the knees and is taken barefoot[1] to a solitary room to remain in meditation for a short while, accompanied only by an initiated guardian. Then the eyes are blindfolded with a black cloth[2] and the godmother puts a coconut under each arm and also under the right arm a bottle of cane spirit, objects which the godson/daughter cannot touch by hand. The godmother has the initiate walk behind her — unguided — to the secret room where the *nganga* lives and where all the *tata ngangas* are waiting.

The godfather, seated before the receptacle, starts to pray or talk with it in the Congo language and to chant,[3] while the rest of the priests form the chorus for the *nganga* son. While the master of the pot prays and converses with the center of force, he cuts the ends of the godson/daughter's hair, rolls them into a ball and puts them in the *nganga;* he then sprinkles cane spirit on several branches and proceeds to cleanse the initiate with them. In some cases, the initiate goes into a trance, signifying possession by one of the dead, and in that case there is chanting and praying to bring the initiate back. The ceremony is suspended for the duration of the trance.

The marking proper starts after the cleansing. Generally, the initiate lies down on the ground — although there are cases when they remain standing. The body is covered up to the neck by a large ceremonial scarf and the godfather makes the marks with a *yúa* or *ayúa* thorn.[4] Three small vertical incisions are made on each side of the chest, though some *paleros* do a fourth oblique incision across the vertical ones; the wounds are dusted with powdered wood and crushed egg shell scorched by fire; sometimes the powdered bones of the *nfumbe* (the dead of the *nganga*) and then wax on top. First the *nbele* (ceremonial machete) and then the ceremonial cowhorn[5] are placed over the wounds. Afterwards, the tongue is marked in the same way as the chest and the powder put on the wounds must be swallowed with the blood.

When the marking is over, the initiate gets up, still blindfolded, and leaning on the godfather, stands at the side of the *nganga,* with the godmother on the opposite side, and a candle is placed in front of the eyes. The godfather asks what it is, to which the initiate responds "a candle". The same is then done with a crucifix.[6]

The marking is over and the blindfold is taken off. The godfather takes the *nbele* and with it hits each side of the back. He then orders the initiate to lift up the right foot, which he also hits twice with the *nbele,* and this is repeated with the left foot.

Finally, the godfather and godmother greet the new initiate with the words: "sala maleco", to which the initiate replies "malecom sala". The other members of the religious family then come to give the same greeting.

After the greeting, the *tata nganga,* standing in front of the pot, says: "mambe", to which those present reply in chorus: "Dio".

"Juramos or no juramos" (Do we take the oath or do we not?), and the chorus replies, "Juramos" (We do). The godfather, accompanied by the godmother, then sacrifices the animals to give food to the *nganga*, in a way similar to that of *regla de ocha ebbó*. In this ceremony, the *nganga* is given the blood of a cockerel and a chicken which must have black feathers[7] — although there are variants on the color of the feathers.

Before the sacrifice, the godfather takes the live animal, hits the new initiate's shoulders hard with it and then drops it onto his head. The godmother then holds the rooster by the legs with its head over the *nganga*, while the godfather bleeds it with the point of the ceremonial knife over the *nganga* so that the blood flows down it into the receptacle. Some of the blood spills over into a gourd containing cane spirit and leaf sap; the godfather has the recent initiate drink the mixture. During this part of the ceremony several songs are chanted in Congo and when the *nganga* has eaten, the godfather chants "agua de musunga".

After the meal, the godmother washes the knife over the *nganga* with brown sugar water. The initiation complete, the ceremony continues with *Congo* chants and dancing, while other *paleros* gathered there may be possessed, make prophecies, etc; festivities could go on for several hours.

Endnotes

1. In all *Conga* ceremonies, believers, initiates or not, must be barefoot.
2. The color of the scarf actually varies according to the master of the *nganga*.
3. These are chants exclusive to the marking.
4. According to some informants, this takes the place of hedgehog spines. Today, a cockspur may be used, or razor blades, etc.
5. This contains several elements of the *nganga* and is covered with a round mirror stuck on with wax.
6. The crucifix would seem to have been introduced after the 1912 colored uprising in Santiago. The *nganga* with crucifixes or Christian elements is described as blessed or Christian.
7. From the start of the ceremony, the animals to be sacrificed are placed in front of the *nganga* by the godfather.

JOEL JAMES

The principle of multiple representation

Excerpts from the essay in **Sobre dioses y muertos** (On the Gods and the Dead), Caserón, Santiago de Cuba, 1989.

To the santeros, paleros, hounganes *and* espiritistas de cordón *in my country who believe in what they do and do it for the good.*

Accepting the validity of what we call the principle of multiple representation in the thick weave of beliefs, liturgy and poetry making up Cuban magical-religious systems, presupposes accepting a priori that these systems are grounded on, and have contained within them, tangible — albeit not theoretically systematized — philosophical formulations.

There is philosophy in *ocha, palo, vodú* and *cordón* beyond the specifically religious beliefs that, with very concrete variants in each case, express a holistic view of the world and man, and the organic relation between that world and man.

In an initial semantic approach to the obviously imprecise, ambiguous statement of the principle of multiple representation, we might reformulate the problem from another direction: What do we mean by principle and by multiple representation? With the sole intention of establishing what we see as urgent methodological factors, by principle we refer to the element that, within a given plurality, organizes or tends to organize that plurality in the form of a system. With no ecumenical pretentions, by multiple representation we refer to that which is represented in more than one way through necessity or convenience.

From this perspective other pressing imprecisions appear: does this refer to the entity that is being represented in multiple forms, that is, the subject of the representation, or the spectrum of what is being represented, which is in the final analysis the sum of the different concrete forms of representation? It refers to what is represented, the different forms in which it is represented and, moreover, the link between the one and the other, which determines that what is represented be represented in not one but multiple ways. It is worth emphasizing that the above mentioned ambiguity between necessity and convenience is fortunate because, in all probability, in the dialectical exchange lie some of the possible explanations for the third side of the triangle of questions we have posed.

It is also important to understand that the principle of representation is the basis of all human praxis. In the act of imagining, or representing, what is going to be done or constructed with a certain approximation, man tends to select a single, or at least dominant, representation due to the imperative nature of the end pursued. The starting point can be multiple representation, but initial propositions tend to be reduced in the very process of praxis. Thus, the initial multiple representation will never be reaffirmative or in the end concurrent, at least with the elements that originally made it up. Herein lies the first distinguishing feature of multiple representation in Cuban magical-religious systems: a reality taken as final, which introduces into these considerations certain disturbing questions that I am not sure I can answer: what is the relationship between multiple representation and pragmatism? Can representations be at the same time multiple and pragmatic? Is there not among multiple representations a selective tension that governs them internally? How do pragmatic components appear and how are they made manifest in Cuban magical-religious systems?

Let us leave these questions aside for the moment and move on to examples which are positive and more reassuring. A wide range of manifestations of multiple representation can be expressed within religious ordering, from visually conceived divine bodies as represented in forms that mimic the human form, to the various ways of naming one and the same mystic manifestation or ritual, and even in the many crystallizations with which otherworldly force presents itself in the believer's waking or sleeping state. Thus, multiple representation is an inseparable element of a whole body of Cuban magical-religious beliefs and, as set out here, is not limited to the phenomenon or element that is present in the multiple forms but rather encompasses those very forms and the nexus binding the two...

Pursuing this line of inquiry, we might approach the magnitudes or components of multiple representation that characterize — if not exclusively primordially — each of the magical-religious systems.

Considered globally within each system, the essence of the principle of multiple representation would be the prevailing forms in which divine or supernatural bodies are manifested within the representation as such, the positions which the practitioner takes within those representations and the communicative quality between the supernatural and the earthly levels.

For *regla de ocha* we propose that the characteristic or most important feature, within the thick web of representations in that system and as far as the divinities are concerned, is the relative ease with which multiple forms of more or less defined anthropomorphism are taken up. The distinguishing feature, as I see it, is that the practitioner takes on the *orisha*, either in trance, on request or as a result of divination.

Depending on its specificities, in *regla conga* the most peculiar element is the all-encompassing, multifaceted quality that magical forces and powers possess, the multiple properties driving them. The position of the practitioner is typically given by the pendular movement toward the *nganga* and vice-versa. The initiate is, indistinctly, at different moments, a person related to the center of the force of magic, and in this ambivalence, over and above the eventual interest of the initiate, lies the *nganga*'s will to survive which is, through this mechanism, the initiate's will to survive in the *nganga*.

For *vodú*, the particular determination of the divinities in the operational framework of multiple representation resides in the many responses of mystical origin occasioned by some deities interfering with others, which in turn have their groundings in the deities' broad freedom of concurrence permitted in the liturgy and cosmogony of *vodú*. The practitioner will always be situated within the representation as an object of risk in dispute with the different deities.

In *cordón*, the outstanding feature of multiple representation, the ordering principle, is the accepted possibility of multiple selection of mediums by the dead for the various representations. The position of the practitioner is commonly dissolved in the mystical collective persona.

Seen in this way, the qualities of the links between superhuman bodies and practitioners or believers, established in representations, is governed, in *regla de ocha* by the need to adjust liturgy to the mutiplicity of human circumstances acting as pressing agents of interrogation on this religious order, which in the last instance is translated into an internal predominance of human demands on divine requests.

For *regla conga*, on the other hand, the *palero's* overriding of the *nganga*, which is the peculiar phenomenon of the link between the one and the other, is the outcome of necessity for this magical-religious system to double back on itself to prevail in adverse circumstances, in the Cuban religious spectrum, with its own profile.

For *vodú*, in the conditioning of multiple representation of the deities and practitioner, the former relate to each other in accordance with the principle of divination by autogenesis which is inherent to this system. While in *cordón* spiritualism the equivalent is governed by an ordering principle that can be expressed as the prevalence of death over life which, curiously, will be the exact antipode, or opposite, of what we formulate for *regla de ascendencia lucumí*.

ARGELIERS LEÓN

Abakuá signs

Excerpt from "Para leer las firmas Abakuá" (How to Read Abakuá Signs") in **Unión**, No. 10, Year III, April-May-June 1990, pp. 10-13.

The *Abakuá* in Cuba have developed the habit of writing down their knowledge in notebooks and, like the old practitioners of *Regla Ocha* (*Santería*)... they write down their stories and talk (*enkame*), as well as their *firmas* (signatures) and *gandó* (signs), in what they call a treatise. Thus there is the Treatise of *Iyamba,* the Treatise of *Isué,* and there might be a section for the Treatise of the River. Each treatise is in paragraphs on concrete actions, like very defined "steps" for the action recounted. The words in those paragraphs are recorded as spoken, with the anarchic spelling of transliteration from oral tradition to the Latin alphabet on the basis of a Spanish language that they speak with the same total anarchy, with often unintelligible handwriting. But the wisdom is very significantly ordered in these "treatises", complemented with illustrations of signatures and signs.

The "reading" of the signs by initiates into the *Abakuá* fraternity is more unitary, because the act of memorizing, or rememorizing, absorbs the totality of the intelligible process and becomes the unifying factor that situates each *gandó* as a text.

Rather than tell a story, that is intelligible and discursive, all the *gandó* pose questions for the reader. In this sense, the reading of a *gandó* approximates to that required by traffic signs, which arise out of the current demands of the road user in today's developed societies...

The reading of road signs is grounded on a knowledge already acquired by the receiver — cultural immersion since childhood — and the existence of an order, historically developed and accepted by consensus, until it is expressed as a legal corpus, called a highway code.

If an arrow, two parallel lines... figures, like the silhouette of a child... can communicate something to a driver, brought up in a city culture, it would mean little or nothing to an Eskimo, a Mapuche, an Itruri pygmy or a Cuban peasant in a remote rural area prior to these 30 years of cultural transformation. And, to ensure that the driver is not illiterate in that reading, society has even created social forms that are "tests" and a "driving licence", a "code" and "traffic police".

A *gandó* interrogates the reader, who may be in two different socio-historical situations. Whether initiate or lay, what the reader has to do in each case is to run his eye over the space in front of him, and the eye will be triggered by the ordering of sign forms, as units that are singularly denoted as semantically concrete centers, and not units that are linked together in a lineal fashion. Vision is held on units separated by the convergence of the strokes of separate figures, which would be a systemic form of ordering a first look at a landscape, for example. In this first articulation, any reader questions. Initiates respond in keeping with the preparation they have received as members of an *Abakuá* fraternity identifying each of the signs, knowing what they refer to, and rememorizing the roles that have to be played according to the visual image received. Lay persons will also stop before these units of meaning and will see in them rectangles, stars, trapezoides, triangles, circles, lines, etc, in accordance with another kind of initiation and another kind of fraternity — a cultural initiation pertaining to a larger fraternity which is their country, their nation. They will be asked to identify each unit of meaning according to their knowledge. They might approach the reading through an erratic eye movement over the space taken up by the figure and retain those identifications.

But in the *gandó* there is another element of structural articulation, which I believe cannot be judged secondary, on a different level from that which we have pointed out as signifying units. We refer to the lineal strokes, which, whether straight lines or circles, arches, snake-like curves, and their ramifications, establish orders of relationships and dependence...

The agent of transmission is now neither weakened nor

remote, much less absent, but rather, through a broad phenomenon of convergence, is a given cultural system which enables and conditions contemplation of the picture, now a complex picture on any hard surface, with a thick line in yellow chalk. The transmitter will impart an eminently subjective message, according to which the strokes will be simpler and rougher, with very personal "contributions" in decorative form, which form part of these *gandó*.

TOMÁS GONZÁLEZ

Sara, one way or another

Taken from **Cine Cubano**, Special Commemorative Issue for "Sarita", 1990, pp.12-18.

Knowing Sara and deciding to surrender myself to timeless love, unbound by the customs of conventional couples, was like opening a casket of joy. From the first seagull winging its magic over the bay, it was simply love at first sight.

Today (because there's not been a single day since then when she's not been by my side) she comes more calmly. Not like then, when she'd catch me mid-dream, when I was three living variants of [José] Lezama Lima, and she'd interrupt my Apocalyptical dives when I stayed over at her place, to rush me with all manner of argument. There was always some interminable speech about a crazy Monday program: visit to the docks, lunch on the Middle Day of an *Iyawó,* singing "Réquiem por Ernesto" to Furé and Sergio Vitier. Then she'd push me into the bathroom, put the toothpaste on my brush (no skimping, of course), only half dry my face, and on the wrong towel...

Now she doesn't do any of that. In the middle of the night if I'm writing she comes ghostlike with the fragrance of cinnamon and old sandalwood fans, she sits on the small rocker, folds her arms above her faint head full of omens, unhurried, and starts to peel off the sweetest and most tormented moments like slowly sucking on amber candy. And nothing can alter this promiscuity, despite being but a vision of herself, a reflection in no mirror, quiet water that nonetheless flows. She tells me how she'd do things if she were in my place. She makes me see that he who has the memory of loved friends is not alone or lost. And I have her, always walking the tightrope of her difficult presence, dressed in all her inner finery, the kind that death above all discloses.

The day we met was like a flash in life. Suddenly, the beautiful clear sky of our days was filled with lightning, and the sound of thunder drowned all other ordinary sounds, of no presence or import.

Someone introduced us. I don't remember who. What I do know is that Sara dazzled me with the unsuspected mystery of her intellect. She shook my hand, not stopping talking for one moment, flirting with her eyes and with her sensual gestures and postures. Her full, well defined lips parted, displaying white teeth in an impeccable smile. Who wouldn't feel dizzy before the overwhelming temptation of her mouth? The short little nose, turned up with the unconscious gesture of a finger of her small hand. Lovely eyes, with those lashes that can only be the daughters of *Ochún Kolé*. Thick, wild eyebrows, like quails in the terror of imminent sacrifice. Her broad forehead a battlefield of mute hope and victory. Her hair would need a chapter unto itself: a strong head of close curls, a thick, black bush of goblins and fireflies. At the time, she wore it straightened, colonial-style. Later, that hair would be the first natural head of black hair in my country. A revolution within the revolution!

She gave me her telephone number. I didn't have time to write it down. I've never been able to remember numbers. I'd even forget my own number and not know how to let people at home know not to wait for me to eat; but I was obsessive about remembering Sara's. Everywhere I went I'd repeat it so as not to forget. I called and we fixed a date, to go all over the place. We went to the cinema, libraries, jazz clubs, the homes of family and friends, parties and just walking.

During all this, as she confessed to me later, she was waiting for something that never quite happened; but the two of us felt it coming.

"Perhaps next time...," we thought.

We were walking on one of those nights when the gardens of Vedado are fragrant with jasmine, though we were too close to notice. Our bodies touched feverishly as we wandered aimlessly, until finally coming to her door. It was time to say goodbye and decide. She was the one who was looking deeply at me. No words were needed. She was free, much more then than later. She had still not married the first time. I was impulsive then, perhaps I still am; and I was crazy about her.

For a long time we just looked at each other without a word. Neither of us dared do anything. The initiative hung in suspense. Putting her two hands on my shoulders, as if she were inviting me to an American country dance, she shook me:

"What is it?" she asked.

I didn't say a thing. My heart was beating fast, clouding my vision, hiding the miracle that was before my eyes, the gift of this life and the other where the gods distribute good fortune.

"How's it going to be with us?" she insisted. "We can be what we want. Lovers without respite or friends without respite. Because I like you a whole lot and I know you want me, too. What shall we do? I can't make all the decisions."

Perhaps to give myself a certain allure, I ranted the words of our poet Emilio Ballagas: "I am your destiny, your invention...," I said.

She heaved a sigh of relief.

"You'll be my brother," she declared, "the brother I've always wanted to have."

She brushed the side of my lips with a kiss and closed the door, not in my face, because everything took place slowly, as if turning the pages of a valuable book.

When I was back home, my thoughts were racing. I accused myself of everything: ... I'd been too smooth. I'd played the Don Juan and made the wrong move, taking the decision out of my hands and giving it to her.

I was desperate, walking shadowy streets, not seeing anything around me. The anguish was devouring my brain. Everything was like a ball of tangled threads. Turmoil.

By a closed café, a telephone. I ran across praying that it wouldn't be vandalized or broken. I put the coin in the slot and it was returned to me. It was broken or full. Then I realized that it was giving a dialing tone. I dialled the number and heard it ring. I had got through saving myself a nickel. One, two rings, Sara was waiting by the phone.

"Yes."

"How do you know it's me?" I asked shakily.

"I know, because it could only be you, my brother, my dear brother."

I knew then how well she had learned the Brechtian distancing effect. Silence. Reflexion. Meditation. No, nothing like that. Something began to relax inside me. My heart no longer beat fast. The sweet name of Sara. Yes, a calm sea. Curiosities of the tropics at night. Blue, the sky was still blue, even at night. And when I looked up for a reply from the universe, I saw Venus, which is her star for me, and in our pantheon would be *Ochún*. We are not Greek; but we have our own, indivisible, black icons that make sense of us...

"Tomorrow, what time shall we see each other?" I asked for the sake of saying something.

"I'll always be waiting for you," she replied.

She didn't wait for me to put the phone down.

That's how it all started and it became a friendship that dodged many pitfalls, survived many shipwrecks and faced all kinds of incomprehension, slander, hatred, blackmail, concessions, lies, separations, births, death.

There was a time when we only saw each other for snatched moments in queues at markets or at the Dime store at La Copa. We lived near each other but didn't visit. She was married. I don't know why we didn't visit each other. Sara was pregnant, and given to eating sweet things and drinking soda pop. It was then I discovered she had asthma, virtually the whole time, but uncomplaining; she handled it as something she had to live with, but as if she didn't want to recognize that she was always out of breath and each day a little more worn out. Sara was the domineering type. She wasn't just capable of domineering others but also herself. She accepted the rules of the game: never to let her asthma get the better of her. We'd be in an emergency room and she'd be clutching an aerosol but still talking about work, people, life.

Sara was always working. She was always mulling over the themes of everyday life that she wanted to get on film one day.

She knew, for example, that a documentary about a factory required a background of the work process and the tools involved. In the foreground were the people and what was happening to them. She didn't sing to revolution, she sang from within, bringing out the anonymous good and bad. She homed in on aspects of the revolution, but with a vocation for truth.

Making a film with Sara was marvelous. She was into everything. She managed the lives of her friends (mainly men, she had very few women friends). If Titón (Tomás Gutiérrez Alea) had some extra rice, she'd have it from him to give it to Yuyo (the mother of the "Guapachá" brothers Amado and Pedrito). If any of us had a bit of money, we were obliged to help someone else who needed it. And Sara's place was like a "layette bank" for any friend who was having a child.

Sara was a natural-born sociologist. She loved poking her nose into the most intricate worlds. Social research was her forte; but with no assumptions. She tried to be objective in her analysis. She let the phenomena under study point to the underlying laws. But she wasn't an empiricist. Behind the craziness there was method, rigor; the ideology shaping her plans was organic, not external. She had been a student in seminars at the Institute of Ethnology and Folklore, along with Furé, Alberto Pedro and Miguel Barnet. After the seminars, she sought refuge in the cinema. And the cinema was the best tool she could have found for her eternal human quest. She sought the truth from behind the lens, almost always a polemical truth, as if looking for trouble. She didn't go for the known; her self-imposed premise was the most innocent "I don't know," and from there she set about finding out from within.

I was swept along more than once on those forays for the treasures hidden within the most ordinary people. She was fascinated by *el ambiente*, the world of the marginal, and wanted to use what she knew about film to leave popular testimony.

But Sara's first step was at home. She was bold enough to take the camera into her own family. Nobody went untouched as she demystified the unholy and told the story of what had been pushed to the back of the closet through mulatto ideology and its petit-bourgeois pretensions. Her poetic **Crónica de mi familia**

(Chronicle of My Family) came from digging into drawers, coffers, trunks and charcoal etchings. Sara bared all that the family had wanted to cast into deep oblivion... There's an aunt, who molds herself as best she can into the new life, with an exaggerated pose that was in part born of violence and in part a defence against being misunderstood: the aunt with the religion of a *santera* and the culture of an ex-prostitute... The scandal it created was a preamble to her next marvelous documentary **Mi aporte** (My Part), a biting attack on class postures, especially those of the petit-bourgeoisie.

One night, almost jokingly, she suggested I write the script for a film, her first feature. We began to put together a storyline and the characters out of our own experiences. She talked about her happiness and difficulties with a lover from *el ambiente*, who was *Abakuá*. She talked about the taboos in the relationship, the *machismo*. I put myself on the line, too. I was familiar with the *machista* woman, who takes on the macho cult, the exclusively male sect and its violence, and manipulates its secrets (like breaking taboos) to keep a lover in tow.

That night we were putting ourselves on the line, in secret play "where only fools tread"; because the children and Germinal, her husband, were sleeping. We were in the living room, plotting the film.

"We'll do a film about a real screwed up couple," she said. "He has to be real marginal, from *el ambiente*. He'll have a gold tooth," she laughed, "and she has to be all screwed up because of her middle-class background. A white woman with a *jabao* (high brown)..."

"Why not black?" I asked.

"It'd be too much," she replied, "and we want this film to get shown, right?"

"How do they meet?" I asked. "It can't be chance."

She's a teacher at the primary school in the neighborhood where he lives.

"Imagination?" was my comment rather than question. "Do you know someone like that?"

"Yes, I know a teacher."

"Can I see her?"

"Whenever you want," she answered.

"Actors?" without believing very much that the film could really be carried off.

"Why?" she asked, inhaling from her asthma spray.

She coughed a little and immediately recovered.

"It's better to know from the start who you're writing for or constructing a character around."

She carelessly moved her legs and put her spray down. Then she stuttered aggressively:

"Yes, yes, I know who you want for the man."

"I haven't thought of anybody," I said, pretending.

"Come on, man, I know you," making me relax. "I know you want Mario for the part."

"It wouldn't be a bad idea," I acted out, "He's a good actor."

"...and your pal," she declared, finishing the sentence for me.

"He's made for the part," I said almost on reflection. "He's also got his ambitious streak. He was born in Carrauao in the heart of Cerro. That's fine: but I decide on the broad."

"Who?" I asked, on guard, because I had my own selection from among several actress friends.

"A cracker. An actress who's a real hustler. She's called Yolanda. She's an invader, she comes from the depths of Guantánamo.

"And if she's a hustler how do we get class?" I asked a bit angry about what I thought was a wild blunder of choice on Sara's part. "How do we convey middle class?"

"She's an actress," she said smiling and undoubting.

That was the first work session for the script of our film **De cierta manera** (One Way or Another). I left Sara's home at about 3:00 in the morning; and yet at 10:00 we were in the Academy of Sciences looking for Alberto Pedro as our researcher.

Alberto Pedro and Sara were to involve themselves with the fieldwork and the many documentary parts to be included in the film. The storyline was mine.

That's how our work team began to take shape. All our friends were to be involved. Germinal, Sara's husband, would be soundman. Amaury Pérez Vidal was still not much more than a child, but was sound assistant. Sergio Vitier would do the music.

At a given point Leonardo Acosta would bring out his tenor saxophone and occasionally light his rational lamp.

Luis García, Iván Arocha, Caíta, Nancy Morejón, Rogelio Martínez Furé and Tomás Gutiérrez Alea would tutor the whole venture. And Titón and Julio García Espinosa would have to do the final editing after Sara died.

In reality, the group was pretty heterogeneous, but what we had in common was the quest for our identity, that identity possessed by the most humble people, the raison d'être of the revolution.

The script was written in record time. There was so much enthusiasm. It was like a party at Sara's place. Sara was making her first feature and who wasn't going to help bring that project to fruition?

Sergio filled the night with great chords from his guitar. He did variations on the theme of **Véndele** (Leave That Man), by Guillermo, ex-boxer, singer, who also acted in the film, with my lyrics. Sergio drank in the depths of popular music with great humility and great love. He let it flow without altering it, with no unnecessary flourishes, unadorned, letting the beauty of it come through. All of this is what made the music speak as a person in its own right, recounting what's happening, knowing what it is saying and why.

We had a real runaround with the film. I don't know where Sara got all her energy and optimism, sure from the very start that the end-product would be good. I think a lot of this was due to Sara not going it alone. Alfredo Guevara, despite being a very busy man, was always there, full of enthusiasm for Sara's first film. I recall he wanted it to be in color and it was Sara who insisted it be black and white. She wanted a film that cost as little as possible.

One Way or Another did not have to go through any censorship committee. Alfredo had passed it no holds barred. Only Julio García Espinosa didn't agree with the ending. To solve matters, in a single night, I wrote ten variations on the ending, which was finally a combination of several. We were in a hurry, we couldn't waste time discussing or theorizing.

Despite the fact that Sara couldn't do the final edit, **One Way**

or Another was a popular film. Neither myself not her closest collaborators were allowed into the editing room. The film that we had conceived for two hours, told in Sara's very particular way, was edited down to just over an hour. Even so, it was saved by the strength and veracity of the images, its solid arguments and its encompassing analysis of the marginal proletariat.

The last time I saw Sara was a few days before her death. Her small son, Alfredo, had happily pulled through surgery. She told me about a dream she'd had.

"I was entering the cemetery with Alfredo in my arms and all the graves were covered in huge white sheets," she smiled gently and sighed. "I know Alfredo won't die; but one way or another I didn't like the dream."

"Why?" I asked, seeing the look of concern on her face.

"For me," she replied.

"For fuck's sake, Sarita!" was all I could shout.

Two days later Sara died of an asthma attack, fulfilled as a black woman, filmmaker, mother, revolutionary.

NATALIA BOLÍVAR

The orishas in Cuba

Excerpts from **Las orishas en Cuba** (The Orishas in Cuba), Unión, Havana, 1990, pp. 22-29, 35-40.

The Yoruba religion in Cuba

In Africa each *orisha* was originally linked to a village or region... In Yoruba land, *Shango* was worshipped in Oyó, *Yemaya* in Egba, *Ogun* in Ekití and Oridó, and *Oshun* in Ijosa and Ijebu. Certain forms of worship, however, extended over the whole region, such as *Obatala* and *Oddua,* king of the founding of *Ifé,* from whom all Yoruba rulers are considered to be descended. The Arara worshipped *Foddun* and the *Fodduces,* deities similar to those of the Yoruba pantheon. In almost all cases they were mortals deified after death, a practice common to the genesis of all religion... Those ancestors with *aché* (power) became the *orishas...* For the worship of the *orisha,* it was essential for family members to establish a base (*odu*): a pot as the receptacle for the support-object for the force or *aché* of the *orisha.* This support-object is the material base for the *orisha,* in which offerings are made and which is sprinkled with the blood of sacrificial animals. Duly consecrated, it becomes the attribute of the god, like the pebblestone on the river-bed for *Shango,* irons for *Ogun,* and the bow and arrow for *Ochosi.*

The orisha is pure, immaterial force, that is only perceptible to human beings when one of the descendants is chosen by the orisha to be possessed. This is the origin of what much later, through the process of syncretization, we would call in *Regla de Ocha* the *hijo de santo* (child of the saint). The relationship which is here spiritual was in Africa a blood relationship. The chosen (*elegún*) are also called *iyawo...* After the ceremony of invocation, the orisha "mounts" the *iyawo,* dances, is welcomed, hears complaints, gives advice, solves problems and gives thanks...

Santeria, regla de ocha, ifa

According to likeness, the figures of [Yoruba divinities] fused with the hagiography of the Church... the figure of *Babalú Ayé* with St Lazarus, *Aggayú Solá* with St Christopher, *Changó* with St Barbara, *Elegguá* with St Anthony, and so on in syncretism. *Santería* was born of a logical, natural syncretization of Yoruba and Spanish Catholic faiths...

From 1568 there were black *cabildos* in Cuba... each with a king, chosen from among the elders of a religious group, or three captains and three godmothers... Each *nation* had its *cabildo* which was at the same time a mutual aid society, school of language and tradition of each African group, especially the worship of certain deities... African religious practices, recognized as such, were officially legal in 1870...

Last century, in Calimete, Matanzas province, lived a black slave named Eulogio Gutiérrez with exceptional religious instruction. When slavery was abolished in 1880, he decided to return to Africa to make contact with his land of origin. In Nigeria he was recognized as a descendant of *obbas* (kings)... Though he was initiated as *Obatalá*, he had to share his venerated *orisha* with the secret order of the *babalawo*, and he *received* Olofi on two occasions. He was respected and lived as a noble. Then *Orula* gave him the unexpected and disagreeable order to return to Cuba, the land where he had been a slave, to install *Regla de Ifá*, the sacred order of the *babalao*. Gutiérrez returned to Cuba and went back to Calimete. Armed with the knowledge of unknown riches, it is told that he became master of the plantation where he had worked as a slave. He eventually moved to Regla, in Havana, and opened a house to *Ifá*...

A *babalao* who came to Cuba around 1860 and was given the name of Villalonga, founded another branch of *Ifá*. He brought from Africa the attributes of *Olofi*, which he concealed for fear of persecution and which remained hidden for 120 years, before being brought out and today venerated in the liturgy. They were the first *babalaos*, who would continue the *Regla de Ifá* in Cuba.

On magic

The principle of like produces like (imitative magic) suggests not only what must be done but also what must not be done: prohibitions or taboos... The purpose of positive magic is to bring about something that is desired; the purpose of negative magic (prohibitions, taboos, etc) is to avert something that is feared from happening. Both the desired and undesired consequences are in accordance with the laws of likeness and contact. For example, an act of witchcraft can cause impotence: ingredients including balsam, and soil from the cemetery, are to be placed in a receptacle with the name of the victim, to induce their effect on the subject through the paper bearing the name... The *guao* (nettle) is, of course, used only for bad effects and bringing on tragedy. It is obvious: contact in itself is irritating...

The problem with magic does not lie in believing that necessary and essential relations exist from which laws can be deduced; the problem is believing that likeness or proximity are relations of that kind, when they are not. Likeness and proximity are chance, contingent relations and cannot constitute the basis of profound knowledge. Magic can work its illusory technique and its mythical domain on fictitious knowledge.

But can an appraisal of the role of magic stop there? I think not. It is correct and necessary to establish a dividing line between science and magic. It should also be born in mind that science has achieved a domain over nature undreamed of by witchdoctors and sorcerers. The reality of numerous parapsychological phenomena has been established beyond reasonable doubt. In centers of advanced research the world over, considerable resources are devoted to the study of telepathy, precognition, clairvoyance and telekinesis. But the brilliant achievements of the natural sciences are nowhere near met by the social sciences. The social sciences barely merit the name before Marx, and the life of that great figure could only lay the foundations.

Our social and individual lives are woven with uncertainty. Chance forms a substantial part of our very nature, in that space of existential anguish of the as yet inexplicable and uncertain, where faith claims its right to help go on living. Doubtless, the path to follow is the hard one of conquering objective knowledge, real control over our environment and ourselves. But while we still cry, hundreds of thousands of years of drum magic will be in our blood.

Pattaki [story] of Elegguá

Elegguá is the son of *Okuboro* who was king of Añagui. One day, while he was still a boy, he was with his followers when he saw a three-eyed bright light on the ground. As he got nearer he saw it was a dried coconut (*obi*). *Elegguá* took it to the palace, told his parents what he had seen and threw the *obi* behind a door. Shortly after, everyone was amazed to see the light coming out of the *obi*. Three days later, Elegguá died. Everyone respected the *obi*, which continued to shine brightly, but over time people forgot about it. Then when the people found themselves in a desperate situation and when the *arubbó* (elders) met, they reached the conclusion that the cause was the neglect of the *obi*. This, in effect, was empty and eaten by bugs. The elders agreed to make something solid and lasting and thought of placing a saint's stone (*otá*) in the place of the *obi*, behind the door. That was the origin of the birth of *Elegguá* as an *orisha*. That is why it is said: "*Ikú lobi ocha*. Death gave birth to a saint."

Elegguá

Major orisha. Holds the keys to destiny, opens and closes the door to misfortune or happiness. Is chance and death personified. He guards the forest and scrub. He is the son of *Obatalá* and *Yemú*. He is the first of the group of four warriors (*Elegguá, Oggún, Ochosi* and *Osun*). He won with *Olofi, Obatalá* and *Orula*, sufficient privileges to be the first: *Okana*. No orisha comes before him because *Olofi* himself said: "As you are the smallest and my messenger, you will be the greatest on earth and in the skies, and without you it will never be possible to do anything."

Olofi also agreed that he be greeted and that he eat before the other *orishas*, as well as be the first to enter the house. It is generally accepted that *Elegguá* has 21 paths and 21 cowries. He is friend and protector of *Ochún*.

In the **Diloggún** he speaks for *Okanasorde, Oggundá, Oddí* and *Ojuani* (1-3-7-11). His days are Monday and Tuesday and all those falling on the 3rd of the month. He is celebrated on January 6 and June 13.

Traditionally the figure of *Elegguá* is very much linked to *Echu. Echu* is the incarnation of the problems afflicting man. He is not exactly a satanic figure because no orisha represents pure concepts and all admit contradictions. *Echu* is not the devil although he is present in all misfortune. He lives on the streets, in the forest and scrub, and if he enters a home, tragedy ensues. *Echu Agroi* and *Echu Afrodí* each have 24 paths and 24 cowries.

The *Elegguá-Echu* pair constitute the mythical expression of the inevitable relation between positive and negative. For the Yoruba, the home is shelter par excellence, the privileged place against the vicissitudes of fate. *Elegguá* lives on the very threshold, marking with his presence the boundary between two worlds: the inner one of security, and the outer one of danger. But there can be no security without danger, no calm without concern, which is why the *Elegguá-Echu* pair is indissoluble despite the opposition. *Elegguá* protects the home and when there are problems it is because the vagabond *Echu* has come in.

Elegguá is known in *Regla de Palo* as *Mañunga,* which is the same as *Anima Sola; Lubaniba,* which is *San Antonio de Padua; Nkuyu,* which is the same as *Elegguá Alagguana,* which is the same as *Anima Sola.* His name in Fon: *Legba.* His name in Haiti: *Papa Legba.*

Receptacle:

Gourd or clay frying pan, which is the most common.

The stone is looked for according to the path marked by the letter (hill, river, forest, etc), and can take different forms, though always human. Generally three cowries form the eyes and mouth. It should be put behind the door in contact with the floor. *Elegguá* has all kinds of natural elements, but they are used depending on the path.

The *Elegguá* or *Erere* prepared by a *santero* can only have rough stone, a sea conch shell and a handful of cowries. The *Elegguás* with human face, laden with mysticism, are the ones prepared according to the oracle of *Ifá*. It should be noted that many *santeros* prepare them incorrectly. *Elegguá* is also represented in a dried coconut.

Attributes:
Elegguá has as attributes all kinds of objects used in children's games: kites, whistles, bowls, soldiers, as well as all kinds of keys, machete, stick, straw hat, fishing rod and tackle, gold nuggets and silver coins, sticks, branches, shotgun and holster, deer horns, decorated dried coconuts, wine jars, goats horns.

Necklaces:
Red and black, representing life and death; beginning and end; war and tranquility; one and the other.

Clothing:
Vest, trousers girded at the knee and a big red hat like a chef's. All in red and black. Sometimes, the trouser legs can be one red and one black, or both striped. Jacket, trousers and especially the hat, are decorated with bells, beads and cowries.

Offerings (*ardimú*):
Cane spirit, tobacco, roasted corn, coconut, smoked fish, dumplings, smoked hutia, palm butter, candles, all kinds of candy (toffee fudge, caramelized coconut, etc). A very special offering is a hutia head or sacrificial rat.

Animals:
Goats and baby goats, chicks (black, brown and red), chickens and cocks, rats, hutias, deer, turtles and for some *Elegguás* (two) pigeons. His messenger is the rat.

Dances:
When this orisha mounts, he runs behind the door which is his usual place. He jumps and shakes like a kid, pulls faces and mimes children's games, like flying a kite and spinning a top. He jokes with the spectators, comes and goes; he's a trickster, always up to mischief, which can be erotic. He is always given a stick to

break through the undergrowth, underlining his role in opening the paths. He often dances spinning round on one foot, as if in an allegorical whirlwind.

We can generally say that the jocular, childish character representing *Elegguá* aims to imitate fate's unexpected twists and turns, the at times happy, at times hapless, alternatives of fortune. *Elegguá* personifies that totally unpredictable character of chance, that opens and closes paths to us arbitrarily and, on so many occasions, would seem to mock us. He has three chants in the *Orú del Eyá Aranlá*.

Afflictions for which he affords protection:
Accidents, fights, death caused by uncontainable hemorrhaging and also caused by betrayal, water on the blood, grief and suffering. AIDS?...

Ewe (plants — popular Cuban names):
Aba, abrecamino, aceitero, agalla de costa, aguacate blanco, ají de China, ají chileno, ají guaguao, alacrán/rabo de ratón, albahaca de hoja ancha, alcanfor, almácigo, atipola, aretillo, aroma amarilla/olorosa, aroma de uña de gato, artemisa, aticuanla, baría, bejuco verraco, bejuco sabanero, bejuco San Pedro, bejuco lombriz, bejuco jimagua/parra cimarrona, bejuco guaro, bejuco prieto, bejuco colorado, bibona, bija, carraspita, caumao, cayaya, crotos, curujey, chamico, chichicate, ébano carbonero, escoba cimarrona, espartillo, espinillo, espuela de caballero, flor de agua, gambuto/gambutera, gatiado, grama de cabello, guabico, guajaca, guaro, guayaba, guayabillo, guira cimarrona, itu, ítamo real, lengua de vaca, maloja, mastuerzo, huevo de gallo, jobo, meloncillo, mijo, ñame, ojo de ratón jurubama/jurubama, pelo diablo, palo moro, palo negro, palo torcido, palo víbora, pastillo, pata de gallina, pendejera, pica pica, picha de gato, piñón crillo, piñón botija, pinipiniche, pinipini, piña de ratón, rabo de gato, raspalengua, raspa barriga, rompesaraguey, Sam Diego, siguaraya, tabaco, tengue, travesura, tripa de jutía, yamao, yerba fina & hedionda/guanina, rabo de ratón/alacrán, zarza blanca.

Godchild:
Intelligent and clever but not always scrupulous. Inclined to depravation and corruption. Swindles, rackets and political

intrigue guarantee success in life.

Catholicization:
Elegguá is syncretized with the *Niño de Atocha, San Antonio de Padua* and *Anima Sola.*

The story of the *Niño de Atocha* is as follows: in the city of Atocha, Spain, there were many Christians taken prisoner during the latter years of Arab occupation. Nobody was authorized to enter the prisons, except children. Mothers and wives of the prisoners, knowing that they were without sufficient bread and water, prayed constantly for their suffering to be alleviated. One day, a child arrived at the prison with a basket full of bread and a bucket full of water with a drinking bowl. The Moors watched with amazement as, after serving the countless prisoners, both the basket and the bucket were still as full as they started. According to legend, Jesus Christ answered the prayers and had come, as a child, to those in need of material and spiritual help. From then dates the image of the *Niño de Atocha,* celebrated on January 1st.

His syncretism with *Elegguá* would seem to be related to the childish nature in which the orisha is represented and to the fact that *Elegguá* speaks in the **Diloggún** in *Ocana,* while the *Niño de Atocha* festivity is January 1st, first day of the year.

San Antonio was born in Lisbon. When he was 15 he became a monk at the San Agustín monastery of secular canons. He preached in several countries; he was in Africa, and eloquent stories are told of him. Arguing with someone who could not believe that the flesh and blood of Jesus were to be found in the bread and wine of mass, he had the mule of the disbeliever spurn a pile of barley, even when it was half-starving, and kneel before the Holy Sacrament. It is also told that on one occasion he began to pray by the sea shore and the fishes came to the surface to listen, whereupon he took advantage of the moment to bless them — which perhaps gave them underwater benefits. Likewise it is said that he spoke to people of different nationalities and that he was understood by all. The celebration of *San Antonio* with *Elegguá* would seem to be related to what is generally represented as a child in arms.

Various paths of *Elegguá,* like *Alona, Lagguama, Echu Bi,*

Baralanube, are reminiscent of *Anima Sola,* of souls who are burning in purgatory and have nobody to pray for their salvation. The somewhat desperate nature of this figure would seem to invite magic. His syncretism with *Elegguá* is supposedly due to the ambiguous profile of both. *Anima Sola* needs help and is not squeamish in tormenting mortals to get that help, which is not as thorny or compromising as turning directly to the Devil. Similarly, *Elegguá* is capable of getting up to mischief without identifying absolutely with Evil.

GERARDO MOSQUERA

Strokes of magical realism in Manuel Mendive

Manuel Mendive has become the single most important Cuban painter today. His work is quintessentially Afro-Cuban, inspired by his own Yoruba family background. The following is based on the article "Manuel Mendive y la evolución de su pintura" ("Manuel Mendive and the Evolution of his Painting") by art critic Gerardo Mosquera in his book **Exploraciones en la plástica cubana** (Explorations into Cuban Art), Letras Cubanas, Havana, 1983, pp. 232-45, 280-82. Mosquera uses quotes on the work of Mendive by Rogelio Martínez Furé and Nancy Morejón. Each has here been separated out, and Martínez Furé quoted at greater length from the original. To bring the overall piece up to date, a fourth part has been added by Pedro Pérez Sarduy.

The real and the magic

Manuel Mendive Hoyo was born on December 15, 1944, in Luyanó, the same Havana neighborhood where Wifredo Lam went back to live for a few months on his "retour au pays natal" in 1942 and where he made his first "rediscoveries" of that visual universe André Breton would later describe as an untrammelled union of real and magical worlds. It is mainly a dock and factory worker neighborhood.

The wooden house [where he was born] was built in 1900 by his maternal grandfather Fermín Hoyo Espelusín, a construction worker... This grandfather is the most direct family antecedent for

Mendive's artistic talent, for he was also a carver and engraver. He would be sought for complicated architectural projects with decorative work and other nonfunctional aspects, such as the "Mudejar Palace" in the Plaza de las Ursulinas or the monument to General Antonio Maceo in the Havana park of the same name. During the building of the latter he was to be blinded in an accident. He was one of those anonymous master-builders who from colonial times spontaneously shaped "the style" of a city "without style" as it was aptly described by Carpentier in a memorable essay on the architecture of Havana; one of those eclectic "naifs" who were bold enough to invent scores of rare orders, with unusual, fancy columns and capitals whose design was hardly ever repeated throughout the kilometers of avenued porchways dating back to the turn of the century...

But it was not only his family. Mendive grew up in a crowded, tucked-away city neighborhood, with little traffic, where there are silk-cotton trees on street corners and yards with banana trees. Everybody knows one another. On Sunday men sit out on the porches in their vests playing dominoes, people chat from house to house across the street, and doors are left ajar, on a hook, so as not to have to go and open them each time a neighbor wants to come in to the living room or dining room or go through to the kitchen at the back for a chat, while children play ball outdoors or mark the pavement with chalk. It is one of those bustling Havana neighborhoods that is at the same time well-ordered and family-oriented, by-passed to a certain extent by the traffic and conglomeration of more hectic central areas. It is a neighborhood where family and group traditions are kept strong.

In this neighborhood, the case of a family like Mendive's, mulatto believers in *santería* or *Regla de Ocha* — the syncretic faith derived basically from Yorubá beliefs — is fairly common... believers don't see a contradiction with contemporary Cuban life, in which they play a positive part. This can be summed up in a strong image to be seen in houses in Mendive's neighborhood, as in Cuban homes elsewhere: an altar to *Santa Barbara-Changó* or the Brown Virgin of *El Cobre-Ochún,* flanked by portraits of Fidel Castro, José Martí, Camilo Cienfuegos, Che and even Lenin...

Santería worship spans a wide range, from the *babalao* and *iyawó* to the non-believer who in a moment of desperation seeks "protection" or makes a "promise", and the Catholic who unconsciously puts red flowers for Saint Barbara and white ones for the Virgin of Mercy, not knowing that they are the colors of African deities, or who worships a mass-produced statue of a leper on crutches, without realizing that it is taken from a parable of Jesus syncretized with the Dahomeyan god *Babalú-Ayé* and not a saint canonized by the Church.

Ever since he was a child, Mendive had shown a natural inclination toward painting and artistic things, and a great love for animals which he always liked to have around him: dogs, pigeons, rabbits, ducks, fish, a peacock, a monkey... He would pass the time painting the altar to Saint Barbara in the living room of his home, and also flowers, cityscapes and family portraits...

He studied up to eighth grade in a state school. When the revolution triumphed he was 14. He enrolled in the Villate Academy to study commercial art, which was in those times a base for the poor with artistic talent. But he was only there for a few months. His painting, his [1955] UNESCO prize for painting, the recognition of his work, and above all, the new climate of support for culture from the outset of the revolution, consolidated a decision on his part to devote himself to art. In 1959 he enrolled in painting and sculpture classes at the San Alejandro Academy...

Paradoxically, at the Academy, the future painter was primarily interested in sculpture... His hands shaped brown and black nudes in a sensual and opulent naturalism, with a baroque concern for body movement... He did of course also study painting. He worked on landscape, portraits, flowers, the human form... He liked to cross the bay to Regla — a town which has its own "virgin", Our Lady of Regla, patron saint of Havana port, syncretized with *Yemayá*, Yoruba goddess of the sea, and where there has been a strong presence of *santería* and *Abakuá*...

... [Mendive] completely identifies with what he paints. He is incapable of painting from a distance, from the outside, not even as an academic exercise. This is very important to understanding his later painting. He paints only people, animals and things that are close to him, that belong to his creative universe. When he is tempted to paint something exterior, he does so by almost forcing it into his personal world, to the point that might seem incongruous, though not in aesthetic dimension. This psychological-artistic device, framed within his wide ingenuity, is what produced the strong images of a cosmic rocket flying among Yoruba deities... or Martí on a small rocking chair with Che and *Oyá*, the orisha of the cemetery, who cuts the flowers...

*Gerardo Mosquera in **Exploraciones en la plástica cubana** (Explorations into Cuban Art), Letras Cubanas, Havana, 1983, pp. 232-245.*

Erí Wolé

"My head is turning" [*Erí Wolé* in Yoruba] ... it's philosophical analysis, thematic renovation and abrupt experience. Here we have the old concept of composition in bands; and yet, they are not absolutely rectilinear but irregular and curved. This new concept of composition allows movement. In each of the bands there is an action as in the early **Birth of *Ochún***, this time tremendously dynamic. The first band shows his ancestors. Among them, mounted on a goat, *Eshu*, spirit of evil and good, with his two faces. The face of good smokes a cigar; the face of evil devours a rat's head.

In the second band is the painter himself and his family; all seated on chairs, they look into infinity. Flying over their heads an eye, a peacock, a hen; and next to the head of the painter's self-portrait, fear in animal form. The third band, in sinuous and triangular form, bounded along the bottom by a large serpent (his constant theme of life and death) takes the form of a bladder engulfing humankind in its chaos. Many rats devour men and women, and near the center, a waning moon and a little man sitting on top. The alienated little man is staring. A man who is madness thrusts a dagger in the moon. All the while each rat eats an arm of a woman to stop her from fighting, the tongue of a man to stop him from speaking, the genitals of a child to stop procreation. In the fourth, main band, huge peacocks fly over a bus. One peacock alights on the roof of a small bus. The passengers can be seen. One is going out of the back door. *Ikú*, blocking the way, barricades the front door. Mendive stretched out on the street, with his right foot under the front wheel, looking at the moon. In the last band are men and women, his friends. At the end of the band, the self-portrait of the painter on crutches. The predominant color is red.

Nancy Morejón in "El mundo de un primitivo" in ***Gaceta de Cuba****, Havana, No. 76, September 1969, quoted in Mosquero, pp. 280-82.*

Elegba

Mendive welcomes us smiling. He is young, but his thick black beard gives him the look of an Ethiopian monk. He has a deep voice and ponders over the questions before answering. In the yard, a peacock, sacred bird of *Oshún* and *Yemayá,* shows off its enormous tail, while some new-born ducklings splash in a green gully. In the distance, the sound of factory whistles.

"You ask why I chose the Yoruba theme for my work. Well, I'll tell you... African traditions that have so influenced our culture have been the medium that has enabled me to express my life experiences. It is the theme I have always used, it is my means of expression, although my style has changed a lot from my early paintings to the present. At the beginning, my work was aggressive in its impact, which produced an ephemeral sensation in the spectator, given the violence of the painting. Now that is no longer a prevalent factor, but rather subtlety of image, which is designed to envelop the same previously aggressive elements in a more suggestive atmosphere."

Mendive's family is one of those typical Cuban families — of which there are so many in the western provinces — who have kept our traditions of Yoruba ancestry strong. His father has been a railway worker for over 25 years. His uncles and cousins are *tamboreros (oló-batá)* and singers (*akpwón*), of that line of Cubans who have handed down Yoruba rhythms, songs and language over the centuries. The mother reigns in this house, moving through her domain with that legendary dignity of the priestess (*iyalosha*) daughters of Yemayá, to give us that cup of coffee or, in her large red-tiled kitchen impregnated with the aroma of herbs, to make us the dishes brought from African lands: *ilá, oshinshín, amalá*. Food for deities and human beings.

Mendive's background is traditional and at the same time modern, which permits him, thanks to his academic study and his contact with other young Cuban painters, to be up-to-date on the latest trends in world painting, familiar with ancient and modern techniques, and also, thanks to his family life, to be deeply informed on the complex symbolism of our myths. There is nothing gratuitous in his work; each color, each form, has a meaning, a precise function...

It is difficult to classify Mendive's work as that of a given school or trend. It is neither symbolist nor primitive, in the European sense. While his inspiration comes from deep national roots and his images from certain paintings and sculpture we can find in Cuban *casas de santos* — especially in the provinces — decorating walls, jugs or items used for ritual, and even holy manuscripts or books, and whose ingenuity is like a last star in the Cuban firmament of the great art of the Yoruba and Dahomeyan peoples of Western Africa, there is a contemporary feel and use of the latest techniques in all his work. In the composition, in the textures he creates, there is always the intelligence of a modern artist, desiring to express his vision of the world and to find a language of his own with its roots in one of the rich traditions of his people...

Mendive lives surrounded by paintings and sculptures. In his room he has some of his early work, done as a student, of which he is particularly fond. He has decorated the walls with photographs of classic African, Greek and pre-Colombian art. The stained-glass partitions are of vividly colored geometric design. And in prominent position, opposite his bed, the first thing he sees when he wakes up and before he falls asleep: *Elegba*. A statue over a century old, inherited from his forbears. A startling head some 45cms in height, carved in coral rock, with cowrie eyes, and the mouth wide open, as if clamoring from the start of time. This *Elegba* is the most impressive image I have seen of the master of paths and crossroads, symbol of destiny, in our mythology...

Mendive accompanies me to the porch. He smiles as he sees me off. As I reach the corner, I discover a huge revolutionary mural painted on a white wall. I am taken by the imagination and rhythm in the ordering of the figures. Thinking of a talented popular artist hidden in the neighborhood, I returned to Mendive's house and asked. He replied with a look of complicity: "Sometimes I go with the kids and the people of the Committee [for the Defence of the Revolution] to decorate the block."

Again there is a smile on his old Ethiopian monk's face.

Rogelio Martínez Furé in ***Diálogos imaginarios*** *(Imaginary Dialogues), Arte y Literatura, Havana, 1979, pp.239-243, quoted in Mosquera, pp. 240-41.*

The painter's castle

Entering the home and studio of Manuel Mendive is crossing the threshold into the magical world of an artist who has gathered within its domain all the elements that nurture his paintings, sculpture, ceramics and "dancing canvases". A colorful menagerie of tropical fish, parrots, canaries, parakeets and dogs of many breeds (including his favorite Alsatian) live harmoniously together with his hens and ducks and aging peacock, sacred bird of *Oshun* and *Yemaya,* the two female aquarian deities in the Afro-Cuban pantheon. They all share the modern studio where Mendive works by day, in the bright sunlight streaming in, uninvited, through the large airy room. They co-habit the yard of lemon, avocado, coconut and orange trees, herbs and wild flowers. At the back, a goat awaits the propitious occasion for a banquet offering.

Leaving behind the noise and artificial smells of the city, Mendive took refuge beyond the city outskirts. He settled in the small village of Santa María del Rosario, in search of a night symphony of crickets and the fragrance of rosemary. Visible from Mendive's roof-terrace, atop the hill, towering over the village, Santa María del Rosario Church, one of the oldest in Cuba, with its gold-plated mahogany altar. It was built by the rich Count of Casa Bayona, a member of the creole sugar aristocracy about whom strange stories have been handed down, not least his relations with his African slaves. The painter found a small, abandoned house made of the best wood, which had been the overseer's home. This house, with its modest but classical appearance, has been painstakingly rebuilt and transformed in the image of the artist, with high tiled roof, two wings, porches, patio and yard. It is Mendive's shrine to the imagination, amidst flora and fauna, where his friends also find refuge. With his now thick gray beard and Rastafarian locks, Mendive has even more the appearance of an Ethiopian monk, receiving visitors, friends or new acquaintances, with a warm smile, recounting stories of the region, which he has also depicted in an enormous mural at the entrance to the village.

Undoubtedly a mythical world. But a culture without myth would be a tree without leaves.

Pedro Pérez Sarduy in ***Water, Fish, Men,*** *catalogue to a Mendive exhibition at the October Gallery, London, 1988.*

MARCELINO AROZARENA

Bembesiana

An unpublished poem read by the poet in March 1992 on his 80th birthday.

Bembé,
I too want to see,
though your
skating on sand pierces my brain.

To me your sound
burns feverish
and makes me tremble.

I tremble like a *chekeré,*
I tremble
not with cold,
or shock,
but sheer pleasure under the *aché* of *bembé.*

I'm sorry
if you see me tremble;
I'm a musical instrument

I tremble like cane in the wind,
like vertical waves,
like that oriental cha-cha, canasta maraca.
Basta!
Never discovering the inner me:
On the inside she chatters, on the outside I *chekeré.*

But I never stop trembling
like a comet's trail,
poetic metaphor likens me to earthquake;
like a whip I see me punish feeling;
I'm the heart metronome of the *bembé*
- *diástole,*
sístole-;
I berth in Pleasure port and load with relish:
creature that I am of rhythm,
with the rhythm I stay.

My *chekeré,* swollen tail-less gourd.
I can't stop shaking it though it shakes me.
Yes,
Shangó on his path of *Aña,*
is out to lash me to the tryptic *batá*:
Okónkolo
Itótele
Iyá.

I take the hollow cedarwood
yet
its mysteries never divulge;
the two tense goat hides
right
and left
receive my drumming,
echos that bring alive the *bembé.*

Enter!
Since the *bembé* is profane
may *Obatalá* open her white dove hands
may *Papá Oggún* let loose his irons and *Babalú, his* dogs,
stay away Lame *Osaín* and his green medicine
for he who comes is lost,
the evil eye is about,
prayers turn to curls.
Anima Sola is animated

Yemayá is unhurried in her
enveloping waves,
and *Elegba* invents a truce reaping paths.
Do you know?
We've reached the critical moment:
Elegbá has the key to break open the *bembé.*

ELOY MACHADO

Asere

Two of the many poems Eloy Machado performs in his Sunday "yard" sessions in Havana. *Asere* is a creole Cuban term in its contemporary usage loosely translatable as "brother", meaning good or trusted friend. It is of *Carabalí* origin, that is, from the region of Old Calabar, today southeast Nigeria. In the *Abakuá* religion in Cuba, as in the *Igbo* religion in Calabar, *asere* was a form of greeting: "I greet you".

ASERE I say

Asere I say
in my people's
tongue
asere I say
I come from
Ethiopia
asere chisel and mallet
saw, hammer and nail
masquerade
of my sweat
asere I say
breathing
the heat of the furnace
reasonably
like the wind
blowing in one direction
I love the sound of *son*
the word people
that's why we are
antero ñaña
the root of the leaf

that's why
in coconut and cacao
where the rumba
was bullets
with molasses
and great feeling
there was I
asere endabio.

I am all that

I am the poet of rumba
I am *danzón,* echo of the drum.
I am the mission of my roots,
the story of my slum.
I am life slipping by,
I am the colors on a string of beads
keeping my roots alive.
I am chili pepper,
I am hot,
I am the step of *Shangó,*
step of *Obbatalá*
laughter of *Yemayá,*
bravery of *Oggún,*
the marble or spinning-top of *Elegba.*
I am *Obbá,*
I am *Siré, siré,*
I am *Aberiñán* and *Aberisan,*
I am reason in the puzzle,
the man who brought light
to *Obedí* the Hunter of doubt,
I am the hand of truth,
I am *Arere,*
I am conscience,
I am *Orula.*

TATO QUIÑONES

Ifa says

Taken from **A pie de obra** (On the Spot), Unión, Havana, 1990, pp 24-27, 51-52.

Ifa says

Blessed be two, not one
That was prophesied to the sea lily
To go to the very mire of creation
The moment of creation has come!
ODU DE IFA

First, it was my mother's belly, its warm juices lovingly enveloping me.

They say the day I was born Havana baked in 40 degrees centigrade and the flies were dropping on the tablecloths and bedcovers, flapping stupified in the August heat.

The first pains came with daybreak. She was alone and afraid, and went to the home of her mother, my grandmother, Obadina, may she rest in peace.

"I think the baby's coming," she said to her.

Obadina kissed her on the forehead and told her to kneel before the *canastillero* for the *santos.*

Shaking bells, rattles and maracas, she invoked them one by one in the name of love and life, *kosi ikú, kosi aro, kosi eyé, kosi ofo, arikú babagua,* so that we should have health, tranquility and a good life and to ward off death, sickness, evil and shame.

Then she vigorously rubbed her body with herbs dampened with holy water; she traced crosses of powdered eggshell and *corojo* oil on the soles of her shoes, and helped her to her feet.

They reached the hospital as it struck noon. By then my mother was in a cold sweat and walked holding on to walls and furniture, and Obadina's arm, hearing her sweet consolation.

She was taken up to the labor room. Obadina stayed below murmuring a rosary.

At four in the afternoon she was still shouting, groaning and crying with each wave of pain.

Obadina's sole thought was that the christian God was not powerful or merciful enough. She stuffed the rosary deep into her pocket, smoothed the folds of her full starched skirt and went to the godfather's, to the house of *babalao* Epifanio Ruiz.

It was a big airy house, with a garden down the side where a peacock was strutting, and a door always open, barely held by an enormous shell.

Epifanio was a black man in his fifties at the time, tall, very thin, with a tired gait and a hollow voice; his look was wise and gentle behind the thick tortoiseshell glasses he always wore.

The *babalao* consulted *Ifá* with the *ekuelé,* transcribing the *Odu* as it was revealed to him. When he finished, he told Obadina that a boy would be born, strong and good; son of *Changó* and favorite of *Yemayá*; that the motto for all his days would be *Obá Ikuro,* The King Didn't Lie, and that any lies he told could become truths, and the truths lies, and having come into the world to win he'd never lose. He also said that the one about to be born should always carry on him a bit of red cloth, and that for the first years of his life he must wear an iron chain around his left ankle so that *Oggún,* who was always jealous of sons of *Changó,* would recognise and respect him. After saying this, he gave her a piece of red cloth and a hen's egg that he had cleansed in *omiero de Oloddu Mare.*

"Now go back to the hospital", he told her. "You must find a way of getting to your daughter and put the piece of cloth on her belly and rub it with the egg. Then you will go out into the street and smash it on the nearest corner; the boy will be born strong and healthy, and you and your daughter will live to see him grow up. As soon as he is born, you must cleanse him with the cloth, and then keep it so that he carries it with him always. Now go, do what I have told you, and may *Olofi* be with you.

Drenched in sweat, wild-eyed, grasping the side of the bed, my mother was almost beside herself when Obadina, nobody knows how, burst into the room, covered her belly with the piece of red cloth and rubbed it gently with the egg.

"Ay, *Changó*," she said. "*Cawo, cawosile* every day! *Oba cozo*, king of kings!" The one about to be born is your son, power and glory be yours on man's earth, help him and help his mother, daughter of mine and most faithful and loving woman of *Oyá*!

Then, without looking or speaking to anybody, she went out into the street and on the nearest corner threw the egg to the ground.

They say I didn't cry. That I had big blue eyes, and short, woolly hair, like an albino.

When Obadina came back into the room, they let her cleanse me with the piece of red cloth that for many years after I would always carry in my pocket, and that my mother still keeps in a corner of the wardrobe, along with other mementoes she considers important.

The cockerel

for Nicolás Reinoso

He who is hungry doesn't worry about taboos.
He who is hungry doesn't worry about death.
He who is hungry will take the money from the offering.

From an Iwi poem

A huge cockerel suddenly appeared in the high window onto the yard. It was a grown bird, sleek and healthy-looking, that jumped in to land on the bare kitchen table.

"Into the pot with him!" I said, catching it.

"Just a moment!", said grandma. "You never know what that bird might have been used for. Who knows what trouble it might have cleaned up and where?"

"Shall I let it go then?"

"No way! You hold that animal there until I find out whether it can or can't be eaten."

So grandma went and opened the little cupboard behind the door for the *Santos Guerreros* (Warrior Saints) and consulted their opinion by throwing the coconut.

Elegguá, Oggún, Osun and *Ochosi* replied there was no problem: the cockerel could be eaten by all in the house. They would only eat the blood, the feathers, the head, the innards and the legs roasted on the grill.

After the meal, when we were all still drowsy with the stupor of soup and fricassée, I asked grandma what she would have done with the cockerel if the Warriors had ordered us not to eat it.

"Don't be asking things that are of no concern to you!" she said. "Sleep tight, and pleasant dreams. There's a new day tomorrow!"

EXCILIA SALDAÑA

Ofumelli

Ofumelli (1967) was published in **Pájaro Cascabel**, Special Issue "En Cuba Ahora", Nos 5/6, January-July 1967, Mexico, pp.43-46.

Don't go and repeat this, my friend; there are those who would make of this my crime.

J.W.Goethe

Achini má achini má
Ikú furé buyée má
Achini má achini má
Ediyó furé buyé má
Achini má achini má
Ogún furé buyé má [1]

For César Calvo

I

Alright, foreigner, I don't blame you for not knowing my language
we shall go
to the sea where all tongues merge
At the
time not registered by clocks, when only
sleepwalkers and blind moths or those who
create love without looking each other in the eye
can feel
Then *Yemayá* enters to order the life of mortals
The earth listens and pays homage
So you, foreigner, surely loved
yet foreigner in this city

where women hang their looks on balconies
and are the ultimate sole repository of anger
so you, if you want to understand why
the parks strip themselves like a new bride
and some trees always wave their arms
in defiance of the wind that goes to die in the rocks
so you will cup your hands
to collect the warm milk dripping
incessantly
from the den of night.

II

The beginning and end of questions and the open sign
The coconuts are face down. The cowries are waiting.[2]
The answer can only come from *Ifá*.
These are his words:
This year tenderness will reign
over walled streets of neon lights
hasty people who let fly
brimming with joy or tedium
young mothers pulling prams who
talk in doctor's surgeries
and mistake melancholy for tonsils
those who put off sleep
or perhaps bring forward the dawn
all lie with the city under the drum call

I shall also be with you
a light shawl round my shoulders
a rainbow of light round my neck
I too splashing your cheeks with my blood-dyed hair
shall be with you
(Letting you be taken in like a child
by this parade of acrobats
you know nothing)
I ask you to take me to the hotel window a while
where you leaned insulting the stars
and forgetting the route that awaits you

where there are only friendly sounds
(there's room for the possibility)
Shall we try a demented way of loving
or might you simply say:
"You see? This is a smile."

The city has no name
it hasn't been baptized in any ritual
and the blacks and the whites argue over it
and the whites and the blacks mount it
up to the orgasm of the last bell tower
and I... I would like to offer you a city
the real hidden city of *Yemayá Oloku*

III

Seven colors watch over me
and the spark in my hand gleams
("God save you and protect you from my hatred
of the centuries and centuries of a fall
God save you")

If only you knew that all paths lead
to striking the unreality of my skin
and your sword can do nothing
against the thinnest of my veins
If only you knew that I have collected the sweat of love
(and on it braided three of your body hairs)[3]
If only you knew that never again can you raise the whip
or sing an unconcerned song
after the holocaust of virgins.

If only you knew that hunchbacks and albinos are sacred[4]
that in the mountain the owl flirts with the thicket
If only you knew perhaps only my name
bathed in sacred plants
you would try nothing
I am
Oyá

goddess and *señora,*
lady and mistress of the cemetery.

IV
Be ready
Prepare your eyelids for the sleep of white vultures
There's no hurry
Forgive yourself.
Meditate a little on the fate of suicides
It's none of your business
Protect yourself
(I don't want to harm you)
I want to lavish dreams on your body
I want to think that all the while I will crumble
bread under your watchful instinct
and that one day you will say to me
"Woman, we have to move quarters, the bedstead grates
like a *charanga*. What the hell's happening to us? Is this
boredom
                    or the love of marmots?"
(I don't want to harm you
but
scratching the rhythm of calm
rarifying the space of a supplication
monstrously volatile
my heralds will follow you
wherever you take your shadow
in all corners of this square world)

Stop

"*Ikú,* follow him for me to the point of hallucination
you have pierced my uterus
like an old sieve
with your hard gums
you have cracked my nipples
I am your mother
nobody but me

can you serve under your spell"

Your body is one of lament
in spite of everything
I don't want to harm you
Listen you, foreigner in my city
it is the women who possess the men
All places are equal
solitude whinnies in any setting

("*Ikú* alight on his head")

Hold on to my gills
know my breathing
they are the death rattles
death rattle
a beach with a single gull
S.O.S.
(save us from the bottles with messages)
Glass
a single drop of salt
"The mirror will reproduce your ridiculous buttocks
the vortex of my thigh has
a dog eternally pissing on it
Foreigner
get up and go
(I don't want to harm you)
Foreigner
tears, Tears. I want to sleep)
I give you the chance to dissolve me
or forget me simply as smoke from the ashes
Get up
I order you
I am
Oyá
a poor woman mistress of the dead.[5]

Endnotes

1. The chant is to ward off death (*Ikú*), grief, crime (*Ediyó*) and evil spell (*Ogún*).
2. Coconuts and cowries are used in ritual.
3. Exorcism used by women to prevent the phallic erection of the man in question with another woman.
4. Hunchbacks and albinos were created by the supreme god *Olofí* one day when he was drunk.
5. The mythical story is that *Changó*, the god of thunder, fire and vanity, the handsomest of blacks, had three women: *Obbá*, his legitimate wife, symbol of conjugal love; *Ochún*, the divine whore, goddess of honey, rivers, joy and sensuality; and *Oyá*, goddess of lightning, who loves *Changó* to distraction, the lover who desires to be his wife, who, knowing the lover *Changó* is, put *Ikú* in the corner of her home so that he would never leave. In this recreation of the myth, death will enter the foreigner's mind. It is a symbolic death, too much love, too much fear, too much solitude.

EUGENIO HERNÁNDEZ

María Antonia

Taken from the Eugenio Hernández collection of plays **Teatro** (Theater), Letras Cubanas, Havana, 1989, pp.94-106.

SCENE III

The Godmother's house and the river

(In a poor neighborhood. A day after the last scene.)

GODMOTHER. (At the door to her house. To the gathering.)

On this day, give us the calm of your grace, in the joyfulness of your steps; the freshness of your love in this river that runs before us, like a happy, contented child. Keep the waters from clouding or running off course. Men strong like the wind, let us take the Virgin to her waters. (A group of men go into the house and carry the Virgin on their shoulders.) Morning water, let us enter you with all our strength on our shoulders. (Singing.)

Oshiminigeee agó-shaworí kokó / agó shaworí kokó / Yalodde apetebí / Orúmila / Agó chaworí kokó.

AKPWON. (Taking up the chant.)

Tonu Mase tonu / Mase tonu Mase.

CHORUS. *Tónashe, tónashe.*

(People, singing and dancing, move in procession to the river.)

IYALOCHAS. (At the river bank. With the words that are repeated at the beginning of all rites.) *Kosí ikú, kosí aro, kosí oyó, kosí efó, arikú babagua.*

IYAWO. (In unison.) Let there be no death, nor sickness, nor bloodshed or evil, nor shame. Health and good fortune, our father!

(The men holding the Virgin enter the water with the Godmother. The *Iyalochas* sound the metal bells.)

MAN. *Oshún morí-yeyeo-obiniose-ababe-orosúm nonicolalague-iyá mi-coyá-soún-yalé carigué ñare guaña-rí-oyalé cuasé o aña Ayuba!*

GODMOTHER. We, who do not enjoy grace, have cleansed ourselves with yours to give us the life and health we do not have. May the evil in which we live end and the *santo* have compassion on our misery.

Iyá mí ilé oddo / Iyá mí ilé oddo / iyá mí ilé oddo / iyá bobbó ashé ishemí saramawó é / iyá bobbo ashé

CHORUS. (Singing)

Iyá mí ilé oddo / iyá mí ilé oddo / iyá mí ilé oddo / ishemí saramawó é
iyá mí ilé oddo

(María Antonia appears.)

GODMOTHER. Daughter of *Oshún*, be joyous with us, dance, queen, that your days be tranquil, woman; may your spirit have good fortune, and your *eledda* be blessed.

MARIA ANTONIA. (Falling to her knees before her.) Be with me and guide me! Cleanse my spirit with your bounty and my shame with your fresh water, mother of mine. Make me new, like the first day I saw your compassionate eyes, my mother.

GODMOTHER. (Cleansing her.) May *Oloddumare* protect your awakening each day. And may night not fall before drying your anguish; may you find your voice and *Elegguá* clear your way; may evil be kept from you always and may good be yours; may your name shine on the lips of those who are gathered here.

AKPWON. (Singing)

Wónlówo unsheke / yaloddo moyébberé.

CHORUS. *Wamilé Osún / Osún wámila / aláweré / wámilé Osún.*

(María Antonia enters the river with the *Iyalochas*, one is mounted by *Oshún*. She faces María Antonia. With the characteristic movements, she invites María Antonia to dance, to laugh, to sing, and to imitate her happiness and sensuality.)

AKPWON. (Singing)

Yalodde koledderún / wedde wedde koledderún.

CHORUS. (Singing)

Wedde wedde / koleddertún / Wedde wedde koleddertún / wedde wedde.

(The procession advances dancing and singing on the way back to the Godmother's house. At the head, María Antonia and the one mounted by *Oshún*, dancing. Entering the house.)

AKPWON. Iyalodde mofinyeo.

CHORUS. *A la mofinyé moró.*

AKPWON. Iyalodde mofinyeo.

CHORUS. *A la mofinyé moró.*

(The dancing intensifies crescendo. *Akpwon* chants persistently over María Antonia, who is on the verge of a trance. To precipitate the possession, he rings a little brass bell over her. María Antonia tries to escape but the *Iyalochas* and *Oshún* make a ring around her. *Akpwón* talks in her ear. María Antonia cries out, roughly breaks through the circle, and flees.

CHORUS. *A la misere misere wolosún.*

(The music loses intensity, to a low murmur that fades. Yuyo follows María Antonia.)

YUYO. (Half drunk.) Whew! It's getting hot round here! Not a breath of air to be had.

MARIA ANTONIA. Nobody's getting my head. See how they were going steal it from me? For a minute there, I thought I'd lost it. *Oshún* can't find a head and is after me, but for the life of me, I'm not going to let her have it. Last night, before you arrived, *Ikú* came to see me; *Ikú* comes after me every day.

YUYO. Doesn't that feel good? (Caressing her.)

MARIA ANTONIA. (Shaking herself free.) Don't you ever do that again.

YUYO. Why not?

MARIA ANTONIA. 'Cos no macho's going to lay a finger on me.

YUYO. Let me touch you, go on.

MARIA ANTONIA. Get away!

YUYO. Just a little. Let me kiss you like last night, remember?

MARIA ANTONIA. Listen, are you going?

YUYO. Let's go to your room again, *negrona*.

MARIA ANTONIA. Do you want me to make trouble for you? Nobody's getting in my blood.

YUYO. Don't you be treating me that way. Be my woman again.
MARIA ANTONIA. It's like their witchcraft at work on me!
YUYO. You weren't like this last night. Now you can hardly look at me. Why?
MARIA ANTONIA. It's not such a pretty face to look at. Get out, get out of here. Go and have some fun!
YUYO. What have I done wrong? I don't deserve this. I've been good to you.
MARIA ANTONIA. Has last night gone to your head?
YUYO. You didn't mean what you said? (María Antonia bursts out laughing. Yuyo confronts her.) I'm macho enough, don't mess with me!
MARIA ANTONIA. And I'm woman enough! I might lie with you but that's not the same as being together.
YUYO. Then, why, why did you do it?
MARIA ANTONIA. I wanted to.
YUYO. That's a lie.
MARIA ANTONIA. Solitude for the dead!
YUYO. And what was it you said to me? Eh? What was it you said to me? That I should leave my wife and come live with you. Don't you remember you tore your dress and we had each other on the floor, María Antonia, we rolled around and the floorboards creaked. You said: hold me! And I held you and you laughed, until the wind outside broke a branch of the silk cotton tree, and you...
MARIA ANTONIA. Don't go on.
YUYO. ...trembled and said: *Oyá* has just broken *Iroko*'s arm.
MARIA ANTONIA. Open your eyes, Yuyo. Last night, I closed them tight, very tight when I was with you, but you'd gone... I hurt so! I wasn't with you, I was with Julián. It wasn't your arms, your breath, your sweat. Julián's my prison. I tried to forget, but couldn't; bury him in the lie, but couldn't; in my kisses, in my caresses. Why did I lie, when all I wanted was to hide in you? You disgust me. Get out.
YUYO. Look, look what you've done to me. Give me María Antonia, give me her all! (He grabs her and tries to kiss her.)
MARIA ANTONIA. (Brusquely breaking free.) What's this? What do you want of me? I'm no filthy rag. Or am I worse? Always the

same old thing. Can't feel myself breath, can't sing a song that's not a lie. I want to forget and be born again. If anyone's listening, before I drown in these words, I can't go on. I'm sick and tired of singing, and rumba, and rotting in this misery; of this body that only knows how to give desire, of being María Antonia, of being what everyone wants me to be, get it? No! How can you get it, when that's what you come for!

YUYO. What are you saying? What's the matter with you? I've got a few pesos still.

MARIA ANTONIA. Go back to your wife.

YUYO. Whatever you want, let's have fun some place, and leave all this. Don't be crazy. A *negra rica* like you! We can't set the world aright, but we can set ourselves right.

MARIA ANTONIA. I've had enough of you and your trouble!

YUYO. *Mi negra,* don't leave me.

MARIA ANTONIA. Look, there's your wife.

YUYO. I don't care. I told her everything.

MARIA ANTONIA. What?

YUYO. That I was coming to live with you and that...

MARIA ANTONIA. What did she have to say to that? Tell me.

YUYO. (On the offensive.) She laughed and said your kind of woman couldn't belong to anyone. You can't leave me; you can't play around with men like that.

MARIA ANTONIA. Go with your wife to the *toque* and enjoy yourself. She's right: a whore can't be a woman even if she tries. We don't know how to build on anything.

MATILDE. (On stage.) Yuyo, come home, come on. Let's go, Yuyo.

MARIA ANTONIA. Do as your wife says.

YUYO. I saw you enjoying it, laughing, beside yourself.

MARIA ANTONIA. Shut up!

MATILDE. Yuyo!

YUYO. You only have thoughts for Julián, eh?

MARIA ANTONIA. Mention him again, and I'll break your soul.

YUYO. But he doesn't love you. If he wins, he'll leave you high and dry.

MATILDE. Come away from that woman!

MARIA ANTONIA. (To Matilde.) Get him away from here or I

won't answer for my actions.

YUYO. That's why you're like you are, all churned up inside. Nobody loves you. A woman like you is good for pleasure, that's all.

MATILDE. (To María Antonia.) What have you done to him?

MARIA ANTONIA. What María Antonia knows how to do to a man!

MATILDE. You've gone and bewitched him, haven't you?

MARIA ANTONIA. I lay with him. I don't know if after that, he'll ever be able to lie with you again!

MATILDE. He's not the first husband you've driven away. You're jealous. He's my husband.

MARIA ANTONIA. Well, there you have him! Intact. Except I forgot to ask to borrow him. It's not my fault he follows me around like a dog. Put him on a leash! (She goes off.)

MATILDE. (To Yuyo.) No, this can't end here. This can't be it, Yuyo. No. Yuyo, why? Why? What does it matter? What does it matter? That slut's no good to anybody. What does it matter? If I'd been a man, I'd have done the same, and then I'd have spat on her butt. So be it, punishment where punishment's due. (Yuyo pulls a bottle from his pocket.) Don't drink any more, man. You've only yourself to harm.

YUYO. Go to hell!

MATILDE. Don't let it be said that a woman like that...

YUYO. Leave me be, Matilde, leave me be; do me a favor, will you?

MATILDE. Come on home. I'll heat some water for you to bathe. Yuyo, listen, listen, do it for your children, not me!

YUYO. Go away!

MATILDE. I'm not going if you're not coming with me.

YUYO. Go away, before I let into you right here.

MATILDE. You'd do that to your own wife?

YUYO. Get out of the way!

MATILDE. Hell, you weren't like that before! You'd come home from work and lie by my side.

YUYO. Yeah, I'd lie by your side in that doghouse seeing the roof coming down over us, and the kids crying from hunger, and every cent I earned I'd give you; it didn't bother you I stank of

rotten potato, there was the water to wash off the smell. You forgot it real fast but...me? I was tired of living in that pigswill! I wanted to live. I've a right to live!
MATILDE. What's that woman done to you? What's it that woman does, Yuyo? Where's it all going to end? Yuyo, don't ruin yourself! Yuyo!
YUYO. (Entering the Godmother's house. With a shout.) María Antonia! (The crowd thins out. The music suddenly stops. Face to face, Yuyo and María Antonia. The Godmother, interceding.)
GODMOTHER. Yuyo, son, go home, don't ruin yourself. Go on. María Antonia, listen just for once. How come your head can't take any advice?
MARIA ANTONIA. Who told them to stop?
GODMOTHER. You'll be killed like a bitch.
MARIA ANTONIA. Like a wild bitch, which isn't the same. You only die once. Go on playing, *Oshún* wants to be happy.
MATILDE. Yuyo, your children, Yuyo!
GODMOTHER. (To Yuyo.) Isn't your wife enough for you? María Antonia likes to tempt death, play with it, run with it. But one day, one day...
SECOND *IYALOCHA*. Yuyo, son, do what your wife says. Go!
GODMOTHER. (To María Antonia.) Spare me this misery, I beg you.
MARIA ANTONIA. If the river has stones, it's not because they've been thrown there; the water knows what must lie at the bottom. Play on! (Defiant, she starts to sing.) *Yeyé bi obbí tosúo Yeyé bi obbí tosúo.*

(People try to take her.)

GODMOTHER. I love her as if she were mine, but I know she has one serious defect: she's too strongheaded. She thinks the world can be shaped to her desires.
MATILDE. *Obbatalá*, break that bad woman! Have her burn in sorrow; twist the paths, that she have no peace or rest.

(Yuyo tries to throw himself on María Antonia.)

1ST MAN. Let her go, man!
2ND MAN. Do it for your children!
MATILDE. No, Yuyo, no!
MARIA ANTONIA. Let him go! If he's macho, let him walk

without a stick!

(Yuyo takes out a knife. Matilde throws her arms around him. He throws her off.)

GODMOTHER. (Embracing him to calm him and get the knife off him.) Wash your head in fresh water and don't stray from the path Elegguá has given you. Shake off the evil from the corners; *Laroye*'s ready to stir up trouble. Bless *Elegguá,* messenger of *Olofí,* who has opened a fresh path where there's no place for misfortune and evil. (Yuyo makes unintelligible sounds.) Go to your children and your wife. And if anyone calls you, bite back your voice and don't reply. *Ikú* is under the sheets until the third day when the new moon comes.

(Yuyo violently breaks loose from the Godmother. He goes after María Antonia. Face to face with her, he lifts the arm holding the knife. A kid shouts from offstage, breaking the tension.)

TINO. (Voice.) Julián won! He won!

MARIA ANTONIA. (To Yuyo.) Go on!

(Yuyo lets the knife drop at María Antonia's feet and people run to Tino.)

MARIA ANTONIA. Never take out a weapon if you're not going to use it! (She joins the crowd.)

GODMOTHER. (Picking up the knife. To Matilde.) Take him away before María Antonia puts him down more.

(Matilde takes Yuyo away. Outside the house, people crowd round Tino.)

1ST *SANTERA*. Fine day that black chose to box.

2ND *SANTERA*. The *santos* protect him.

1ST MAN. Well, are you going to let him speak or what? Come on Tino, tell us how it went.

TINO. Great fight! It was the fourth round. Spider had him up against the rope. (Acting it out.) Right, left, right, left; an upper cut and he threw him against the rope. (He makes out he's been beaten towards the imaginary ropes of the ring. There's an exclamation of disapproval.) Spider moves in for the kill. Then they get into a clinch. The referee separates them. A left hook to Julián's head, another hook, another...

YOUTH. Stop, man, you're killing him!

TINO. Julián was bleeding like a bull. Spider started throwing out punches. (He starts spinning around.) One, two, three, four, five, ten jabs to the face...
WOMAN. Animal! Can't you see you're killing him!
TINO. A tremendous right and Julián fell to the canvas,
IST MAN. My money!

(They begin to whistle.)

TINO. Go to it, black man! You're big enough! Get up, champ! (Acting the referee.) One...two...three...four...
2ND *SANTERA* But, what happened, for God's sake?
2ND MAN. Shut up, woman! Can't you see he can spin a story? He's a performer!
3RD WOMAN. I'm getting tired of this! What did that black do? He didn't kill the other?
2ND MAN. Shut up, woman, calm down! Have a bit of patience.
TINO. ...eight...nine...nine and a half.
OLD MAN. Stop, man!
TINO. (As if it were the bell.) Clang! Clang! Clang! (People sigh with relief.) The bell rang. Julián went to his corner. His eyes were closed, like a Chinaman. (As Julián.) I only need one blow!
OLD WOMAN. Get on with it, you little son-of-a-bitch!

(People begin to whistle.)

1ST PERSON. Where's that rat from the square?
2ND PERSON. His bravado's gone!
3RD PERSON. Here's where you have to be, champ!
4TH PERSON. I'm played up to my butt, and if that black lets me down, I'll have no place to sit.
5TH PERSON. Julián, show this fat-lipped trash what you're made of.
6TH PERSON. Bust his guts, champ!
7TH PERSON. Better get his skates on!
8TH PERSON. Looks like he's in the wrong business. Should've been a runner, not a boxer.
9TH PERSON. Let a hen go!
10TH PERSON. Let María Antonia go!
11TH PERSON. Your *ashé*'s not here, champ! That's why they can break you!

TINO. (As Julián.) You'll be champ! Don't send me any more messages.
1ST MAN. Want me to throw you the towel?
TINO. If you do, I'll finish you off like a dog.
2ND MAN. Don't talk so much, you'll lose your breath!
TINO. That's it! (Like a bell.) Clang! Clang! Clang!
PERSON. Big as hell, stop playing around and fight!
1ST OLD WOMAN. It's your mother's heart'll be playing around!
2ND OLD WOMAN. Cool it, woman, cool it!
TINO. Julián was covered in blood. They began to fight. He had Spider up against the rope. They fell in a clinch. The referee separated them.
2ND MAN. Come on, Julián, eat that fish!
3RD MAN. Now I can sit, champ!
4TH MAN. *Viva* Julián!
5TH MAN. Finish him off! Give him a finishing punch!
TINO. Julián started hitting out with his left: one, two, three lefts on the nose. Spider was bleeding; a hard hook to the pit of the stomach.
1ST PERSON. Have his head!
2ND PERSON. For the neighborhood's honor, champ!
3RD PERSON. Finish him off!
TINO. (Throwing frantic punches.) One, two, three, four lefts...
3RD OLD WOMAN. Stop dithering and finish him off with your right.
TINO. He had him up against the rope again.
2ND WOMAN. And he didn't break him in two?
TINO. Julián spat out the sponge... Ash! Cuash!... And with a tremendous... (the boy gave a Tarzan shout)...he slug a right and... Spider was left without his web.
VOICE. *Viva* Julián!
ALL. *Viva*!

(The crowd, jubilant, carries Tino off as if he were Julián. They show him off. Tino, as Julián, puts on a great display greeting people. María Antonia, watches from the side.)

1ST OLD WOMAN. (To Second Old Woman.) And he got up?
2ND OLD WOMAN. Don't be stupid? Didn't you hear?
1ST OLD WOMAN. The kid goes so fast.

1ST *SANTERA*. That's all blacks are good for. It didn't occur to him to be a doctor or anything like that. I'm not going to clap till I see a black up on a cloud.
2ND *SANTERA*. Well, your hands are going to rot, my dear. Be satisfied with a boxer or a musician.
2ND MAN. All the same, he's got to learn how to box; he can't win a fight with only his right. If he goes on like that, he'll wind up a punching bag.
1ST MAN. And Joe Louis?
2ND MAN. That was something else. Joe Louis knew how to box and was clever. The American black thinks, legislates. Julián doesn't think. His idea is to ride everything roughshod.

(People drift to the dancing. María Antonia and Tino are left facing each other...)

MANUEL GRANADOS

Adire and broken time

Excerpts from **Adire y el Tiempo Roto** (Adire and Broken Time), Casa, Havana, 1967, pp.72-74, 170-174, 227-230, 271-273, 335-338. Editors' subtitles.

Julian...

When they went in there was so much noise and confusion that nobody noticed. She walked in on Antonio's arm, curious and expectant, but a bit scared because it was something she'd never seen before. People she didn't know were walking about the house. There were some women dressed in white, but most were in brightly colored skirts, and men with necklaces added to the colorfulness of the place.

She recognized Andrea, the godmother of Manana's son Julián, who looked at them in amazement, mouth open. She smiled. The woman turned on her heels and went off shouting:

"Manana, Manana, praise God, you've got some fancy visitors!"

Manana was surprised, too, and very pleased, hurrying over to them:

"But Miss Elsa, you here! I didn't think you'd like this sort of thing, really when you told me I didn't believe you."

"Girl, don't be silly," said the godmother. "Here, if you've no Dinga in you, you've Mandinga."

"Sssh, woman, we'll be making them angry!"

"No, man, no," said Elsa, laughing placidly.

"And who might this fine gentleman be?"

"My fiancé."

"Pleased to meet you, ma'am," said Antonio trying to be pleasant.

"But come through to the yard," said Manana. "It's cooler and there's a good spot waiting for you." They went through to the yard of the big house: dark faces, hair straightened with hot combs, grotesque movements, strange figures dancing, and a horrible smell: seasoned with the vibrant rhythm of beating drums.

She spotted Julián across the other side of the courtyard and went dizzy at the sight, regaining her composure only after a great effort. His shirt vulgarly unbuttoned, he was pouring something into a pot that was slowly cooking on an iron grill. She instinctively hung more tightly on her fiancé's arm.

"Look miss, look mister," said old Moisés. "I have these seats for you. It'll soon be 12:00 and this'll begin..."

"Thank you, old man, thank you," they replied in unison.

"I'll bring something to drink," added the old man. He went off graciously, stooping a bit from all the cane spirit he'd had. Gradually the chant went up:

Elegguara Elegguara
Asokere keré meyé
Elegguara Elegguara
Alagguana kilá mosá é.

The air was broken by the chorus voices rising higher and higher, driven by mystic forces deliriously seeking absolute liberation, while a black man with a deep metallic voice led the singers, chanting something in an exotic language.

The noise of frenetic drum beats bounced back off the walls, the notes spread like seismic waves. Julián had taken the batá drum and was playing it in front of the couple. He spoke for the *Orishas* and for her, as he anointed the hide of the sacred drum with sweat, pride and tears. He thought of the maiden who was given the great *Abakuá* secret, according to a story Moisés told. She received the strangest declaration of love. Not in sweet, trite words, but ones that went in through her ears, ran through her veins and became terrible, sensual hands taking her by the waist and opening her up, and she adored the fire burning inside her. Caught, beside herself, exalted in mystery, she watched the hands of the man breaking in the hide and thereby nurturing the barbaric substance: "Everything's on fire... I'm falling straight down dark precipices. I'm falling, I'm falling, I'm falling, I'm falling."

She shouted:

"Take me away, Antonio!"

"We're leaving! I've had enough, that black boy's done nothing but look at you."

"Yes, let's go," she said as she felt herself faint.

And Roberto

...Roberto and Julián felt anxiety and fear on finding themselves in that silent crowd, casting around senselessly, trapped by their inner panic, beyond reason.

They found the place. There was a park nearby, overlooked by the terrace of what appeared to be the best hotel in town. From the park bench they could see gentlemen in impeccable guayabera shirts and white suits, and green bespectacled military men on the terrace. Flash cars with official license plates were parked in front of the building, and helmeted soldiers bearing rifles strolled by in twos. Some had their hands theateningly ready, carrying Thompson and German machine guns. Over by the plainer-style City Hall, policemen in blue patrolled the street with guns. Men with cameras and reporters walked from one side to the other hunting for news. The air was tense. The young men realised they wouldn't blend in; there were few in civilian dress and they certainly weren't civilian, because pistols stuck terrifyingly out of shirt and guayabera. They decided to leave, going up Aguilera Street:

"How much money have you got?" asked Roberto.

"Almost 400 pesos, and you?"

"About 50, I had to leave money in Santa Cruz."

"I know, I would have given you some."

"It's OK, they'll have enough."

They took a left at the corner:

"Look, it's in that house, I was told the telegraph post was outside the door, and it's the right number."

"It's closed," Julián observed.

They went up to the house. Roberto knocked hard with his knuckles; from the pavement Julián tried to see the back of the Cathedral. The door opened. The young woman, around 20 years old, very white-skinned and with delicate gestures, gave them an odd look:

"Yes?"

"We've come from Santa Cruz...and..."

At Roberto' words, she gave a startled look into the street, and taking a step back, said:

"Come in, please come in!"

As they did, they had the impression they were in the home of well-to-do people. Everything was arranged exquisitely, in provincial good taste. Julián noted the tiled hallway, the shine. He tried to remember but couldn't place it. He had the feeling he knew the place, but convinced himself to the contrary on discovering that the floor had a crack running the whole length of the house that was poorly covered with a layer of white cement.

"Sit down, please, sit down. I'll let them know and be right back."

The young men sat on two plush armchairs. Julián went on thinking about a similar place: "The floor, the tiles, the shine."

They heard steps; the young woman came back with an older woman and a man of around 30, according to the black man's calculations. He wore thick glasses, a casual short-sleeved shirt and modern trousers.

"What's your name, my son?" asked the lady affectionately, speaking to Roberto:

"Roberto, I'm the son of..."

"Yes, I already know," interrupted the lady:

"And you?"

"Julián, at your service."

"Well," said the woman, seemingly tired, "we start over again. Will we never rest? And what in heaven is this?... Make yourselves at home boys," she said going off to the bedrooms.

"Feel at home," the man repeated. "Would you like to rest

before talking? Make yourselves comfortable... Look, come over here, it's safer, we've everything prepared."

They went through the house to a beautiful patio of ferns and tarro plants hanging from the eaves; placed haphazardly they appeared well cared-for. On the other side of the patio was a recently built stone construction; it was a small room, behind which there was a wall covered in wild flowers, a small communicating gate, presumably with another patio which couldn't be seen:

"The lady is Aunt Mary Luisa, the young woman is called Dina and is my sister, my name is Jorge. I hope you're comfortable, you'll be living here for the time being."

The light flooded in through the open door. Julián didn't miss a detail of the man in front of him, nor the place. The portrait of a dark-haired young man with thick eyebrows, almost joined together, and a penetrating look, made him stop to observe even longer: "He looks familiar." Despite the hard look, there was a calmness about the face in the picture:

"Who is he?" I asked.

"David,"[a] said the man without looking at the picture. "Sleep now. You might not realise it, but you need to rest; if you need anything, just call," he said, as he took his leave.

"What a time to come!" said Mary Luisa, when Jorge came in to the kitchen, "right now, when things couldn't be worse."

"They were lucky," exclaimed the man, adding, "it's right that innocence is a saving grace."

"They have to be gone quickly, there've been too many of them... anyway, we're in trouble," said the woman and whispered: "Glory to the Father, to the Son and to the Holy Ghost!"

She closed her eyes, in prayer, running her fingers through a rosary tucked in her pocket.

"What are we going to do, Aunt? We've not been told what to do with them. I thought the black boy could go to the car repair shop, he'd be better off there; he can sleep and eat with us, no one will know any better, and hopefully they won't be in Santiago long. We'll have Roberto here, we'll say he's one of the family, a cousin, your godson... What do you think?"

"Thank God nothing happened; it could have been worse!"

"I'll go and check things out in the street."

"Go by the Alcochas' house to see if they've any news," said the woman going in to the back room.

"Good-bye!" said the man, ill at ease.

"God be with you, son!" the woman murmured. "May the Lord's wrath be stayed."

Cira and Juan

"I'll walk four centuries of madness, from beyond inconcrete but real limits, where there have only been voices, burning hide and whiplash. Oh no, they've always stank to me; I have to eat and sleep. If Lola could only see, I can sense her laugh. I do it for the bed I'm going to sleep in, for the plate of hot food, not for the rough hands that will touch me... and still, I'm better, better."

"What's your name, doll?" asked the black man.

"Cira, and yours?"

"Juan de Dios."

"You talk real strange... Are you from here?"

"From Santiago, why?"

She looked him over minutely. He was by her side completely naked: "He doesn't stink", she thought, laying her head on his strong chest. She said tenderly: "You're a beautiful black man."

"Do you like black men?"

She didn't answer, but turned her face to look at the floor. A cockroach was working its way to the door. She thought of the third-rate hotel she was in. In her time, before the fall, she wouldn't have gone to a place like that for anything, least of all in the company of a black.

"Are you an athlete?" she asked.

"I'm a boxer."

"I thought so... And what's that?" she said, pointing to the leather bracelet around his dark wrist. "What is it?"

"An *iddé*," the individual answered, lightly kissing her ear. She felt herself liking it and let herself go. The heat of the man by her side gave her morbid pleasure: "The skin, the laughter, the freshness, unknown boundaries, distance. Is there no limit with a whore, are a black and a whore the same?" She had been wrong;

she didn't feel nauseous.

"I fought Kid Gavilán."

"Is he a champion?"

"A champ," affirmed the man.

"What's an *iddé*?"

"It's to do with *santería*; I'm the son of *Changó*," said the black man, winking and watching her with distrust. "You have a problem with me?"

The rough voice shook her. The man realized and smiling, pinched her breast.

"Don't be afraid," he said.

She felt her strength go and on top of that felt an impulse to show no interest. She couldn't, the presence of the man stole life from her, was pleasurable.

"You've never been with a black man?"

"Never," she confessed, faint, trapped in a moment of desire, wanting to give herself totally. He moved back a bit to take a better look at her. She breathed more calmly.

"I think the blacks are always *ñáñigos*...something bad."

"Being *ñáñigo* isn't bad," he said, losing interest. The cockroach now slid across the door frame and reached the wall.

"Tell me about it, Juan de Dios."

They had taken a bottle of Bacardí matured rum with them to the room. The black man took a good swig from the bottle; he clicked his tongue and enjoyed the acerbity of the liquid; with a fixed look, he seemed to be ordering his thoughts:

"I was studying, I wanted to be a violinist, when I went into boxing," he exclaimed with melancholy, grabbing the bottle again.

"Did you like it?"

"I've always thought that anyone who's in fighting is an animal, but well, it was three pesos a fight; I had no money for food, and I did it."

"Just like whores," she thought, trying to squeeze a spot on his broad back. His breath wafting the smell of alcohol over the room made her deliciously dizzy.

"Things got worse and now I'm not a violinist, or a surveyor, or a boxer."

"So you wanted to be a surveyor... and what's that?"

"Measuring land... Don't you know that?"

"What land?"

The man noticed the cockroach and following it with his eyes shrugged his shoulders. Smiling, he took the woman by the armpits, and bit her on the face:

"I don't know, land, that's all."

Her body was excited again. She felt like a weak tree, lashed by a sudden gale, bent by an implacable wind forcing her branches. She kissed the earth, letting her leaves drop and they fell on open fields. Her body damp, the trunk gave in to the big broad universe, mystic black abyss, bees and lemon trees. She received him, for a second time; she received him:

"Tell me, go on," she almost begged...

Sierra Maestra

"How many hours have we been walking?" Julián asked.

"Including the rest, about seven," replied Roberto.

"I'm lost now... Have you realized something about the sun?"

"What," he asked, taken aback.

"The sun's back to front, what's south seems north to me."

"I thought that, too."

"Halt! Who goes there?"

The voice coming out of the thicket shook us; startled, we look into the trees; nothing:

"Frank País!" we both shouted at the same time. Seconds passed, it seemed an eternity. We couldn't say exactly where they came out from; they were simply there in front of us, four of them with copious beards and long hair, one of them with it tangled and hanging dirty down his back, all with the red and black armbands of M-26-7. We'd packed enough of them during our time in Santiago. Two came over to us while the other two kept their rifles trained on us:

"Put your hands up!" one of them shouted, aiming at us; that annoyed me. Weren't we all revolutionaries? Without a word I put up my hands leaving the briefcase on the ground. They searched us meticulously, one of the rebels took the briefcase without opening it, and spoke:

"Where are you going?"

"Frank País," I said remembering the driver's instructions.

"Where are you coming from?"

"Frank País," this time Roberto and I said it together.

Stepping aside, the bearded rebels signaled us to walk towards the wood:

"We'll see, get going," said one of them. In the wood, the terrain was flat, and we were surprised by how high up we were. But I was completely taken by surprise to see a jeep, with two uniformed rebels complete with cartridge belts waiting for us... The bumper on the jeep read: "Rebel Army"... On the canvas, I read: U.S. Navy. The jeep set off. Trying to get my bearings, I recognized the feeling; we were going some place. I remembered the journey with the soldiers to Contramaestre del Sur...

The blue gel stuck deep in my subconscious delighted in a far-off vision of peace, whose lines of unknown form were a sedative in the mist but also caustic, sowing calm and insecurity. I had taken the first steps, and couldn't flee from such a magnet. "Is what I see real, or is only what I don't see real? If I can explain something, give it shape, recognize it. Am I passing it through filters, that were in turn imposed through the power and pressure of alien filters? If I can logically explain things, are they real? When Manana is Manana... Elsa is Elsa, and not Manana of her father, her mother, her class and her time, and Elsa of her mother, and not Manana of her father, her class and her time, and Elsa of her mother, her father, her class and her time? Damián no, Damián is atemporal, he was without meaning. Damián is not. Used to the coming and going of thoughts, I suffered no possible escape. What greater suffering?

"Julián, you're shit black..! I can have a son, but not yours!"

What greater sorrow?

"He was called Damián because an old black man selling oranges in Santa Rosa Square identified him." What greater scepticism? "I'm tired, here at least we have a place to live." What greater hope? "Roberto." What greater knife-edge to enclose humankind? "In the final analysis, some have their fate written." What greater weakness? "I'm frightened, very frightened, I don't want to be alone!"

"Can you hear me, Julián?" Roberto asked.

"What d'you say?"

"You fell asleep, don't you see we're there."

The rebels sitting in the back had got out; guns across their shoulders, they watched us with mistrust.

V

"Everything's in order," said Captain Narciso. But remember, you're not detained but retained; you can go wherever you want within camp boundaries, except the armory and quartermaster corps, for the rest you can consider yourselves comrades.

"For how long?" I asked, mortified, feeling like when I was in the Contramaestre garrison.

"I can't say, we'll hurry things along, Santiago has to answer a few things; it's regulations."

Disgusted, we left to look around the camp. Some rebels with thick long beards, sitting on the ground, looked at us with no interest at all. After wandering around for a good while we came across the river. A rebel in underpants, up to his knees in water, was beating a pair of trousers with wood to wash them. The place was exuberant and had the fresh fragrance of wild flowers. I took a deep breath of natural enchantment and made straight for the water looking for somewhere to swim.

"You're new?" said the rebel looking at Roberto.

"Yes..." Can you tell?

"You're clean-shaven."

As he said it, a broad smile spread through his thick black curly beard.

Carlos Mora

"To where?" asked a voice at his side.

Caught unawares, he realized he was sitting next to a very black young man. He was dressed in a fine wool sweater in subdued colors and very tight trousers; he looked foreign. The young man smiled at him, showing clean well-cared-for teeth; with a friendly gesture, he added:

"It seems you were thinking out loud."

"Yes, so it would seem."

"My name's Carlos Mora, I'm a repatriate."

"From where?"

"New York, United States."

"Is it long since you came back?"

"Since the first days of the triumph."

"You feel good?"

"Yes and no. Sometimes I'm afraid."

"Of what?"

"I don't know... Don't you feel the same?"

"I can't be afraid, nobody who's free feels that way," I answered a bit mortified.

"Not only afraid," said the young man, "it's that... I can't explain."

"What's bothering you?" asked Julián.

"I've always had to do what I don't want."

"Why did you come?"

"I don't know, but it's awkward now."

"It's your mind that's afraid," declared Julián scornfully.

"Could be," said the other, shrugging his shoulders. "But I began to be afraid here, in the country of liberty."

He finished the sentence with irony, and looking straight at Julián said with a certain tone of desperation: "I don't understand anything!" He went on, keeping his eyes fixed on Julián's face: "I don't know you, I'm not your friend, but no matter, I'll tell you anyway. There, the enemy's one, easily identifiable, white, and walks on the opposite side, may wear the ministerial trappings of the Ku-Klux-Klan, and not all belong to the John Birch Society. He looks at you with hatred and spits when you pass, but you see him. He's an assault on your epidermis, he wants to exterminate you physically or make you his servant. You have only to accept, resist, defend yourself or kill him: eye for an eye, tooth for a tooth."

"And here?" asked Julián, interrupting him, wanting to know more.

"Here, it's different. It's not created by you, it's outside and at incredible speed bombards your brain and enters your mind. It's so strong, it doesn't matter whether you're asleep or awake, and like the billboards, radio, cinema or television, only other slogans, other words: it's an official who looks distrustingly because you wear blue jeans, you like jazz and miss Camels; a typist who stops typing to chat out loud about the last voluntary work stint, and you're interested in saxophone more than the balance of forces and surplus value. Then, careful, you might be a reactionary, you don't like collectives, and though you help, they know intuitively that you don't like it. I'll always be alienated... aren't you?"

"No." Am I?

"I'd go back, even to live in Little Rock," continued the repatriate, "or whoring in New York. Tell me honestly, what do you think?"

"Not me!", Julián answered airily. "I'm made of different stuff, I know what I am, what I'm made of! You're shit!"

The young man got up and took a step back. Ready to attack, he clenched his fists. For a second, Julián felt the weight of his hostile look, slowly got up in front of him, leaned back with fists clenched, and was ready.

He had a world of lava gushing through his fingers. He was a young volcano on the verge of eruption, color of years, centuries, time: "What was a leopard from temperate Africa going to do on the flat-topped Kilimanjaro,[b] what did he see, what did he see." He needed to be fired, to scatter, to burn and leave behind the smell of scorched flesh, sterile land, bones in the sun, minds downtrodden, bodies disintegrated: silence, non-existence. Absolutes! "Absolutes?" he thought. "I know why the Cubans leave. It's not the shortage of food or the fact they can't buy cars. People don't want the responsibility. Am I responsible?"

He waited with inexplicable anger for the blow, so that he might return it. Surprisingly, the young man unclenched his hands and smiled. Laughing almost cynically, he said:

"You're gross. Forgive me but what you have said so clearly makes me laugh: I'm shit and you're a man. That's a laugh, a real laugh!"

He ran off. Julián was rooted to the spot, and watching the other running down, exclaimed: "To hell with him, he looks like a queer!"

Then he slowly went down to the road: "Destroyed, atomic dust, but never beaten."

Everything was green, and from the depths of the plastic substance came a primitive, guttural noise: "The first call, the first demand... How many classes of alignment are there, I'll always be afraid, what must he be made of... and me? Why do these things happen? Somebody said it, I read it and thought it: this will never go back to being a hybrid, even though the corn's totally American."

Editors' notes

a. David was the nom de plume of Frank País, key leader of the July 26 Movement in Santiago de Cuba, who was killed in the struggle.

b. The meeting takes place outside the Hemingway Museum, and the reference is to Hemingway's writing.

PART 3

Redrawing the line

WALTERIO CARBONELL

Birth of a national culture

Excerpts from **Como surgió la cultura nacional** (How the National Culture Arose), Crítica, Havana, 1961, pp. 10-12, 17, 18-20, 21, 23-30, 107-111, 37-38, 46-49, 51-55. Editors' title and subtitles.

Rescuing Africa from oblivion

Of all the countries of the Americas, Cuba, throughout the period of the slave trade, was one of the richest sources of information on Africa. To have an idea of the vast wealth of knowledge that Cuba possessed on Africa, suffice it to know that between 1800 and 1850, the majority of the Cuban population, calculated at between a million and a million and a half inhabitants, were African; that African religions had many more followers than the Catholic religion; and that African music was more widely played and admired than Spanish music. Little was known about China or India, etc. Africa was the passion of the planters, the traders, the colonial authorities, the bankers and the priests, and all those guided by a lucrative spirit. By day and by night, priests and bankers would anxiously await the arrival of slave ships. Colonialists in their political circles, in the Havana City Hall, in the Consulate, in the Sociedad Patriótica de Amigos del País (Patriotic Society of Friends of the Country), debated the fate of sugar, coffee and public works should England succeed in blocking the slave trade. These gentlemen's conclusions were very pessimistic: if the trade were blocked, the outcome could only be their ruin.

Planters were knowledgable about African culture; they knew which of the African races were the strongest for agricultural work, which the most bellicose and also the most docile for slave labor, and which were the most apt to provoke anti-slavery uprisings. They knew many characteristics of the peoples of Guinea, Nigeria, the Congo and Río de Oro. Africa was of such interest to them that it was not by chance that the most important book to be written during the three and half centuries of colonization was called *Historia de la esclavitud de la raza africana en el Nuevo Mundo y en especial en los países américo-hispanos* (A History of the Slavery of the African Race in the New World and Especially in the Hispanic-American Countries) by José Antonio Saco, a book that by one of those rare coincidences historians rarely cited and intellectuals never read.

The end of Spanish colonial rule in Cuba cast a cloak of oblivion over the African continent. Africa was no longer of interest economically, and so there was no need to obtain new cultural knowledge. Slavery had ended; Africa was of no more interest. Politicians and writers during Spanish colonial times frequently invoked Africa, but politicians and writers of the bourgeois republic never once recalled its name. What for? The bourgeois republic didn't need Africa. It's a curious fact; the same planters, traders, bankers and priests who during the colonial period suffered nights of insomnia waiting for the slave ships with their human cargo, were the first to forget the African continent when Cuba became a republic. Africa became a disturbing word for so-called educated people. Africa was a kind of Babylon whose name evoked lust. And they were right. Africa was lust in both senses of the word, in the lewdness and material appetites of those Pharysees on the plantations and in the churches. They turned the male into a material thing, a trade object, a commodity; and the female, into an object of double possession, a possession for work and a sexual possession. Those who in Spanish colonial times accused the few who did speak out against the slave trade of being enemies of the King, property and religion, were the ones during the bourgeois republic to proscribe the name of Africa. Africa was the source of wealth on which the bourgeois republic was later built. But its name evoked the abominable origins of bourgeois wealth and as such had to be erased from Cuban political and social life. Its religions, music, habits and customs, and all its cultural values were as prohibited as in the colonial period...

The bourgeois republic only had a memory for recalling its own past sufferings, not those of the slaves... All that might damage bourgeois morale was silenced... Its morale was very fragile, because its past morale, its colonial morale, was founded on the enslavement of blacks...

While bourgeois rule is a thing of the past in our country, it is a very healthy sign for the people that Fidel Castro should recall the past of the former ruling class. It is very healthy because the prejudices and vices of past social conditions live on in many people's minds. We would do well to recall the real history of the bourgeoisie, a history falsified by politicians, professors, historians, because the bourgeoisie grounded its authority not only on economic and political power but also on the power of lies propagated by its educated men. And, moreover, many of those lies are upheld today as truths, even by those who are revolutionaries, who have contributed to the liberation of our country from bourgeois rule but who have been incapable of liberating themselves from all the ideological power of the bourgeoisie. We have to create in people an historical awareness of at least 150 years... One of the tasks of the revolutionary writer today is to clarify our historical past... While confusion reigns over our ideological past, we will suffer, as Karl Marx said with respect to the 1848 Revolution in France, not only the ills of the present, but also those of the past.

The Africanization of Spanish culture

Cuban history was made by two peoples from two different continents: Africa and Europe. Thanks to the feverish heads of thinkers during the bourgeois republic, they were reduced to the history of one people alone: Spain. That is, to the history of the people who came from Spain, the least European of Europe. Put another way, to the history of the whitest people of Africa. Anything African they could not hide, they classed as barbaric, like black music and religion. But history has more lives than a cat...

Already long before the triumph of the revolution, the

bourgeoisie was profoundly debilitated by imperialism, not only in terms of its economic power but also its cultural power. Its cultural values had also been undermined by the traditions and manifestations of the blacks. Thus, African musical rhythms considered savage by the bourgeoisie up until 1930, were in the end adopted by them. The musical rhythms of the slave quarters, rhythms for which slaveholders punished their blacks with a hundred lashes of the whip, became the musical rhythms that entertained the bourgeoisie. The music of the colonial white population disappeared and the vaccuum was filled with black music.

Another symptom of the weakness of bourgeois culture was the contagious nature of black religious beliefs. Savage gods who devoured children, *Changó, Obatalá, Yemayá,* were civilized and possessed the spirits of the wealthy, not to devour them but to cohabit with them, to help solve their love problems, their aspirations to hold high government office, or get them out of trouble in business.

Africa was present in their social, artistic and religious expressions, it influenced the bourgeois republic's social and public life, without its name being uttered. Its saints were not banished, because the bourgeoisie continued to worship them. Its music was no longer savage, because the bourgeoisie, musically orphaned, danced to black music in the clubs. In the end, it was all mixed together; it was, as we'd say today, a great *pachanga*. But the *pachanga* was greater in music, religion and the psychology of the blacks than in their social situation. The black continued to be discriminated against...

It should not be deduced from this that black religions were not weakened. African religions lost ground even among the black population, the majority of whom were won over by the religion of the ruling class. The phenomenon is a little similar to that of the Roman Empire when the religion of the poor and exploited, Christianity, became that of the dominant class. The main difference between Rome and Cuba is that the bourgeoisie never made the African rites official.

It is really interesting and contradictory that the cultural baggage of a subjugated people became part of the cultural baggage of the dominant class, became ideological superstructures of the class in power... Had their power been all embracing, the bourgeoisie would have furthered industry and science against which the African religions of Cuba's black population would not have been able to survive. But since the bourgeoisie did not rule, since it became a class ruled by Yankee imperialism, since the weakness of its economic system facilitated the survival of African religious beliefs, they survived to the point of undermining the very religious beliefs of the bourgeoisie. Its Catholicism became "Afro-Catholicism." Economic instability produced social instability. Its religion was not sufficient to explain the causes of its instability and it appealed to religious beliefs that were alien to it to solve its economic and psychological problems...

The revolutionary present is decisive proof of Africa's contribution to Cuban culture. If the Church could not move a single one of the popular sectors — as it might have done in Spain, Mexico or Colombia — this was because African religion dominated among the working classes of the country.

The revolution has been able to transform the structure of the country without great obstacles of tradition, customs and life style, because the Cuban people have assimilated important aspects of the African psyche... Africa has facilitated the successful social transformation of the country. This does not mean Spain has disappeared. Spain has been Africanized.

The progressive role of African religion

Despite miscegenation and Spanish acculturation, in 1850 the Africans were still a people in captivity, with their African languages, psychological and cultural traits, and religions. Thanks to their rigidly secret religious organizations, part of their generation's experience was preserved and passed down into what we today call national culture.

Religious organizations prevented Spanish colonialism from destroying their wealth of experience, and played a positive role in preserving African culture, as well as a progressive political role. Thanks to the vitality of religions, black music was preserved, the music whose rhythms gave birth to Cuban music, the highest expression of national culture.

I have said that the religious organizations played a progressive role in our nationhood, politically and culturally. This might surprise many since up until now the opposite view has been held, which is, that black religions are a form of barbarism. However, that was the thesis of Spanish colonialist ideologues and the reactionary bourgeoisie.

The silence of certain revolutionary writers on the political and cultural role of African religious beliefs is also a little suspect. Do they fear that prying into such questions might be sensitive to the black population? All that can be learned from their writings on religion is that Catholicism was an instrument of the dominant classes. No judgment is passed on African religions; it is not to be learned from them whether these beliefs played a progressive or reactionary role in the social conflicts of the 19th century. Perhaps because Marx said: religion is the opium of the people?

Generations of Marxists have interpreted this mechanically. They have repeated it without reflection, because religion is opium when it is an instrument at the service of the dominant class, when the dominant class uses religion to make people dormant and exploit them mercilessly... African beliefs in Cuba were the beliefs of the most exploited sector of the population. Only Catholicism was opium, because it was the religion of the colonial state in the interests of the slaveholders, merchants, traders, clergy and the stinking people of the colonial apparatus who killed, tortured, maimed and exploited the slaves. Catholicism was the opium of the people, in whose name the exploiters opposed the first great freedom to be won: that of the slaves...

The religious organizations of the Africans in Cuba were not only the most effective instruments for preserving the cultural traditions of the blacks; they also functioned as political organizations against slavery. The clandestine, religious nature of these organizations concealed their real political role. They had no written program, but in practice functioned as an underground political organization. Aponte didn't create any special organization; his most effective revolutionary instrument to fight Spanish colonialism and the slaveholding system was none other than the religious organizations...

On national culture

Marxism attacks interpretations of a people's culture based on four or five eminent individuals, seeing this as an artistocratic view of culture, negating the role of the masses in the creation of cultures. To our misfortune, it is idealist theory that has prevailed here as regards so-called national culture. Not even in the capitalist countries do bourgeois intellectuals interpret the national culture of their respective countries through four or five figures; such an approach is outdated. But in our country cultural idealism is still in place even with a socialist revolution. Hasn't there been talk these days of reviving national culture? Hasn't the talk been about four or five pro-slavery writers, because they are national culture? Since the people do not write pro-slavery tracts, then the people do not produce culture.

For the idealists, people who have no writing have no culture, they are primitive, and belong to prehistory. And since they are primitive, everything that is said and done against them is more than justified. The colonizations of early capitalism were effected in the name of civilization. And the imperialists of today try to justify their colonial rule in America, Africa and Asia on the basis of cultural superiority. It is to be regretted that the colonialist concept of culture should still hold among us. What past are we to revive? The political counsel of panegyrists of slavery? Is it the case that our cultural inventory comprises the body of reactionary ideas of Arango y Parreño, José Antonio Saco, Luz y Caballero and Domingo del Monte? Do these four or five mystics fattened on the colonial slave apparatus constitute Cuban cultural tradition? Is not popular culture, whose strength lies in black tradition, not also cultural tradition?...

What was our culture born of? Of the Spanish and African cultures within the colonial system. Where did Saco and Varela belong? To Spanish culture... What factors contributed to Spaniards and Africans being stripped of their psychological and cultural background to acquire a new psyche and culture and be described as Cuban? This is the question that has to be answered to understand how the nation and national culture were formed, and to know what is authentically national and what isn't... The new generation of revolutionaries... must start by studying social relations under slavery from the 16th to the late 19th centuries...

The greatest contribution to shaping a national culture was the Ten Years War, which was led by slaveholders. But as for the creation of a culture different from the Spanish or the African... the conflict between slave and slaveholder and the conflict between their respective cultures are what most shaped a national patrimony...

Over recent years, the conflict between the black and Spanish cultures appeared to have ended, because the two cultures met, unexpectedly, under the pressure of North American culture, and that of other countries. The interdependence between nations, the subjugation of certain nations to others, wrought as one of its consequences, the internationalization of cultures. Colonial and neocolonial countries are the ones that have suffered most the effects of internationalization. With the birth of imperialism, cultural nationalism was no longer possible in the way Europe produced cultural nationalisms from the 16th to the 19th centuries. When our independence came about, the age of closed economies and cultures was finished... Colonized by North America and influenced by other cultures, in an atmosphere of internationalization... Cuban culture became less and less Spanish. This was particularly evident from 1936, when the *Orígenes* group were inspired by Valéry and Mallarmé; painters looked to Paris and New York; and black music was infected by North American music, not imperialist music, because the imperialists have no music, but black North American music.

We were a people open to the influences of foreign cultures, not only because of the neocolonial state of our economy but also because of the weakening of our national culture. We started off with cultures borrowed from Spain and Africa, which were not originally of our making, and this was to our great disadvantage. Language, the most important medium for cultural communication, was not the making of our people through a historical process, like the French, English, Arabs, Nigerians and Senegalese made theirs. Black music was not created here, but brought by peoples imported from other centers of culture. And since we did not live through a long process of authentic cultural creation, like the Arab, Chinese, Indian, African and European cultures, in which each people created its own language, its own music, its own painting and sculpture, each different in its conception, each with its own unity of style, that in the last analysis is what characterizes an authentic culture, we, in our cultural weakness, were more susceptible to penetration than the cultures of other countries...

Are we radically different from Africa or Spain? No, in our culture there is more of Spain and Africa than what is authentically ours. Even in music, which is the most developed form of cultural expression in Cuba, the African element is stronger than what has been added. Of course, there are new elements in music and in poetry, and social psychology, that did not exist in Spanish and African culture, and it is because of the appearance of new cultural elements that a national culture is said to exist. But it is a national culture in embryo, a far cry from an authentic culture.

To comprehend how our national culture was formed, we must first know what it is that has given it shape. Principally, we must study the content of African cultures that took root here, because they are the most popular, belonging to those most exploited. It should be noted here that those who speak of the formation of a national culture, refer only to Spanish culture, that is, they take it as the only basis from which ours was germinated. They have a bookish concept of national culture. Without detailed knowledge of the African cultures that influenced us, it is not possible to understand the process which formed our national culture.

REYNALDO GONZÁLEZ

A white problem: Reinterpreting Cecilia Valdés

Excerpts from the book **Contradanzas y latigazos** (Contredanse and Whiplash), Letras Cubanas, Havana, 1983, pp. 22-6, 109-113, 165-7, 170, 174. The page references in the text are to Cirilo Villaverde **Cecilia Valdés** (2 vols), Arte y Literatura, Havana, 1972. The novel is set in the period 1812-1831. Parts of the novel were published in 1839, but it was not published in its entirety until 1879. Editors' title and subtitles.

Cecilia

In 1966, gathering information on Cuban cultural traditions for the journal **Pueblo y Cultura**, I attended a gathering of troubadours in Santiago de Cuba. Virgilio Palais gave an informal talk, interspersed with songs and citations and his proverbial hospitality. We listened to songs by Sindo Garay, Manuel Corona, Eusebio Delfín, Graciano Gómez and many other composers of the old guard of troubadours; they took on new life in voices which, though ravaged by time, were among the few that could convey the atmosphere and intonation of what was by then a definitive part of our popular musical heritage.

Among the countless curious bystanders at the door — to what was half a store, half the front room of a house, and was to become the Santiago de Cuba Troubadours' House[a] — someone insisted on wanting the Cecilia Valdés song. The singers and musicians, immersed in their chords and their couplets, paid no attention. The man was not to be put off. He wanted to hear the

Cecilia Valdés song. In my mind I went over all the troubadour songs I knew and couldn't come up with any dedicated to the character of Cecilia created by Cirilo Villaverde — except for the contredanse "Caramelos vendo" (A candyseller am I) that José Dolores Pimienta dedicates to her in the novel. I thought he must be referring to part of the zarzuela by Gonzalo Roig, which was far beyond the scope our hosts. In the course of the evening the singers inevitably got round to the number requested, which turned out to be none other than "Santa Cecilia" (Saint Cecilia) by Manuel Corona.

For that man there was no doubt that the many compliments in the song were not inspired by a saint, not even the patron saint of music, and, if dedicated to a woman, that woman could only be Cecilia Valdés. The "Arabesque Indian goddess statue", "model of a sculpture", "the languid looks of deep eyes","the sensitive provocative love of your ivory breasts and gentle body" must, in his opinion, pertain to Cecilia Valdés. Who but Cecilia could be described in such terms as "harmonious ensemble, imperious beauty and female virtue"? When the voices died down and guitars were being tuned, he explained to me that Cecilia Valdés had been queen of the *bailes de cuna*[1] in her time and that many musicians had been inspired by her unequaled beauty. He had read it. The descriptions "virginal" and "celestial" in Corona's lyrics meant nothing. Wasn't Cecilia Valdés called "the little bronze virgin"? He'd read that, too.[2] In short, the literary myth corresponded to the past but it lingered on in the present. That song had to be sung to the same woman who inspired Cirilo Villaverde, a man he already saw as a hapless *mulatero* (mulatto-lover).

What happened with the troubadours was one more piece of proof to me of something that is common knowledge: Cecilia Valdés is a literary figure who has acquired an infinite importance among Cubans; for better or for worse she has come to epitomize feminine essence and presence. Those who know the typical Cuban family — black, white or mulatto — will appreciate how Cecilia Valdés has become a myth unto herself, representative of collectively accepted values, on many occasions far removed from the anecdote of the novel. This is because the fictional character embodied concepts deeply rooted in people's knowledge and convictions. When this occurs — and it rarely does — the book acquires a worth that transcends the artistic and throws into relief weighty elements of collective wisdom.

The novel **Cecilia Valdés o La Loma del Angel** (Cecilia Valdés or Angel's Hill) is rightly considered a monument of 19th-century Cuban literature, first and foremost because it captured an era and a conception of life in its most contradictory detail. Those of us wanting to know about our colonial past before the independence wars, those of us wishing to reconstruct customs and follow the thread of historical coherence in Cuba, are indebted to that book. Its protagonist, the *mulata blanconaza* (the mulatto woman almost passing for white) who was queen among the *pardos y morenos* (mulattoes and blacks) of Angel's Hill, with all the aggravating circumstances of history, has transcended her literary origins. First, she was an archetype; now she comes before us as a breach through which we can pass into eventful 19th-century Cuba. What is more (and this explains the amorous fixation of the music lover in the Santiago de Cuba Troubadours' House), the literary character takes on the quality of an effective symbol because of the historic reiteration of the reasons for her misfortune. Although Cuban society made the transition from a slave colony to a bourgeois republic, precisely because that change was not a total reality, the circumstances that were propitious to stories like that of Cecilia Valdés persisted among us, subtly disguised.

With the disappearance of slavery as an economic system determining institutions in the Isle of Cuba, with the wars of independence over and the republic in place, what was posed through the character and the story spread like a latent imposition in ethical positions and prejudices that gained legal ground under the aegis of our dependent bourgeoisie. Cecilia Valdés continued to epitomize pejorative concepts of *mulatez* (brown-ness) that obstructed racial assimilation as a defining trait of our culture and nationhood. From literary personage, she came to represent sexist manipulation and all that the dominant (white) culture labeled bad in mulatto woman: a danger to established matrimony; the white man's seduction and loss of sense; the ability to attract through sensuality, but an irresolute and sly demonic angel; the ever latent possibility of a second love to come, to be enjoyed, but not in marriage — like Leonardo Gamboa's mulatto concubine in the novel.[3]

Creole femme fatale

Cirilo Villaverde gave literary form to an already existing myth in the social world-view of his time: the *mulata*. Cecilia Valdés, "lovely, sensual, frivolous woman, all sex and no brain, vain from top to toe,"[4] that was the myth. What we receive when we read the book is far superior to any discriminatory definition or facile psychology. As we turn the pages of the novel we find elements to understand the complex situation of the mulatto woman and her mulatto condition, even when the author is unable to clear his vision of the prejudices prevailing at the time. A synthesis in herself, but laden with symbolism and prejudice, the *mulata* Cecilia is one and many: we see her as lover, drawn by a passion that comes as a fact of her beauty and society's conditioning of her psychology; the author depicts her as coarse, aggressive, resentful in her uncultured state; we know her to be conceited and indolent; we would like her to be sensitive to the feelings of those around her; but at the same time this comes over, we also get the accumulated wrongs that circumscribe her false motivations.

It is quite apparent that the above observations are not without a marked moralism, in line with the novelist's aim. Sometimes humble, sometimes haughty, contemptuous or seductive, Cecilia Valdés used her feminine charm as her only tool, tacitly resigned to the limitations society has imposed on her. Unlike most literary characters, she is the sum of a plurality of intentions: she is at one and the same time victim and victimiser. Her historical context is surpassed by the transcendance of her myth and the value expressed therein. The repercussions are understandable knowing that, in and beyond her time, she — or another Cecilia — appears to "punish" in her wake and merit *guarachas*[b] like that popular on the streets of Havana between the years 1815 and 1820:

Mulatto woman would have me dead.
Won't they arrest her, I said?
Man alive can there be
if she who kills roams free?[5]

How many mulatto women and how many *guarachas* like these have had their effect on the streets of Cuba? We have before us a kind of femme fatale, as projected by the so-called cultural industry, only ahead of her time. Cecilia loved and wanted to be loved, but her sensual prowess impeded the awakening of lasting sentiment; she was defeated for embarking on a love relationship forbidden by society. Leonardo Gamboa loved her, but distrust always accompanied his feelings: "And it seems to me that you would be capable of loving any man to make me jealous", he says to her.(II:309) His own father accepts that "she is well brought up and honest in life... she has not as yet caused any talk," but there is "reason" to suspect her morality: "she's of a hybrid race; there can be no trusting in her virtue. She's *mulatilla* (little brown), and it is common knowledge that the child of the cat, kills the rat, and where baby goat leaps, so also the nanny."(II:328) The experienced *mulatero* Cándido Gamboa knows that Leonardo's intention is "to take her as his lover." "It doesn't even occur to me that my son's infatuation should lead him to the point of taking Valdés for his wife; what I fear, what I see as a disgrace for the family, is that he will take her as his lover." (II:332-333)

From the start of the novel, there are concepts of fatalism, predestination, and insurmountable barriers at play. Tracing the character of little Cecilia, the novelist includes elements to sow concern: she already showed "more voluptuousness than firmness"(I:105), "more cajolery and conniving than to be expected in a girl of her age"(I:117); and if the whole were beautiful, "for perfection all that was missing was that her expression be less malicious, if not malignant."(I:105) The reader can observe how the girl becomes a "proud and vengeful *mulata*"(II:380), carried to the point of fatality and capable of dragging an honest man into crime."[6]

Cecilia is described by her grandmother:

> Her figure and looks will be the end of me before long. And although I shouldn't be the one to say so, she is the prettiest woman seen on earth. Nobody would say she had any color in her at all. She looks white. Her prettiness has me crazy and beside myself. Keeping her from the white gentlemen who pursue her like flies after honey doesn't allow me to live or sleep. (II:19)

Born in a neighborhood of *pardos y morenos*, she was so markedly different, the author tells us, that "it was pitiful to see her among *morenos*," (II:69-70) for she had "perhaps the prettiest face of any woman in Havana at the time." (I:228) Though such an assertion would be seen as racist today, making out that blacks do not merit beauty, in those times it was taken for granted by *arriviste* mulattoes like Cecilia and by a good many of her kind. She did not consider herself destined for blacks and, with a marked predilection for whites, chose as the object of her love the son of a slavetrader millionaire. Her predestination, "cleansed" by her miscegenation and her beauty, is reiterated throughout the story, and is underlined, as Villaverde compares her influence over Leonardo and the weak sexual attraction of Isabel Ilincheta, white, rich and cultured, but with less charm:

> On seeing her, although the eyes of the *mulata* sent out rays not of love but anger, Leonardo was completely overwhelmed, and forgot Isabel, the balls at Alquízar and the walks along palm-lined paths and through orange groves on the coffee plantations. [While the description is charged with sensuality when trying to represent Cecilia:] burning tight lips; blood near bursting in her round cheeks; her full breast straining at the stays of her dress. (I:228-229)

It is accepted that the beauty born of her racial mix was eminently attractive: "There was none more beautiful nor more capable of unhingeing a man in love. She was tall and slender... for the regularity of her features and symmetry of form; her narrow waist contrasting with broad, bare shoulders; the amorous expression of her head; and the light bronze color; she could pass for the Venus of a hybrid Caucasian-Ethiopian race... The women were all eyes looking at her, the men stood aside for her, making flattering and vulgar remarks, and in an instant the low murmur of 'The little bronze virgin, the little bronze virgin!' ran from one side of the ball to the other." (I:142)

Convention is crossed

The balls were usually held during festive periods; "they were open to individuals of both sexes of the colored class, and young whites who honored them with their presence were not turned away either". (I:134-135) In Villaverde's observation here we find the beginnings of fusion with the white. Generally, those of "superior" race attending were poor, with nothing much to lose. Although social precepts discriminated against *pardos y morenos*, in popular neighborhoods this didn't apply to all, nor were they taken as irrefutable: poverty unified more than ethical concepts. Villaverde makes it clear that the balls attract all the neighborhood, including many whites among those knocking at Mercedes Ayalá's door in curiosity, especially women, "mute spectators" who observed how "young creoles, of decent, well-off families... were not embarrassed to brush with people of color and took part in their most typical form of entertainment." (I:136)

Presumably it was easier for a white man than a white woman to cross that threshold at that time.[7] Undoubtedly, the poor whites of the neighborhood didn't get the same treatment from their mulatto lady hosts as the rich young men; the exceptional nature of the latter is underlined by the narrator, indicating that "some [were going] out of interest, others for motives a less little pure." (I:136) The rich young men went fishing in muddy waters and promised destinies as bait, knowing that their presence was welcome. The *pardas y morenas*, like Cecilia's grandmother, took it for granted that "white, though poor, is good for a husband," but all the better if rich. They offered themselves as "husbands," but lending the term limited meaning, wholly unrelated to the officialization of a carnal relationship. Their attraction to black and brown women was proverbial; they want to the dances to meet them and court them, not out of friendship with men of color, though they maintained cordial relations with them. The manifest animosity of Leonardo Gamboa toward black and brown men was undisguised when he censures Cecilia for her affectionate relations. At the dance, "there was a dividing line between colored and white men that was tacitly, and it would seem effortlessly, respected by both one and the other" (I:155)...

In terms of ethnic exchange and integration, it is not easy to attribute the definitive role to one element or the other, components of that "new individual category in society"; in their surrender they move toward what was to become a "living symbol of the fusion of two races." "This encounter implies no determinism of one blood or another, but a purely cultural integration, that gives birth to an existing reality on our continent."[8] With their capacity for cultural survival, those considered inferior, through persuasion and perseverance, ended up possessing at the same time as they were possessed, dominating at the same time as being dominated. The rules of the social and economic game were made by the dominant culture, but were never played to the letter, nor did they continue as they had been laid down at the start. The dominant took on ways of the dominated, removed from the patterns of their own forebears, in a transplanted African setting and a process of inadvertent creolization. The mixing of skin color was translated into another more definitive mix. Despite the shades and colors, the idiosyncracy would become one...

The progressive mulatto-ization, generation by generation, became a recurrent aspiration. "I would die of shame if I married and had a *throw-back*." (II:62) The **sub-text**: the growing mulatto-ization, the fears and myths engendered in members of a stratified and unjust society... The author puts an equally sarcastic and practical version of this in the mouth of Uribe, the tailor:

> Do you like me less because I am colored? Folly. How many counts, lawyers and doctors are there who would be ashamed that their father or mother sit by them in their carriage, or accompany them to the audience of the Captain General on the Days of the King or the Queen

> Christina? Perhaps you are not as knowledgable as I because you do not brush with grandeur. But reflect a little and think back. Do you know who the count's father was? Well, he was his grandfather's butler. And the marchioness's father? A saddler from Matanzas, blacker than the wax on the thread he used to sew the harnesses. That the marquis of wherever keeps his mother hidden from his visitors at the Cathedral palace? And what have you to say about the father of the high-class doctor? He's a butcher round the corner... Well I don't have to hide my ancestors. My father was a Spanish brigadier. I hold him in great esteem, and my mother was no slave, or woman of *nation*. If the fathers of those gentlemen had been tailors, they would have passed, because it is well-known that H.E. the King has declared our skill a noble art, as also that of cigar maker, and we can use "esquire"... (I:231-232)

Aristocratic mixes and consideration for coloreds, by royal recognition or blessing, inform us of intermediary strata in the superstructure of colonial slavery. They are an antecedent to our 20th-century "hidden grandmother." Behind the humor or badmouthing, a constant drama of many Cuban families, concealing features that show them to have a touch or two of African ancestry; a desperate attempt to look white at all costs, to reach a racial parity that would enable them to leave the economic periphery.

Endnotes

1. Gathering of creole coloreds to dance and often gamble: private house, few musicians, harp and guitar, small and without etiquette. Esteban Pichardo **Diccionario provincial casi razonado de voces y frases cubanas** (1836), Ciencias Sociales, Havana, 1985, p. 200.
2. Attributed by Villaverde to admirers of Cecilia Valdés. According to Esteban Rodríguez Herrera, its origin is a poetic composition of last century entitled "Mulata":

    Bronze Venus, like the very bronze
    that two different metals make,

that two rival principals color,
two antipathetic beings engender.(I:142-143)

3. "The one who marries Isabel [Ilincheta] can rest assured that he will have no headaches, even through he be more jealous than a Turk. With women like C... [Cecilia Valdés], the danger is constant, like walking on tinder. It has never passed through my mind to marry her, or any like her, and yet, here I am, in a sweat whenever I think she might be flirting right now with the mulatto musician [José Dolores Pimienta]. In Havana she [Cecilia] will be my Venus; in Alquízar [Isabel] my guardian angel, my Ursuline nun, my sister of charity."(II:108-109)
4. Elías Entralgo "El capitalinismo habanero," Prolog to Lolo de la Torriente **La Habana de Cecilia Valdés (siglo XIX)**
5. Alejo Carpentier **La música en Cuba**, Lux-Hilo, Havana, 1961.
6. On José Dolores Pimienta's aptitude for the assassination at the ending and his unconditional love for Cecilia Valdés, see the reply of Manuel de la Cruz in the polemic with Manuel Fernández Junco, in **Cuba en la UNESCO**, p.78-84.
7. It was customary for people to be gathered outside the house where the dance was being held, and this is referred to in travelogs of the time (see Juan Pérez de la Riva, p.126)..[also] **La moda o Recreo Semanal del Bello Sexo**, Havana, January 16, 1928:169. In the description of the dance thrown by Mercedes Ayala, Villaverde narrates that there had been showers in the afternoon that had left the ground wet and "the streets impassable... but this didn't put off the inquisitive... who thronged the door and window, blocking almost half the narrow, winding street."(I:135) A ripple went through that chorus of onlookers as they clapped the arrival of Cecilia Valdés.
8. Miguel Barnet "La cultura que generó el mundo del azúcar", **Revolución y Cultura**, Havana, June 7, 1979.

Editors' notes

a) There are Troubadour Houses in towns and cities throughout Cuba where street musicians and singers go.
b) The *guaracha* is a popular Cuban dance rhythm.

SALVADOR BUENO

The black and white in the narrative of Alejo Carpentier

Taken from **El negro en la novela hispanoamericana** (The Black in the Hispanic American Novel), Letras Cubanas, Havana, 1986, pp.249-60.

Ecue-Yamba-O!, published in Madrid in 1933 by España Press with the subtitle "An Afro-Cuban Story", was the first novel of an unknown author: Alejo Carpentier. Two years previously, an excerpt from that work had appeared in a journal of which Carpentier was editor in chief, **Imán** (Paris, 1931); only one issue of this journal sponsored and managed by the Argentinian writer Elvira de Alvear was ever published. At the end of the Spanish edition of the book was this note: "First version: Havana Gaol, August 1-9, 1927. Final version: Paris, January-August, 1933."[1]

The famous author was repeatedly to criticize his initial work, pointing out what he considered to be its substantial faults and limitations. The first time was in his essay on literary criticism "Problematic of the Contemporary Latin American Novel"[2] which, by way of clarification, he begins with a quote from Goethe: "We have just arrived and we know not how. Do not ask me where we come from; suffice it to know that we are here." The author himself refers to the genesis of his work:

> In a period of great interest in the Afro-Cuban folklore recently "discovered" by intellectuals of my generation, I

> wrote a novel ***Ecue-Yamba-O***!, whose characters were rural blacks of the time. The reader should know that I grew up in the Cuban countryside in contact with black peasants and the children of black peasants; that later, very interested in the practice of *santería* and *ñañiguismo*, I attended innumerable ritual ceremonies... After 20 years of research on the syncretic realities of Cuba, I realized that the most profound, authentic, universal world I had set out to depict in my novel had remained beyond the scope of my observation. For example, the animism of the black peasant, the black's relationship with the forest; certain initiation practices that had been cleverly and disconcertingly kept from me by practitioners.[3]

Earlier in the essay, Carpentier synthesizes his appreciation of what he calls "the naturalist-nativist-typicist vernacular method" which, when applied to the Latin American novel, "has given us a picturesque regionalist novelistic tradition that in few cases has reached deep into the transcendental nature of things." Taking these two points of view as our point of departure, we can attempt to evaluate the *negrismo* in this, Carpentier's first narrative. Since the novels and short stories of this author broach a multitude of problems, diverse in form and content, we shall here only be analyzing them in relation to the significance of the African presence in the New World as a constant thread in his work.

The very title ***Ecue-Yamba-O***! (which in Lucumí dialect means "Praise be to God") underscores the importance of the esoteric, and within that the magical elements of *santería* and witchcraft; that is to say, the peculiar religious syncretism among the Cuban population of African ancestry. Fernando Alegría points to this as "a quasi-documentary novel about the magical primitive world of a sector of the black population in Cuba".[4] In this vein, the first Madrid edition included photographs and illustrations of religious symbols, ritual objects, drums and invocations. The work paid great attention to ritual formulas, initiation ceremonies and other manifestations of a magical-religious nature.

Cuban intellectuals of Carpentier's generation, coming into

public life in the decade of 1920 to 1930, turned to the discovery of national roots deformed by imperialism and stumbled on the manifestations of African cultures transplanted to the island, studied for years by Fernando Ortiz (1881-1969):

> A process of rapprochement with the black took place, especially as writers and artists of the cosmopolitan period had closed their eyes obstinately to the presence of the black on the island, ashamed of the fact... Now, as a reaction to that discriminatory spirit, the black was taken up with almost excessive enthusiasm, seeking therein certain values that were preferred to others, perhaps more lyrical, but nowhere near as strong.[5]

Those young men of Cuba in the decade 1920-1930 were very informed of the most up-to-date literary and artistic fashions of the early post-war period. They were the nucleus of the Minorista Group, which in 1928 declared the struggle against Yankee imperialism for Cuba's economic independence, and defended avant-garde art and dissemination of the latest artistic and scientific doctrine. Among them, Carpentier was one of those to push for a renewal of music; in 1927 he organized the first concerts of the "new music" with works by Stravinsky, Ravel and other contemporary masters.

> Those already familiar with **The Rite of Spring** — the great banner of revolution at the time — rightly began to draw attention to the fact that in Regla, on the other side of the bay [from Havana], there were rhythms every bit as complex and interesting as those Stravinsky had created to evoke the primitive games of pagan Russia.

He concluded:

> That was how the Afro-Cubanist current came into being and would for over ten years nurture poems, novels and folkloric and sociological studies. It was a trend that in many cases never went beyond the superficial and

peripheral, to the "black under sun-drenched palms" but was a necessary step to better understand certain poetic, musical, ethnic and social factors that had contributed to shaping the creole physiognomy.[6]

Ecue-Yamba-O! was a culminating point of this narrative trend. Following the nomenclature that made Wolfgang Kayser fashionable, it has been considered a novel of space. Different settings are laid out for the reader: rural settings, a sugar mill in the early decades of this century, town festivities and miracle-making ceremonies through to the urban area, the capital, the Havana gaol, as we follow the life trajectory of Menegildo Cué, the novel's protagonist, from birth to death. He leaves a son of the same name who will run the same existential cycle. Opposition of spaces — as Pedro Lastra has said — which serves as an aperture to other oppositions of spaces in Carpentier's later work.

Ecue-Yamba-O! is a novel that is advanced for its times. While its perception of reality corresponds to *criollista* techniques prevalent during that period, there is also an avant-garde aspect to Carpentier's work. The language of the characters is reproduced as phonetically deformed in the style of *criollistas* and *regionalistas*, but we find at each instant images and techniques that are evidently avant-garde. This confluence of expressive formulas reveals the contradictory structure and execution of this novel, a true example of the transformation that was already taking place during those years in Hispanic-American narrative. We find incorporated into the text many popular songs, sayings and expressions. But alongside them germinate overtly futuristic metaphors and similes, even resonances of the grotesque style created by Valle Inclán. A contrast is thereby established between on the one hand an approximation to the latest avant-garde techniques — a breath of cosmopolitanism — and the contribution of certain typically picturesque, rough and rugged, folkloric elements.

In an essay drafted in prison, Juan Marinello appraised the merits of the novel in which the author showed himself to be "as avid for primitivism as slave to refinement". In his opinion,

Carpentier bears no testimony to the social reality of black Cubans:

> Neither our blacks nor our people show their stature in ***Ecue-Yamba-O***! Menegildo could have conveyed the troubles of a man hemmed in without detracting from his person, and the peasants of San Lucio likewise the anguish of eviction. Despite the beauties of the novel, it remains a book of episodes, when it could have been one of essence.[8]

Nonetheless, the economic and social conditions of the neo-colonial republic were not forgotten by the young novelist. The progressive predominance of U.S. companies, today called "transnationals", the exploitation of peasants, not only Cubans but Haitians, Jamaicans, etc., and the pseudo-democratic politicking all reveal the economic and cultural underdevelopment of Cuba at that time. In its anti-imperialism, its denunciation of latifundism and sugar, Carpentier's first novel takes a stand on collective problems, even though the author observes them as elements within his aesthetic perspective and does not make proposals to transform that socio-economic reality.

This first attempt to broach the social reality of the continent does not situate Carpentier among those who crystallized their observations according to the polarity of "civilization-barbarity" originally put forward by Domingo Faustino Sarmiento and which found resonance in **Doña Bárbara** (1929) by Rómulo Gallegos (1884-1969). Carpentier's interest — albeit epidermic — was to unravel the culture of "those from below", without disdain and without glossing anything over. Social stratification was represented through the exploited: the Cué family, whose ancestors were brought violently from Africa to be thrown into slavery, and who, in the novel's present-day, suffer class extortion. With this positive sign comes the protagonist's discovery of syncretic beliefs; his mother, "Salomé had not neglected his spiritual life", "she had initiated him into the mysteries of 'great things', whose obscure designs go beyond man's comprehension." Because man can direct these invisible forces:

> Just as whites have filled the atmosphere with ciphered messages, the times of symphonies and English courses, men of color capable of keeping alive the great tradition of centuries, a science passed down from fathers to sons, kings to princes, initiators to initiated, know that the air is subtly interwoven with threads which transmit the forces invoked in ceremonies whose function, deep down, is to condense a higher mystery and channel it in favor or against something.

Carpentier broaches syncretic beliefs with the curiosity of the researcher, but does not miss the fact that these dark-skinned people represent the nucleus of autochtony, the very essence of nationhood under siege from deforming foreign forces. "Only the blacks, Menegildo, Longina, Salomé and their offspring, jealously maintain a Caribbean character and tradition". As in the early work of Nicolás Guillén, **Motivos de son** (1930) and **Sóngoro cosongo** (1931), the black constitutes the specificity of the Cuban broken by the economic rapacity of imperialism and by foreign ideas and customs: "The *bongó* antidote to Wall Street!... No hot-dogs with the *santos de mayeya*!"

Ecue-Yamba-O! is structured around the life journey of Menegildo: the novel is divided into three parts or sections titled "Childhood", "Adolescence" and "The City" (that is, the adulthood of the protagonist). Each of these three phases corresponds to the progressive approximation of Menegildo to the world of magical beliefs of African origin. In his childhood, he discovers "gold and brightly colored statues" and learns about the witchdoctor Beruá's therapeutic powers. To win Longina's love, the adolescent Menegildo turns to those mythical forces; Beruá prepares the *embó* along with the "bigger things" of the gods. When Menegildo flees from the city accused of murder, he is helped and advised by his cousin Antonio, who makes him understand the importance of *ñañigo* powers, one of which comes down to an initiation ceremony which is one of the most successful passages of the novel. Insisting on his rejection of **Ecue-Yamba-O,** Carpentier confessed:

> ...it is perhaps a failed attempt for its abuse of metaphors,

> mechanical similes, images of abhorrently futurist bad taste, and for my generation's concept of nationhood. But not everything about it is deplorable. The chapters on the *ñañigo* "breaking in" salvage it from disaster.[9]

The three chapters on the initiation ceremony complement another salvageable part of the novel, which is the part in which, as a child, Menegildo discovers unsuspected sides to reality, crawling under the furniture in his peasant home, a part that has its similarities with the later short story **Viaje a la semilla** (Journey to the Seed, 1944). It is not particularly successful in its minute description of tropical nature; the description of a hurricane fails for the mechanical profusion of avant-garde imagery. The return of Longina, a widow, to her home, the birth of a new Menegildo who repeats the same adventures as his father, paves the way for another twist of the spiral, the apparent recurrence is none other than a new cycle to be traveled by the impoverished. This is a first sign of what would be a similar confrontation in processes in the future narrative of Carpentier. As Carlos Santander T. observed, **Ecue-Yamba-O!**:

> puts forward two basic ideas that the author would continue to develop in his future writing: one, that America is the continent of magical reality, though without the generalization that comes in **Los pasos perdidos** (The Lost Steps), since [in the former] the magical reality is Cuban; the second, that syncretism is the essential form in which magical reality presents itself. Those who would separate this, Carpentier's first novel, from the rest of his literary production, are therefore mistaken.[10]

Magical reality exists for those beings who "had a concept of the universe which accepted the possible magical quality of any phenomenon"; they "turned to ancient tradition... which allowed man, bared before a land as yet unrecovered from recent convulsions, to find within him instinctive defences to the ferociousness of what had been created". They are "blacks", looked down upon and exploited, violently uprooted from their native lands. "And what was wrong with the blacks? Weren't they men like the rest? Was a black worth less than an American? In the face of such total plunder, they found energy in the forces of magic and myth, finding 'true pride in primitive life, full of small complications and magical arguments that men of the North could never understand'." And so, magical reality was not an intellectual concept Carpentier learned from civilized Europe; it was life on the American continent immersed in a mix of cultures, beliefs and superstitions — overlapping and transcultured — that enabled the young writer to take up the latest in European culture and, at the same time, assimilate the African witchcraft transplanted to Cuba without taking more than a few steps from his Havana home, and without being torn in two.

Endnotes

1. All the quotes from **Ecue-Yamba-O!** are from the España edition, Madrid, 1933.
2. Alejo Carpentier **Tientos y diferencias**, Autonomous University of Mexico, 1964, pp. 5-47.
3. Ibid, pp.12-13.
4. Fernando Alegría **Literatura y Revolución**, Fondo de Cultura Económica, 1971, p.96.
5. Alejo Carpentier "Variaciones sobre un tema cubano", **Américas**, March 1950, p.14.
6. Alejo Carpentier **La música en Cuba**, Fondo de Cultura Económica, Mexico, 1946.
7. Pedro Lastra "Aproximaciones a *Ecue-Yamba-O!*" in **Asedios a Carpentier**, Universitaria, Santiago, Chile, 1972.
8. Juan Marinello **Literatura hispanoamericana**, Mexico, 1937, p.175.
9. "Confesiones sencillas de un escritor barroco" in **Homenaje a Alejo Carpentier**, New York, 1970, p.22.
10. Carlos Santander T. "Lo maravilloso en la obra de Alejo Carpentier" in **Homenaje a Carpentier**, New York, 1970, p.123-124.

MIGUEL BARNET

Runaway story

Taken from **Living Memory** (La fuente viva, Letras Cubanas, Havana, 1983). Editors' title.

Before defining what I understand by the testimonial novel, allow me to to tell a brief story.

My incursion into this terrain was purely by chance. I always loved adventure stories, biographies and autobiographies, true stories like the epic tale of the African warrior Soundyate, the sinking of the **Titanic** or the Boston Tea Party. And the memoirs of the slave Manzano or those of Isadora Duncan. I remember how reading **Cecilia Valdés** revealed a world that I found much more fascinating than the one in Salgari's novels. For years I would walk along Inquisition Street and Machine Wharf; I would stop on Angel's Hill in a youthful attempt to reconstruct the last chapter of Villaverde's novel. It was for me a cult of the strange, mysterious past, that led me to ethnographic and folkloric research. I always felt a pressing need to understand this country, especially social relations. One day I laid my hands on **Juan Pérez Jolote**, the study of an indigenous community through Mexican anthropologist Ricardo Pozas' conversations with a Chamula Indian. I was struck by the strong story and credible prose. The book was effective, sociologically and artistically, and made a deep impression on me.

I had been working with Esteban Montejo on a monograph on Yoruba funeral cults and social life in the slave barracoons. Esteban, the runaway slave, was one of my old informants, but his life stood out, filling in unknown chapters in the history of Cuba. His life experiences were, it can safely be said, unique. I saw the possibility of doing a book along the same lines as

Ricardo Pozas, and didn't stop to think twice. That's how **Autobiography of a Runaway Slave** came about. But, since each of us "goes to market with a different basket", so each has a different book, and I set out to do something different, though along the same basic lines. That's how I started out working with the ethnographic story, the novel as reality and testimony. I found the term novel constraining. There were times when I wavered in my intentions, because I didn't want to write a novel. What I wanted was an ethnographic story, which was how I subtitled **Runaway Slave**.

The idea of what I wanted to do took shape in the practical work of interviewing, indexing and transcribing recordings. It was not by chance that I had chosen an ex-slave, a runaway and *mambí*. Esteban could fill certain lacunae that existed in Cuban history with his singular exploits, his years of solitary life exposed to the elements, his recollections of ethnic relations in the barracoons, his knowledge of the island ecology. Esteban, moreover, had been party to the most significant events during successive periods of his life: from the hoe and shackles of slavery to the machete of the Independence War. He had also witnessed other equally important events.

Esteban Montejo's whole life was atypical, marked by the sign of a singular destiny. When Graham Greene described that life as unique, I took it as an exact description; it was not banal praise for the work, but an intelligent observation. Not all subjects bear those characteristics, which is why **Runaway** is an ideal type in its genre.

As I organized the data, based on my interviews with him — lasting five or six hours a day — I realized what I wanted to do and the structure I would give it. The first decision was that the testimonial novel would be a text like a fresco, reproducing or recreating — and I would emphasize the latter — social developments that were landmarks in a country's culture. And that the protagonists of the testimonial novel would refer to them, reflecting on their importance and value, or simply making them known through their own part in them. The events would not be trivial, although presumed triviality can be very eloquent in this kind of story, because the insignificant can take on magnitude, especially when the "insignificance" has to do with the character and subjectivity of the informant. But I preferred the historical facts or moments to be ones of radical change in national culture, leaving their mark on the spirit and idiosyncracy of the people.

Thus, the runaway, after a slave childhood amidst pigsty and whiplash, embarked on a profligate life on the run; then he became a wage laborer and finally *mambí*. That's to say: slavery, *marronage, patronato* and Independence War. Each and every one of those periods has left a deep imprint on the Cuban psyche, helping shape it and give it a history. And they are not marginal occurrences but social upheavals, collective epic events that can only be reconstructed through historical memory. And for this, what better than a representative protagonist, a legitimate actor. This example serves to demonstrate the first characteristic I believe the testimonial novel must have: that of deciphering reality, taking major events that have helped shape a people, and describing them through the words of an apt protagonist.

I think that in Alejo Carpentier's **Kingdom of this World**, Ti Noel serves this purpose. He is the people, the 'us' that speaks and appraises events, having been witness to them. Naturally, he is a literary witness, an invention of Carpentier. He is not real but he plays the part of a *griot*, of a protagonist in a testimonial novel. Ti Noel, or rather Alejo Carpentier makes Ti Noel the narrator witness who, like *Elegguá*, sees all. Runaway and Rachel are unwittingly real witnesses, sociological rather than literary, because despite the fact that they are my literary recreation, manipulated by threads of fiction, they are flesh and blood human beings, both real and convincing.

This brings me to a second point I believe essential to the testimonial novel: the suppression of, or perhaps more fairly put, discretion on the part of the writer or sociologist as to the "I" form and the presence of the self. Not disappearing Truman Capote-style, dissipating all semblance of imagination and opinion, but letting the protagonist be the judge. Of course, Truman Capote didn't believe in what he said, proof of which is in his novel **In Cold Blood**, where he sides throughout with Perry, the tender, melancholic assassin.

This does not mean that the author, at a given moment, is not so into the mentality, the psychology of the characters as to judge with their values, speak through their mouths, because there has to be a strong and deep bond of identification and sympathy between author and informant. Individuality must be cast aside to take on that of the informant and the collectivity being represented. Flaubert said, "Madame Bovary, c'est moi." The author of a testimonial novel must say together with the protagonist: "I am the times." That has to be a hard and fast premise, an arrow on target...

The solid works of our continent have only two great exponents: those who go beyond their times, who introduce a new style and a new, original, personal, whimsical vision of the world; and those who want to take on the values and psychology of their peoples, who will be the ones who capture their times, or return to the past to explain the present, not least to themselves.

The great masters go beyond self, intuitive of popular wisdom and the future. Their secret, their knowledge, stems from a deep understanding of the people and their expressive forms: one might mention José Lezama Lima and Nicolás Guillén. And in Mexico, Juan Rulfo, who through dream, through the image reflecting memory, delved into the collective mind, the anguish and aspirations of his people. When Miguel Páramo goes in search of his dead father, is not the world shaped around hope that of Juan Rulfo?

"That's why I came to Comala, because I was told my father lived here." I know few novels as credible as Juan Rulfo's **Pedro Páramo**. The work of the artist, Eliot said, is a continual sacrifice, a continual extinction of self.

It is in this depersonalisation that art comes closer to science. And for that art not to be a failed hybrid, it must chart a different future, along new paths. The artist must be a visionary. The artist who works with the materials of brute reality must do so to the best advantage, dissecting them, extracting from them what is new, for the future.

That is a difficult task, and there are times when the writer runs the risk of getting lost in the sand. But if we didn't dream that what we argue today will be accepted tomorrow by the sociologist and the historian, then our effort would be short-lived.

Some might tell me that's tantamount to believing that if you've got God by the beard, then you've absolute truth, but that's not the case. It's simply to further our knowledge of a reality, and if this isn't done with conviction and the necessary balance, our work will be like jelly.

To further our knowledge of reality, to impart on this a sense of history, is another crucial feature of the testimonial novel. Furthering knowledge of reality is wanting to free the reader from prejudice and atavism. The reader must be equipped with an awareness of the past, given a myth which is both positive and useful as a model for categorization. This model, it should go without saying, must be relative and ambiguous; it can't be static or definitive, but only a starting point. That is what I wanted Runaway and Rachel to be, starting points for knowing a period, an historical era. Such a knowledge of reality is far removed from the gray didacticism that has blocked many, especially post-war, creative efforts. Knowledge of reality implies knowledge of self. The reader should be able to find himself in books, as if he were one of the characters moving, gesticulating, imagining, writing, judging. I believe literature should give man critical faculties, leaving a margin of doubt for either contradiction or affirmation.

In **Rachel** I have used the technique of counterpoint or Rashomon system: looking as if through a concave mirror, for the reader to identify with the book, whether that be for or against Rachel. In Estenoz and Ivonet's race war, she took the position of the government and the hordes who went into the hills of Oriente to put down the explosive rebel uprising of the Colored Independents. Here, Rachel is the extreme type, taking sides because that is the measure of the most exacerbated form of racism. Later she becomes paternalist, wants to understand... But what is important is that such an attitude isn't only Rachel's, but that of many Rachels. And the model has to be extreme so as to shake the reader. There are other characters with different points of view on the same event, among them Esteban Montejo, who defends the 1912 War to the hilt. And this is just one example of a knowledge of reality, that is, the phenomenon, but behind it there is a viewpoint, or various viewpoints.

NANCY MOREJÓN

Race and nation

Excerpt from **Nación y mestizaje en Nicolás Guillén** (Nation and Miscegenation in Nicolás Guillén), UNEAC, Havana, 1982, pp.19-31.

Tracing the term *transculturation* and applying it to the poetry and journalistic or literary prose of Nicolás Guillén (b. Camagüey 1902) undoubtedly leads to considerable conjecture. The reader might immediately question the link between that term and a poetic and literary output that is of its own right inserted in the classical values of contemporary Spanish language. And yet, as one becomes more familiar with the author's extensive secondary bibliography, due attention to this concept is inescapable. One of the distinguishing traits of Guillén's work is the place of nation. Who today would not subscribe to his being defined as Cuba's national poet? That condition goes beyond a mere label to an invaluable essence. In the context of the Caribbean, nation can never be grasped in its totality, as an integral, dynamic category, unless we bear in mind a whole process of transculturation which has brought it into being. Cuban culture, as an integral part of the culture of the Greater and Lesser Antilles, stands out at the present time for a national awareness only conceivable thanks to the determining action of a socialist revolution. That awareness is discovering popular roots nurtured on the ancestral wisdom of two basic components: the Hispanic and the African, both of which determine our social and psychological being. It is no secret to anyone that Guillén's poetry as well as his articles and short essays, on diverse topics, proclaim more than explicitly an undeniable vocation for analyzing and legitimately taking on the specific nature of our culture. But in Guillén the mere fact of perceiving our culture accordingly is not sufficient. He has not only given form to and dissected such elements; he has also sung to the process of transculturation. Let us look without further delay, therefore, at the background to the term.

The Cuban scholar Fernando Ortiz, whose multifaceted writing was the very font of inspiration for our anthropological, linguistic, historical, ethnographic and sociological study, was the one who passed on to us the word transculturation, but it already had its own history. It was not his invention, but he was the one who, with his indescribable love for what is Cuban, with his striving to discover the truth behind the largest of the Caribbean islands, molded it to our requirements, peculiarities and needs. Today, when there has been so much navigation in veritably putrid or uncertain waters around what is taken to be identity, it is impossible not to recognize the effectiveness and validity of Don Fernando's study of the process of transculturation.

The uprooting of large populations and the consequent cultural changes (or clashes), the impact of one civilization on another, was given a common label, the disadvantageous notion of *acculturation*. The Bronislaw Malinowski school welcomed this term until the innovative *transculturation* was coined by Fernando Ortiz. The introduction of this technical word in sociological and anthropological studies is due to him. But it is impossible to understand the term precisely and in its true dimension without first analyzing its antecedent: *acculturation*.

A term valued by U.S. scholars, it is, in the first instance, eminently value-laden. Today it would not be improper to associate its elementary meaning with the concept of assimilation that Frantz Fanon applied to our Caribbean societies (so as to refute it). In that cultural encounter, clash or change, as it has been termed, one of the components becomes acculturated, that is, assimilated into the other; such that one remains dependent or, what is worse, inferiorized, minimized, before the strength of the other. Someone comes out on top. From the outset, we are faced with a process that, as Malinowski points out, is basically Eurocentric. And if we cast our minds back, this acculturation is generally directed at the immigrant and presupposes a considerable degree of barbarity. The indigenous "savage" from overseas is accultured, assimilated, "Christianized", "civilized".

When we mention Eurocentrism, we simply refer to a key phenomenon in the most sadly celebrated theory, spread like a stigma and outrage, of what in reality is far removed from the great western culture.

Acculturation, then, signifies becoming the other, casting aside one's own personality which has been subordinated, through force or improbable persuasion, to adopt a set of totally alien, virtuous, superior values. It is supposedly the conversion of a savage into a civilized being. But that phenomenon cannot be reduced in such simple, partial, normative fashion. It is not a matter of adaptation. It is not water from one glass poured into another, that is boiling, to mold it to the drinker's taste, but rather a process of enormous dimension, rich in alchemy, agent and receiver, conditioned, naturally, by long-accepted laws of class struggle. In our lands of the Americas, Europe not only shaped and influenced us but has also been influenced and shaped by those lands. Its food, its music, its customs, its language, its religion are its own not insofar as whence they originated but in the way they were molded and given new shape...

Transculturation signifies constant interaction, transmutation between two or more cultural components whose unconscious end is the creation of a third cultural whole — that is, culture — new and independent, although its bases, its roots, rest on preceding elements. The reciprocal influence here is determining. No element is superimposed on the other; on the contrary, each one becomes a third entity. None remains immutable. All change and grow in a "give and take" which engenders a new texture. Who could argue today that the Spaniards who came to the West Indies weren't transcultured? As time passed, in the literature of chroniclers and that of the conquistadors, we see an unpredictable influx, first dazzled by, and then feverishly coveting, not only those fertile lands, those rivers of gold, but also the spirit and form of their inhabitants...

"The true history of Cuba is the history of its intricate transculturations."[1] Don Fernando's proposition carries us to a plane which is only viable through an elucidation of our cultural past and its progressive composition. Initially, there is our first, indigenous component, which suffered the violent impact of

Conquest after Discovery. Its physical disappearance led to its total elimination from the nation's cultural panorama, especially in contemporary times. Then, we have the constant immigration of Spanish conquistadors. Andalucians, Portuguese, Galicians, Basques and Catalans came to Cuba, as well as other immigrant groups from ancient Mediterranean cultures, of similar racial mix.

> While some whites brought the feudal economy, as conquistadors in search of booty and peoples to subjugate and make their plebians; others, also white, came driven by the already dawning economy of merchant and even industrial capital.[2]

At the same time, one has to be willing to understand where these white immigrants were coming from; although they *all* came from the Iberian peninsula, we know that many cultures went to make up the incipient Spanish nation. This controversial nation, coming out of a medieval lethargy, did not present to the New World a homogeneous, exact, defined profile. On the contrary. A range of peoples and their respective cultures — and rather than peoples we should think of ethnic groups — swelled the ranks of those who would be transplanted to American lands. How can we not think, then, of the dual impact, the dual clash for these men, uprooted from their native lands and the cultural plurality of their home, to a new social reality where they would encounter not an abrupt, hostile nature, exuberant and antagonistic to their own, but the immense jungle of new races, new customs, new religions, new sexuality?

The other component came from a diverse source of slaves, brought from the West Coast of black Africa. To the islands of the Caribbean, and especially Cuba, came Africans from Senegal, Guinea, the Congo and Angola, on the Atlantic, to Mozambique on the East African Coast. All the groups of African slaves brought from the West Coast had very different tribal and ethnic origins. They spoke evolved languages — some with grammar, others without — but they were all linguistically distinct from one other. The black cultures were also diverse in differing degrees. Those that had already been inserted into Iberian culture were brought by the conquistadors and showed infinite signs of miscegenation. We were peopled by the Mandinga, Yelofe, Hausa, Dahomeyans, who brought agriculture, currency and trade, though never their institutions or governments. They came with no writing. Of course, in that period, the concept we have today of nation was uncertain and unknown. It did not exist. Thus those men also entered into a role they never imagined and that was not in their plans or designs.

The African slave, while also an immigrant, did not arrange to meet the Spanish conquistador. What differentiates one immigration from the other is the basic function each was to have with respect to the other. While the former came to these lands of the New World to seek fortune, with the spirit of adventure of those times, infused with a thirst for gold of the Indies; the latter were brought by force, prisoners in body and soul, to a condition subordinated to the economic designs of their buyers. These two functions would then become the nature of each of the components, bearing in mind the dialectic of time and the incidence on each of the phenomenon — or rather, law — of class struggle.

The basic components were the Spanish and the African; but we cannot ignore other cultures, other components which, in intermittent, minority waves, set down many roots on Cuban and Caribbean soil, to mold the basic component parts of the majority substratum. And here one would have to make a digression.

While in Cuba, the largest of the Greater Antilles, we see that the Spanish component is strong and dominant, we are sure that in the Lesser Antilles the equivalent component would be French, English or Dutch. From this it would have to be inferred that, in general, the culture of the islands is irremediably based on a component of European origin, whether as a nation at the time of appearing on the panorama of the New World or as yet to be forged. Added to that European source, and the African, there were discrete but strong elements of Indian, Chinese and Jewish cultures. In Cuba, the Asiatic element, mainly from Macao and Canton and other regions of the Chinese Empire, has been of considerable importance, though never as great as the basic components. The Chinese, brought to the New World in a supposedly "new" coolie concept of slavery, soon felt the opprobrium of slave exploitation. Imagine, then, for a moment, what the New World culture is: a heiroglyphic of races and cultures, a fresco, smoked glass, in the burning veins of men and women, uprooted like the colts of José Martí in **Our America**, whose manifold revolutionary stock would nurture a new race, a new culture.

The historical and social evolution of the Cuban people rests on this "give and take", in that welcome common denominator in all our culture: miscegenation. It is impossible to perceive or conceive of Cuba's national identity ignoring or even downplaying its essentially miscegenous condition. The diverse formative elements of the Cuban nation are fused in a single substance, precisely that which seeks a face in legitimate national independence.

In the framework of this context common to peoples of all the Caribbean islands, Cubans are characterized for having sought to build a nation that is homogeneous in its heterogenity, defined by a political end beyond any cultural or racial controversy. Whence, the rightful application of the term *transculturation* to our cultural history. We have not been assimilated, that is to say, acculturated to Spanish or African culture; with a highly creative spirit, in a constant quest for nationhood, we have produced a mixed people, who inherit and embody both components, no longer either Spanish or African, but Cuban.

Did we have a stone age? Yes and no. Our archaeology still calls for new thinking about the indigenous cultures on our soil at the time of the arrival of Christopher Columbus and his three caravels. Even today there is no general consensus on this. Yes, there were Indians whose cultural evolution was much less advanced than that of the great cultures on the continent, in Mexico and Guatemala, Peru and Bolivia. A glance at any bibliographical index of the pre-Columbian cultures is astonishing with regard to the magnitude and especially the vibrancy of those cultures in the contemporary world of today's Latin America. In this sense, Cuba, as part of Caribbean and Latin American culture, is an exceptional case in so far as the indigenous element represents neither a strong nor current component in its culture.

As Fernando Ortiz put it, "a cultural hurricane"[3] hit ours and that of the neighboring islands. In a historical second, we were witness to the arrival in unison of compass and horse, money and Church, ammunition and the word, all the components working together to the eventual liquidation of the Indian.

A Cuban of whatever background, of whatever social class, bears the distinctive trait of cultural miscegenation. With his typically creole humour, Don Fernando wrote: "There are Cubans so dark they seem black and there are Cubans so light they seem white." This incisive phrase alludes to an underlying circumstance of our island, and we might do well to remember that popular saying: "If you've no *Congo*, you've *Carabalí*." A Cuban, though racially he may look Yoruba or Catalan, responds to a national character. Over and above any contingency, he is, feels and proudly proclaims himself *Cuban*. The sense of nationhood presupposes a melting pot of races and a mixed culture. And not a melting pot of races and cultures as in other countries of diverse culture, that is, not transculturated.

The cultures that formed part of the process of transculturation in Cuba suffered vertiginously. Over four centuries, a national spirit has been fashioned from cultures deposited here in diverse states: the conquistador with the common denominator of attack and power, avid for possession and adventure; the slave levelled down within the very regime of slavery. Some came to work; others came to be prisoners of work and swell the coffers of modern capitalism. Some of their own free will; others by force. Crossing the ocean was never the best of experiences for humankind and the world. And yet, the very dissociation reached conquistadors and slaves. Some in positions of superiority, others under the yoke of submission; all alienated, beyond themselves, in the frenetic category of transculturation.

The poetry of Guillén and the thought implicit in it, as well as his journalistic prose, are a clear and conscious manifestation of the concept of transculturation we have been exploring up until now. Guillén's late, and even early, work, is indebted to this notion, and while not setting it out in any planned way, exemplifies the subtle nuances of the neologism brought into being by Fernando Ortiz and baptized by Bronislaw Malinowski.

If we take just two texts: the poem **West Indies, Ltd** and the prologue to **Sóngoro cosongo**, we can see at a glance the link or interrelation between the two, and, at the same time, the connection between the two texts — of differing genres — and the concept of transculturation. Let us take sections of the first part of **West Indies, Ltd** and we shall see how the images the poet chooses describe the immensely rich and diverse composition of human beings peopling the island with their respective cultures:

This is a dark smiling people
...
humble, gentle folk, descendants of
slaves
and of that uncivil riffraff
of various breeds
whom in the name of Spain
Columbus kindly ceded to the Indies

Here are whites and blacks and Chinese and
mulattoes
They are cheap colors of course
since through trade and indenture
the dyes have run and there is no stable
tone.
He who thinks otherwise should step forward
and speak.

West Indies, Ltd [4]

Without wishing to gloss over the basic overriding anti-imperialist sentiment to this great flowing poem[5] — whose prime message is directed toward denouncing the omnipotent presence of U.S. capital in Cuba and the islands of the Caribbean as a whole — it is obvious that Guillén's general conception of history and the nature of the Antilles is based on an acceptance of the phenomenon of transculturation. It would, on the other hand, be absurd to attempt to constrain the incommensurate reach of this grand fresco, this pathetic monument to a moment in Cuban life, to the whole notion of a term. It could even be justifiably argued that this poem is very specifically Caribbean and that this is a limiting factor to our argument. But I believe that precisely because it is Caribbean it registers, like none other, the Cuban cultural condition as an integral part of Caribbean culture. If Guillén captured the inner gleam of our islands it is, undoubtedly, because Cuba is an integral part of them.

The image of the islands constituting a single, indivisible, multiple whole, formed by destiny and beset by cultural changes, is key to an understanding of Guillén's poetry and even his aesthetic. Based on the concept of transculturation, that aesthetic is perhaps the element that unequivocably characterizes and defines the work of Nicolás Guillén in relation to that of many who were writing at the same time throughout Hispanic America and the Caribbean — including the English-, French- and Dutch-speaking parts — as well as the infinite contemporary African literature.

The "Prologue" to **Sóngoro cosongo** (1931) is even more explicit:

> I should say finally that this is mulatto verse. The same elements are present as in the ethnic composition of Cuba, where we are all a little brown. Does that hurt? I don't think so. It needs to be said regardless, lest we forget. The African injection in this land runs deep, and so many capillary currents cross and crisscross our well-watered social hydrography that it would take a miniaturist to unravel the heiroglyph.
>
> I therefore think that for us, creole poetry would not be complete without the black. The black, in my opinion, brings solid essence to our cocktail. And the two races that surface so distant one from the other on the island, throw out an underwater hook, like deep tunnels secretly joining two continents. And, the spirit of Cuba is mulatto, and the definitive color will come one day from the spirit to the skin: "Cuban color."
>
> These poems want to bring that day forward...[6]

Looking at the concept of transculturation so explicit in Guillén's work, it should be said that this current paved the way for the creation of an essentially Cuban poetic language. If we return to the crucial contribution of the black to our culture, we should refer to something Guillén himself said with respect to the situation of the Cuban black: "Even after 1880, when the blacks attained their freedom in theory, yet still disputed, the Negro remained absent as such from Cuban poetry and art, and the same occurred well into the Republic." It needs to be said that through the expression of the black it was possible to reach an expression of the Cuban. That is the prime importance of this poetry. Its destiny has been none other than to lay the foundations of a more fitting and more integral vision of the factors that, through a process of transculturation, make up the nation:

> In this mulatto land
> of African and Spaniard
> (on one side *Santa Bárbara*,
> on the other *Changó*),
> always a grandfather missing
> when there isn't a Don too many
> with titles from Castille
> and kinfolk in Bondó:
> better be silent, my friends,
> and not ask the question,
> because we've come from afar
> and go in two by two.
>
> **Song of the Bongó** [7]

Endnotes

1. Fernando Ortiz **Contrapunteo cubano del tabaco y el azúcar,** Introduction by Bronislaw Malinowski, Consejo Nacional de Cultura, Havana, 1963, p.99.
2. Ortiz, op.cit, p.101.
3. Ortiz, op.cit, p.100.
4. Nicolás Guillén **Obra poética (1902-1972)**, 2 vols, Prologue and notes by Angel Augier, Unión, Havana, Vol. 1, 1974, p.212.
5. Other poems show the same, including **Balada de dos abuelos** and

Son número 6.

6. Guillén, op.cit, Vol. 1, p.176.
7. Guillén, op.cit, Vol. 1, pp.178-9.

ALBERTO PEDRO

Rethinking the plantation

Excerpt from "Cultura y Plantación" (Culture and Plantation) in **Del Caribe**, 16-17, Year VI, 1990, pp. 28-30. This was originally a paper given to the International Seminar "Seeds of Trade: Cultural and Economic Exchange in the Caribbean" organized jointly by the Smithsonian Institute in Washington and the host Casa del Caribe in Santiago de Cuba. **Del Caribe** reproduced the papers and debates. Editors' title.

The conceptual error of describing the plantation as a political institution undoubtedly has its genesis in the real and incomparable political influence plantation owners had. Their power came naturally from their lucrative business and, as a rule, the administration of the country protected their interests. But it is an exaggerated simplification to think that the plantation takes the place of government in its political functions despite the influence these plantation owners have and even when they themselves are governing, which is frequently the case.

However, in the colonial situation, the government of subjugated countries prioritizes the interests of the metropolis over and above those of the plantation owners. Nor is coercive authoritarianism exclusive to the white colonialists; rather, history has shown it to be present among all races. Moreover, in those multiracial empires where the colonizer was white, the colonizer exercised authoritarianism over the colonized of all races, including the white. "No taxation without representation" was the motto for the revolution of the Thirteen Colonies against Great Britain in the late 18th century. When Latin America waged its early 19th-century wars of independence against Spain, Simón

Bolívar drew up the Jamaica Charter, decrying the fact that the metropolis denied (especially white) creoles access to colonial government. Not even plantation owners went unaffected by such policies.

As far as internal politics were concerned, there were often rivalries between different sectors of the same ruling class, within the plantation society, and the contradictions between the groups influenced the administration. Thus, in the case of the former French colony of Saint Domingue, whose policies were formulated on the other side of the Atlantic, the Black Code of 1685 under Louis XIV stipulated that the *affranchi*, or freed slave, held the same rights inherent to the French citizen. When in the 18th century, the white sector of the oligarchy wanted to oust the black or "colored" sector of the same class, the influence of the two groups caused a long antagonistic politico-legislative process. For many authors, this process was one of the main causes of the slave and colonial uprising and the rise of the Haitian state in 1804. The protagonists of the parliamentary phase of that process were the planters, with all the political influence derived from their economic power, but none could resolve the problems from within the plantation.

There are also more recent examples. When in the early years of sugar expansion in Cuba, in the first quarter of this century, the plantation owning companies announced they were going to bring in Caribbean labor, reactionary sectors in Cuba were greatly opposed. Plantation administrations, in need of labor, then began to wield their influence; they requested special permits from the government and these were granted but only partially. Without a doubt the government favored the interests of those large companies, but did not dare revoke all previous racist provisions prohibiting the entry of those laborers until a 1917 decree introduced an open-door policy.

This is not the same as saying that the plantation owners usurped the functions of state or government. Without reaching the absurd anarchy of as many states as plantations, within the territorial limits of a single country, the excesses of usurpation must have been very frequent in plantation economies during the slave period. During the bourgeois period of the Republic of

Cuba, there were plantations with their own policing and where there was widespread payment through chits or tokens. And yet, from the late 1930s on, the development of the labor movement enabled workers to campaign for better living quarters on the plantations and to pressure government for money wages.

Neither the political influence of the owners nor the usurpation of those functions make the plantation a "political institution". In reality, when such usurpations took place, they were due to the deficiencies of state, government and the labor movement, if this was already in existence.

In turn, the idea of the plantation as a "socio-cultural" system comes from the objective fact that the conditions of manual labor in the primary sector required a comparatively large human settlement, often with the owner resident and where there was always an administrative body that was in co-habitation with the direct producers (slaves or proletarians); there, mutual relations were established through a socio-cultural system, as is always the case with human settlements. But that system was tied to, and inseparable from, the wider society of the given plantation. In this sense, the plantation is no different from the large or middling estate. In effect, every historical community (tribe, nationality, nation) is at the same time a socio-cultural community comprising an aggregate of economic units, institutions, social groups, etc. The concept of "socio-cultural" system runs the risk of artificially and methodologically isolating the plantation from the society to which it belongs.

Paternalism is also part of this discussion. The slave system the Europeans imposed on the Americas — not the plantation — was the source of the paternalist tradition in inter-race relations. To say that the ideological foundation of slavery presented the false argument of white supremacy and black inferiority would be mere reiteration. Cuban historiography, for example, shows that in 19th-century Havana, certain masters of the creole nobility were very tolerant with their slaves; they permitted their antisocial attitudes and even protected them from repressive authority. Racism, which is also a component part of the dominant ideology during the capitalist phase in multiracial societies, caused the emergence within non-white communities of the ideal of finding a white godfather or protector. Everywhere — not just on the plantation — Uncle Toms emerged who were a blot on human dignity, whether black, white or the colors of the rainbow.

During the capitalist period, there were substantial changes in paternalist relations. At this time, racism didn't disappear but the labor movement came into being. It is not surprising that in countries with a plantation economy rural workers became the main faction of the proletariat. If the absenteeism among plantation owners during slavery was striking, under capitalism the proliferation of limited companies would make it even more notable; and an additional economic feature was the plantation that expelled the workers from its grounds during a large part of the year. New social relations thus came into being, a different form of living, and culture aborbed new content. The labor movement, along with economic, political and social demands, formulated anti-racist programs, pushing back paternalist relations and paving the way for egalitarian relations within the ranks of the proletariat.

For the author of this paper, plantation defines the agro-industrial system whose workers are subordinate to a unified, centralized production control for the external market. Plantation is only a methodological concept. In objective reality, it always appears within the confines of a concrete given society and is at the same time part of the productive relations of that social system. Hence, in each historical period the plantation is qualitatively transformed. Which is why statements such as the links between culture and plantation or politics and plantation will remain very vague if there is no reference to the economic base or structure of a given society. The nature of the dominant productive relations in each case determines the structure of society and, in turn, the internal structure of the plantation; this gives rise to peculiarly complex forms of slave and capitalist plantations.

In the countries in question, the plantation is at the center of production of material goods essential to guaranteeing the very existence of the society and its historical continuity. The plantation has imposed demands on all aspects of social life in those countries as it has also wielded enormous influence over material and spiritual elements of their respective cultures. Its success on the international market is the component most relevant to the formation of the internal market community, the consolidation of the nation and the unification of the culture of each and every one of those peoples; accordingly, that dependence is the driving force behind the commercial economy of the country, which can bring about impressive achievements and serve as a stimulus to urbanization, services and education. It is, in effect, a question of the relationship between this whole multifaceted process and the economy, in the sense of possible financing, which, in the conditions of the plantation economy, the country in question needs to generate through those means and, with alarming frequency, finds itself unable to do so. Each case, whether a type of slave or capitalist plantation, has its own varying peculiarities.

PABLO ARMANDO FERNÁNDEZ

Matilda

Taken from **El vientre del pez** (The Belly of the Fish), Unión, Havana, 1989, pp. 234-243.

She would never have understood her people who spoke the same language, but with such varying accents, pronunciation and vocabulary that it was difficult at times for them to understand each other. The differences were determined by the social background and home country of those migrants from Jamaica, Saint Lucia, Antigua, Trinidad, Tobago, Saint Kitts, Tortola and Barbados, islands as remote as the world of industry and commerce, schools and recreation centers, cities and families Matilda couldn't even innocently imagine. This was because everything in those nights of melodious conversations, became fabulous stones and metals with a shine so bright and distant like that of the stars, always fleeting and deceptive, dimmed by clouds or rusted by rain, until left like those bits of old metal scattered in the alley or piled up in a crumbling heap. Over the years they ended up talking a slang that was half English, half Cuban.

If it hadn't been for Mom [Foster], she would have gone on thinking that the promiscuity in relations between men and women in the yard was natural. Women conceived, gave birth and brought up children without them knowing their real fathers. Matilda didn't know who her own might be, or that of her sisters, and what his absence might have meant to them, but personally she felt the need for affection and shelter other children had from their fathers. Isabel took on pregnancy as if it were self-fecundation: nobody knew who her lovers were. She accepted pregnancy, all the responsibility fell on her weary shoulders, and she wouldn't have accepted help out of sympathy or commiseration. She gave birth to go on in successive germination:

it was her way of conceiving resurrection.

Matilda always felt orphaned and attributed to this her shyness and a certain wanton sourness that made her detached. She confessed to Mom that others had been cruel to her; as a child she had been taunted for having her mother's surname. According to Mom, the proper response was beyond that kind of people's comprehension, because the circumstances of her birth and that of her sisters was simply a reflection of the nature of the society into which she had been born. She sensed that Mom, trying not to touch the scar of what was for her a sensitive wound, avoided giving details of those circumstances. Contrary to what she expected, Mom praised Isabel, counting her virtues: Isabel showed courage, independence, self-respect and admirable devotion to her children, because with the work of her untiring hands she gave them more than the bare necessities... Matilda listened in dismay. From the apparent seclusion of her home, going about her housework, Mom, with her piercing eyes, had penetrated the gaudy tumult of the yard.

It was true that, despite the poverty, helplessness and utter desperation in which they lived, Isabel would make a great effort to dress her daughters decently: on Sundays, clean, shod, seated on stools or benches, at times in silence, at others infectiously happy, they would receive, along with other children in the neighborhood, lessons of religious and general instruction, the latter rudimentary but effective.

The reading and interpretation of biblical texts was undertaken by Dr Patterson, president of the British West Indies Progressive Association, who had received his theological education at the most illustrious Cod-ring-ton Col-lege, he would spell it out deliberately, having his students repeat it after him without making a mistake, to then add with unrestrained delight: a College founded in 1710, which is affiliated to the University of Durham... Reading, writing and arithmetic classes — the three basics — were given by Mistress Alleyne. The children paid respectful attention and feigned interest in the lessons.

Isabel would get them up in the early hours of the morning. After washing their hair with lots of water and soap, she would sit the children out on the central porch in the morning sun to dry their shiny woolly hair. There she would plait their many braids, crisscrossing them over parceled-out square lots of their cranium, like flowerbeds of pink and yellow busy lizzies in dark foliage. She would bring them in for breakfast, and then, with a clap of her maternal hands, they were off out; this time, across the north porch, where the morning light was softer. Both porches were like the deserted protestant churches that she, Matilda, had engraved on her memory from looking at the pictures on the wall: a pointed, tiled roof, supported at the front by six tall columns, embellished the desolate aspect of the rectangular quarters. Sitting quietly, under the severe eyes of Dick Flemming, they waited for "the holy lessons and science lessons" of Dr Patterson and sweet Mistress Alleyne, chosen of our Lord "for evangelical work in the science of language and numbers". Dick's easy rhetoric, though familiar to the children's ears, made it difficult to awaken in them any sympathy for the language of their elders.

Mom was certainly right. Isabel was an excellent cook and her fame as a confectioner did not detract from the excellence of her food. And what of it? Who might be interested? The North Americans of the mill, who wouldn't make use of her services? The wealthy Cubans or those with a regular income, ignorant of the wonders coming out of a pot or pan under Isabel's direction? Could it matter to her daughters? For a whole week they only drank muddy colored, sickly-sweet, warm sugar water, that swamped their innards and produced nausea and colic. Isabel was an expert seamstress, the garments fashioned by her hands could be bettered by none skilled with scissors, needle and thimble. She turned cheap remnants into splendidly made clothes, better than those on display in the windows of El Encanto and Almacenes Inclán in Puerto Padre. And what did that matter? What use were these exceptional talents, except to repair what was worn out through use or frequent washing, or to sew a tear in her daughters' Sunday clothes?

In Delicias, there must have been other girls without fathers, but she had nothing to do with them. Her world was confined to "English alley", their room in the yard and the Fosters' houses. Presumably her father was any one of her mother's friends, of those men who spoke her language and sat on the benches drinking until late, each one facing their room, after the lights were turned out in the big hall, when the North American, English, Greek, Swiss and Norwegian sailors had gone back to their boats in the port, and clean washbasins had been put away, and sheets put on the beds, and young white or brown women would put bills or coins in their hands, depending on the night's activity, and leave a bottle of rum next to the bench, and would go to other rooms where they lived with young white or mulatto men. Then, sitting on their benches, they would share their bottles with the women in the yard, talking about their lands, lost lands in those nights on the Caribbean sea, as distant as the years in which they came as young men, some accompanied, others alone, for a few months to cut cane or do other such lowly work that not even the most needy Cubans in town would have accepted. James Holliday, in his droning — half lament, half frenzy, like feverish ramblings, as incoherent and terrible as a nightmare in which before the danger of death you want to shout, and throat, tongue and lips won't let out the shout that sits in the pit of the stomach — fragmented the episode of seduction, conquest and submission exerted over the imagination through the mouths of contract workers exhibiting gold-filled incisors, canines and molars in display of the wealth of the new Cuba: liquid, sticky, granulated gold in the sugar.

Offices sprang up on all the islands for seasonal contract work on Cuba's sugar mills: "Go to Cuba, Canaan of the West Indies" read the billboards. The promise of fast easy money spread through town and countryside and the males of impoverished families began their temporary exodus. There were also the young in search of adventure; young lovers running away from family opposition; young non-conformists, idealists, and rebels; young people with a sound and progressive education. And the boats lifted anchor at dawn, or at midnight, with their enthusiastic, hopeful, illusory cargo.

And as a girl Matilda would lie awake at night because of the heat, the humidity, the mosquitoes and the stench of her sleeping sisters' bodies, one up against the other, in the iron bed with sagging springs and improvised mattress of sacking, soaked with sweat and urine, while those solitary men, in casual labor or totally unemployed, rapidly growing older and sicker, recited bottle in hand a long shared monolog, as the various members of the gathering told their part...

The rough intonation of John Jasper evoked in them the early mornings of his country of blazing woods and cold peaks: the snow shines on the Great Ridge and the Great Cascade and the undulating flight of the goldfinch sings on the air; the iguana rustles through the thick scrub; the quail rakes through the dry cane leaves and the crickets sleep. John, too; the rum has gone to his old head. The oxen bellow. Tame tenor, the old ox, awakening these parts of the countryside for man to eat his human ration. Goldfinches, iguanas, oxen, ants and worms feed, and working man, who wants to and can work, cannot find occupation for his worker's hands. John Jasper and his brother would like to melt the snow that froze their stomachs and they fled to Port Royal, to the boat... to Pito Cuatro... to the grimy Delicias yard.

With the yelps of an animal trapped by another more voracious and fierce, the voice of Dick Flemming remedied the misfortunes of the crossing, the overcrowding, the promiscuity, the lack of food and the confinement on arrival until the doctor certified that the blacks weren't bringing epidemics in with them. Her race crossed the sea again only to be newly enslaved!

That long, so often reiterated, night oratory did not become clarified in her mind; on the contrary, it confused her so much that it left a bitter feeling of neglect and a desperate need in her heart to belong to somebody, something. Matilda felt like one more thing among the scrap Isabel collected, making the room even smaller. Her own mother was transformed during the hallucinatory performance, and Matilda's ears, listening to her, pinned themselves back in fear: shuddering, frightened that Isabel might go crazy or get drunk. Many times she wanted to jump out of bed and run to the door and the passageway, to stop her suddenly ailing delirium, worsening by the second. And then she would put both hands on her mouth so as not to shout, and her drowned sobbing would dissolve into tears...

On those nights, Isabel would distinguish herself by her diction and the deep tone of her voice would rise to sharp notes when she wanted to pinpoint or emphasize something especially important. She seemed to imitate Gervese Dean or some other lady seen in the cinema; because Gervese was a lady; not even those who were ignorant about what a real lady was could be in the slightest doubt about that. A lady in her looks, her manners, her diction and with the unmistakable walk of a real lady.

Matilda couldn't stop crying. Those damned voices kept her awake and she felt a hunger through her flesh and bones. She cried for her mother who pretended out there in the hall, like a film star, to be a lady, something she wasn't and probably never had been, but with that way of talking and laughing seemed to be. When day came, she would tear off each of the pictures of natural and preserved fruit, cakes topped with cream and giant red strawberries, like the red camellias growing in the Fosters' garden; resplendent golden roast chicken, like that little star fading in the darkness; cold meats, cheeses, crackers and cookies of every flavor, shape and color; candies, vegetables; the entire range of industrial processed meat: ham, sausages, bacon... She felt hunger devouring her with pointed shark's teeth, crushing crab's claws, or the wild boar's fangs: Mama, don't go on, please don't go on, don't...

And that crazy bird Isabel with her crazy feathers and crazy beak, her agitated crazy wings of irridescent sheen, could be heard warbling, humming, twittering, chirping in her damned folly though the wooden walls. What was she doing there jumping and flitting about? If only she could take flight, calm her headlong wings and set off for the coasts of Antigua; reach home, her father's strong embrace, her mother's sweet kind breast; the table. An Eden in Babylon, where birds dreamed of another life, free from the morning clucking, the amorous posturings of the corral, to wander through gardens and fields at whim: their own spent existence nurturing others of unforeseeable transcendence; and where the water sprinkles diamonds on the delicate glass; ripe fleshy fruits; tender vegetables, meat seasoned with fragrant spices; roasts, cold cuts, chilled oysters; pink snapper swimming among slices of apple and potato and green parsley seaweed; delicacies from the oven, the pantry and the ice box; Chinese salads made to enrage his holiness the pope; sauces and creams, desserts a delight to look upon and a surprise to the palate; bottles of sparkling, bubbly rosé and white wine. And the bread, wonderful crusty white bread! A fitting supper for the prodigal daughter! Let everyone come, let nobody miss welcoming her! And her father thanks the Lord and her mother quietly cries. The chandelier and wall lamps light up the porcelain and silver and glass, on the home-embroidered tablecloth, sewn by girls from a good family; the red brown mahogany and velvet of the furniture. And it is all reflected in the dresser mirror. She herself is the mirror, a magnificent, dazzling vision. Damned pictures that have made her hungry mother go mad! For God's sake, mama, don't go on! My own dear mama... sobbed Matilda on the wire springs: the sacks had rolled up under her sisters.

That crazy bird Isabel, exhausted, lost her way; her wings beat over dark, dark water, and the immense sea drowns her last sigh. If it hadn't been for that fool Jeremy Wood, if she had not listened to that idiot who left her in Pito Cuatro, with a stunted girl in arms, sucking the little blood she had left, and another on the way, in a shed in the middle of the canefields next to the railway line, which he walked off along one night to get the midwife, never to return. Jeremiah Wood, may your bones burn in Hell forever so you can feel the burning you left in mine! If she hadn't listened to that lazy good for nothing, she wouldn't be in this rotten room to which John Jasper brought her, where it was hunger by day and bad dreams by night... Isabel had stopped singing. All the bitterness that had left her lips minutes before turned to tenderness. She had heard her poor little girl Matilde fighting a nightmare. She wanted to go in and wake her up. To tell her pretty little girl that she loved her a lot, but it's better to sleep and have a nightmare than be awake and hungry. And she had turned to raise her voice, Miss Lavinia Maud Pearson, only daughter of the most prosperous jeweller in Saint John, educated in dance and music, could commit that impiety. Matilda, on the verge of shouting, heard the door open gently... very gently. The oral symphony had finished. A chill air of rain came in through the window. Hush, hush! Tiptoeing, slowly, slowly, Isabel came over to her bed. Hush, hush! She never knew whether it was the rain or her mother's tears which fell on her damp face.

PEDRO PÉREZ SARDUY

The maids

"The Floral Dance" and "Alicia in Siguaraya Land" are two chapters taken from the unpublished novel, **The Maids**, based on the life story of the author's mother Marta. In the first, the maids go to the Floral Dance, the annual spring ball in central Santa Clara, the author's home town. The setting for the second is the Menéndez family household, which symbolizes the aspiring white Havana lower- to middle-class, often attempting to live beyond their means, and employing black serving staff. There is a popular song named after the *siguaraya,* a gnarled wild tree which is sacred in Afro-Cuban religion and whose leaves serve medicinal purposes. Whenever something in Cuba happens that defeats rational explanation, the joke is: What can one expect in 'siguaraya land'? In this story, Alicia has her fifteenth birthday, which, in Hispanic custom, is an essential part of a girl's 'coming out'.

The floral dance

It was on a Sunday, May 15th, as we were crossing Vidal Park in Santa Clara that my brother-in-law, Antonia and the two of us decided to go and have breakfast at the Café Parisien. It was odd that although we'd had a lot to drink, we were only slightly tipsy and were having fun, chatting about the dance and singing some of those popular songs that were becoming all the rage again thanks to Isolina Carillo. My sister-in-law and I exchanged a glance, and began: "Two gardenias for you, to tell you I love you, I adore you, my darling... Take great care of them, they'll be your heart and mine. Two gardenias for you, they'll have the warmth of a kiss, of those kisses I gave you, kisses that could never have come from another."

We liked to sing, especially after a couple of drinks. Orlando and Rey hummed the chorus and laughed as they listened to

Antonia singing the second part: "They'll stay by your side and talk like when you're with me and you'll believe they're saying I love you. But if at dusk, these gardenias of love fade, it's because they know you have betrayed me with someone new..."

I looked up at the Town Hall clock — it would soon be six in the morning.

The Floral Dance was the one all the young people, especially newly-weds, looked forward to each year. For months and months, girls would be planning what to wear as if it were their wedding day. I remember that that year, 1949, my husband Orlando's brother had married Antonia, a servant of the Trimiños. They were a very well-known family, five of them were classical pianists and violinists and what is more they had the best drapery stores in Santa Clara, Cienfuegos and Sagua la Grande. Antonia was slim like me, but taller, and we always went shopping together, as we did that day for the cloth to make our dresses for the dance. We had various outfits we'd worn to previous parties, but wouldn't even think of going in the same clothes as the year before, least of all in those we'd worn for the December 24th dance in Placetas, where Benny Moré played.

My mother, Alberta, always managed to please all her dancing daughters. She herself sewed our evening gowns, and on many an occasion, while we were still single, would be our chaperone. But that was a thing of the past for me, since I'd been married for seven years by then and I was lucky in that Orlando, like his brother Rey, was a very good dancer. That day the two of us went to Trimiño's store round the corner from Vidal Park, because there were great reductions on good quality cloth and we bought what we wanted. I fancied making myself a full dress of pink and white taffeta. Antonia had still not decided how to make hers. She wanted it strapless, but the white satin she had chosen was very difficult to sew and it needed "bones" to hold up the bust without revealing the seams. But there was time and, when she came by car to the house on the night of the great occasion, I was surprised to see how well the dress fitted her, with her shoulders completely bare and a light, black, hand-knitted stole round her arms and back.

"What do you think, Marta, how do I look?"

"Divine, woman!"

The two brothers, my husband and hers, loved to see us well dressed and we worked all year to please them because also, the truth was, you had to see the way they dressed, too. My Orlando, all in white like his brother, didn't like drill, but preferred gaberdine for summer and pin-stripes for winter. That year he wore a brand new, well-cut double-breasted suit that had everyone talking. He had all his best clothes made by Cordero, a very good tailor married to Florinda, both of whom were good friends of ours. Since Orlando was a shoemaker, he had made a pair of white patent leather shoes that were every bit as good as the best "Florishen", American shoes that everyone wanted. They stood out wherever he went. Rey, also dressed in white, but in an expensive drill suit, joked as always with his brother, saying that the suit made him look like a bag of bones.

The two liked to party and to spend wildly on occasions such as the great Floral Dance of the Bella Unión Society, which was for colored people. That day there were festivities throughout Santa Clara: at the Grand Maceo Society, for mulattoes and certain wealthy blacks; at the Spanish Casino, the Vedado Tennis Club and at the Lyceum, facing Vidal Park, where the wealthy whites held their celebrations. But we weren't bothered with those festivities, because the members of the Bella Unión did everything possible so that ours should be the best organized and with the best bands. The hardest to get were Aragón, Benny, Fajardo, Arsenio Rodríguez and the Orquesta América. That year, the Bella Unión had signed up Aragón, the famous band from Cienfuegos who were all the rage countrywide.

Rey had agreed to pick us up in the carriage at 9 in the evening, and the two of them were there on the dot impeccably dressed in white. Antonia looked really exquisite and I was her match; my brother-in-law's teasing remarks had us in stitches: "'Sis, leave that old man behind, I'll go with you too. Can't you see that little stick he has hidden there?"

Rey, who worked as the private chauffeur of a well-known architect, was five years younger than Orlando and was always joking about age... who was born first, who was shorter, fatter, who drank more and things like that... making us laugh, infected by the irrepressible guffaws that singled him out wherever he went. We used to hire a carriage which would take us around the city center for an hour or so, throwing out streamers, sounding rattles and cardboard horns — and later as the whole city was festive, people would set off for their great dances in convertibles, hired cars, or horse-drawn carriages along the cobbled streets of the city, which would let off fireworks at midnight from its tallest buildings — to leave us finally on the corner of Lorda Alley and Independencia Street to make a triumphal entrance into the Bella Unión with everyone watching. There was always a huge crowd outside hanging around to see the clothes of the dancers, especially the women's gowns. It was unforgettable, especially when you knew that what you had on was worth a year's work, because sometimes the gowns could cost up to 100 pesos and the dances took place three or four times a year, and, like I said before, you wouldn't for the life of you go to two dances wearing the same outfit. Least of all the great Floral Dance, which welcomed in the spring and the summer season. It used to coincide with the celebration of independence on May 20th, but the Bella Unión wanted it to be dedicated to the flowers, and so it was. Sometimes it coincided with Mothers' Day, which is the second Sunday in May, or with my birthday, as it did that 15th, or that of our first son, on the 13th. Ramoncito, who was just six, was at his grandmother's, with her and his aunts who lived near us, and we knew he was happy for us to enjoy ourselves, as long as we took him some candy the next morning. Our only concern was that my mother- and sisters-in-law spoiled him so much.

We greeted our friends as we entered the great ballroom of the Bella Unión and then went up to the second-floor hall where tables were reserved. We sat while our men ordered the first drinks, cider and Pedro Domecq cognac, for our special cocktail: Spain in Flames. Antonia didn't drink much, though now and then liked a glass of good cider; but she didn't even have time to taste a first sip before the band struck up: "Aragón, Aragón...If you hear a sassy *son*...take it it's Aragón..." It was years since we'd danced to that band because, as members of the Society said, it cost too much, especially now they were cutting albums and touring both at home and abroad. But the young committee wanted to hold a great dance and Aragón was what was needed to show that all the effort put in by its members had paid off.

We got up feeling very happy and went down the stairs on the arms of our partners to enjoy an extraordinary night. A night that as it turned out was the first day of my pregnancy with Teresita, according to the calculations of my gynecologist, Dr Celestino Flores.

The first number was the *danzón* **The Magic Flute,** with flutist Richard Egúes putting on quite a show as a soloist, competing with violinists and dancers trying to perform the most daring and at the same time most graceful pirouettes. Dancing the *danzón* was not easy. Not everybody could do it. You couldn't be jumping and throwing your body about like in a mambo; it had to be based on turns, pauses, graceful steps and so on. That's why they played the number that goes: "No, little black lady, no... don't go on dancing the conga... No, little black lady, no, I belong to the Society... If they see me dancing as in Manglar, my fine black reputation will mar... No..." When Aragón played that, it was wild, everybody was singing. A well-coordinated dance partner was the best thing one could have on such an occasion, and my Orlando and his brother were simply unique in their dancing. My Orlando took me by the waist and I felt as if I was dancing on air. Tall and slim as he is, nobody could suspect the firmness with which he led me round the floor.

I remember that we met at a dance. I can't deny I was dying to dance with him since I first laid eyes on him. At the time, the three of us who liked to go dancing and weren't yet betrothed were chaperoned by my mother. It was a dance in Ranchuelo with the Arsenio Rodríguez Band. We'd gone there on an excursion in a bus hired by the Society for its young lady members. Ranchuelo was known for having very good carnival parties and had its own first-rate, very well-organized Society. People in the town had money because everyone worked at the Trinidad y Hermanos cigarette factory. There was a Lyceum, a Spanish Casino and a colored Society which was the envy of the whole of Las Villas province.

The night I saw Orlando dancing I couldn't keep my eyes off him; my mother pinched my arm more than ten times to calm me down. Finally the inevitable happened, our eyes met at a moment when my mother was paying attention to my younger sister Millito, and Orlando came across to my mother and asked for permission to dance with me. My mother had no alternative but to give her consent, what with the flattery of Orlando's words, which still seem so contrived to me today. "Madam, I would like the pleasure of a dance with you, but first I would like to dance with one of your daughters", he said to her, gesturing toward me. "And who told you I danced?" my mother replied. "These *danzones* make even the tiredest feet in the room move." My sisters and I looked at each other along the backs of the chairs and burst out laughing, but our mother didn't think it at all funny. I'd never seen her dance, though she was always singing old *santo* chants in African tongue, but she had never been seen to move so much as a foot in a dance hall. That's not to say that she didn't like to take us to all the dances we wanted, because they were definitely the best place to meet a good man and I know that was what our mother had in mind. So, it goes without saying, that was how our relationship began, and four years later we were married, but not before dancing our way through many dance halls, with our mother always chaperoning right up until the moment we married, on February 15, 1942, when I was almost 19 and Orlando was nearly 25.

The clock bell in Vidal Park, Santa Clara, began to strike and I looked at the watch Orlando had given me for my birthday. It was indeed 6 in the morning and the birds in the trees, having spent the night startled by the fireworks, were preparing to fly off to the savannah, until their return pilgrimage at dusk, as they did every day of the year.

Alicia in Siguaraya land

Alicia, *caballero* Alberto's daughter by his first wife, had a boyfriend of about 17 but who looked a lot older because he was a heavy-built sporting type who took part in the Vedado Yacht Club regattas. He was as ugly as sin, but his family had money.

Ali, as everyone called her, was very nice, wide-eyed and studious, and she'd taken to me as I had to her.

Her father loved her to distraction, and so did *señora* Ofelia. She spent almost every weekend at her father's and her boyfriend would come to visit.

One night, on my way back from visiting one of my sisters, I caught them locked together on the steps in the dark. Ali was really taken aback: "Ay, Tata, where have you been at this time of night... it's so late?" That was all she could think of to say. "I've been out", I replied curtly and I stopped for the great lump of a boy to let me pass. "And what are you doing with your boyfriend on the steps at this time of night?"

Ali wanted to exert her rightful authority as lady of the house, but could never quite carry it off. At the same time, she was with her boyfriend who was looking everywhere except at me. *Señora* Ofelia was very insistent that Orlando, whose father was a cattle rancher, would one day marry Alicia, and I was sure she had come down to say goodbye with her consent.

The following morning, which was a Sunday, Alicia told me her boyfriend had said I'd had a cheek, and she'd replied that if anyone had a cheek, it was her, because she had no right to ask where I'd been at that hour.

"Then, Tata, he said he couldn't stand you, that if you were a maid in his house he'd throw you out himself." "Well, tell him not to worry or waste his time on such evil thoughts because I wouldn't even go to his house to pay a visit. He's rude, and parents who put up with that kind of behavior are as bad if not worse than their children."

He was so disrespectful and slovenly that even in his girlfriend's house he'd take off his cowboy-boots and unbutton his shirt, saying he was too hot. He was always throwing his visits to Miami in the poor girl's face. He went two or three times a month to visit relatives who lived in some place with a name like an American filmstar... I don't remember it right now. Well, Ali wasn't up to that, though her parents were thinking of giving her a little surprise.

Caballero Alberto once told Alicia that if she carried on like her stepmother there was no telling where she would end up, and that her boyfriend Orlando couldn't continue coming to the house, no matter how many cows his father had. "We're not rich, even if Ofelia would like to think so. She puts up with that oaf's bad behavior just so she can say your boyfriend is the son of Mr. so-and-so, the cattle rancher."

That only made things worse. A week later they had a fight and she sobbed her heart out.

Señora Ofelia wasn't ready to give up yet and consoled the girl with promises of a reconciliation. She did her damnedest to talk to Orlando in private, though she never mentioned anything of what was said.

Less than two weeks had gone by when Alicia saw Orlando in a Miramar club and was disillusioned yet again.

"Wouldn't you know that he was there with another girlfriend, and said to the other girls that I couldn't mix in his circles because I was very poor."

A week later, the family went to a fifteenth birthday party at the Country Club and there was Orlando again. He went over to Ali, took her by the arm, pulled her roughly to him, and said: "Just don't let me see you dancing with any of those other guys, you hear!"

Ali was very pretty, probably one of the prettiest little white girls in Havana. She was like a doll, but compared with her friends, or those *Señora* Ofelia wanted for her, she was poor.

Ali's mother had a really good job as a long-distance operator with the Cuban Telephone Company. Her parents divorced when she was just three years old. *Caballero* Alberto never referred to her by name, but said 'Ali's mother'. She was also a beautiful woman, young-looking and shapely still, as far as I could tell from a photo Ali had. She would put it on her dressing table when she was home. But, well, to go back to the girl. Ali was very pretty and aroused a lot of jealousy. People would say: "What a shame, so pretty yet so poor!" Some would actually say to her face: "So, you might be very pretty, but you can't show off a new dress every week like me!" And Ali would cry a lot. I'd console her: "Don't be silly, girl, calm down! How can you think that because you can't wear a new dress every week it's worth shedding precious tears?" Look, they have a dress every day if they want, but they don't have your figure, they don't have your natural finesse, they don't have your education or morals." Then she'd say to me: "Tata, I don't know why you always say they've no morals." "Look, my girl, it's really none of my business, but if you'd done what Orlando wanted, he wouldn't have left you high and dry. But since you were careful and I know full well what he wanted... That's why he lashed out at you, I know. You don't realize it because, although you're nearly 15, you're still a baby. I've been around longer than you and you can't teach an old dog new tricks.

Alicia didn't realise how lovely she was, and if she did at least she wasn't vain like her friends.

When her 15th birthday came round, it was out of this world. It was the first time *caballero* took pleasure from getting into debt, to give his eldest daughter a fantastic party... to the extent that it was mentioned on the **Diario de la Marina** social page. The orchestra alone cost 500 pesos, and all they played was the waltz and four or five other numbers. Then the Riverside Band with Tito Gómez played for an hour, and finally a rock n'roll combo played through to the end of the party, into the early morning hours.

The boys were all in black tie and the girls in long flowing gowns and adorned with really expensive orchids from Goyanes! Even we maids who were helping to serve all had brand new uniforms ordered for the occasion by *señora* Ofelia. There were 35 of us, mostly servants of families who were friends of the Menéndez, offering our services by way of a gift to the birthday girl, which pleased *señora* Ofelia enormously.

When the girl appeared at the top of the Miramar Yacht Club main staircase and came down to the rhythm of 'japi-beidi-tuyu' (happy birthday to you) and all the fanfare of the orchestra, I can still hear people's exclamations. "What a doll!" was the most sincere. Others, who called themselves *señora* Ofelia's friends but were always into gossip, said: "Just look, who can they have borrowed from?"

The party was marvellous and I was in charge of all the servants... organizing the drinks: champagne, beer, spirits ... and cocktails for special people. A four-tier cake and the finest pastries you can imagine were made by the owner himself of Sylvain, the French patisserie. Three pink cadillacs were hired to bring the girls for the waltz! There were cars coming and going! It was all done on credit. "What for?", I too asked myself. To keep up with people who had a lot more than they did, Country Club, Yacht Club, Casino Español and Centro Gallego members, people who were really loaded.

Señora Ofelia got what she wanted. Everybody was talking about Ali's "fifteenth". Even years after I'd left the house, my best reference when I was looking for a new position was to say that I had been head waitress at the Menéndez girl's 'fifteenth'. And when people wanted to make a comparison, they'd say: "Ah... yes... it was good but not like the Menéndez girl's 'fifteenth'!" Everything was before and after Ali's fifteenth. This won *señora* Ofelia *caballero* Alberto's forgiveness for all her previous waywardness.

***

Around that time *señora* Ofelia took the children's godfather as a lover. He was one of the owners of 'Los Amigos' car dealers. She was one of those mistresses, like many others, who made out they were so refined, but given half a chance were hotter than a heifer on heat. The majority of them put on airs but didn't have any morals.

Señora Ofelia and the man would talk on the telephone in English. She kept me away from the phone, taking me for a fool.

"Martucha, don't you answer the phone, I will, understand?"

Of course I understood! So, if I was near the phone doing my cleaning, the telephone would ring, she'd hurry to say: "No, no, don't go, Martucha, I'll take it!" It was totally out of character, because she was so idle she would ask me to fetch her even a glass of water. Now, if the phone rang, she wouldn't let me answer it, when she had told me at the start that this was one of my household duties. When she finished talking and the phone rang again shortly afterwards, then I was supposed to answer it.

"Martucha, see to the phone, please!"

One day I made a remark and she realized I sensed something. I played dumb and said with a smile:

"Mistress, is there a problem? It seems when you talk in English as you do on the phone, I'm not supposed to answer it."

She threw me a dark look and walked away. The months

went by and February 14th, Valentines Day, came round.

"We'll give the house a good clean."

I looked at her and laughed.

"Ay, *seño,* you've a sense of humor! What you mean is that I should fix the house up for you, right?"

"That's right. I want you to fix up the house as if you were expecting your beau."

"But I don't have a beau, *señora*!"

"No, it's just a way of saying that you should make a special effort and fix it really well."

Tico and Cuqui, *señora* Ofelia's two children with *caballero* Alberto, often went out with their godfather, who looked more like their great-grandfather, though he looked fine from a distance. I would get them ready and he would come in his big car and drive them round Havana. He'd take them to the shops and they would come back laden with gifts. Only once did *señora* Ofelia refer to the man as 'the children's godfather', but that was early on. Later, it wasn't even that.

One day *señora* Ofelia called me to say:

"Martucha, when you've finished in the kitchen, close the door. I won't be needing you for a while."

I knew he must be coming that day, if only for an hour. But I wasn't going to get involved. *Caballero* Alberto was about his business, the children were at school. When I finished my work around 2 in the afternoon, I closed the kitchen door and went to my room to rest without worrying myself with what was happening on the other side.

A couple of hours later, because I'd even had a nap, *señora* Ofelia and I crossed paths in the corridor leading to my room and I saw from her expression she was looking fraught. Later I learned they'd had fight that very Valentines Day. She realized I'd guessed something. Female intuition had told me what the final outcome of this relationship would be, for better or for worse, though it was none of my concern and, when it comes down to it, this is white folks' business.

It had to happen. Near the end of February, she called me to say that I couldn't go on working for her because the situation had taken a turn for the worse. The thing was that *caballero*

Alberto had found out — not surprising really, because the whole neighborhood knew. What's more, he was on the verge of going bankrupt and they were about to separate. But she didn't tell me anything.

"You know, Martucha, I can't go on paying you 35 pesos a month. You know that last year we had to let Edelia go and now I can't offer you any more than 25 pesos a month."

She was pushing me because she knew full well that my work was worth a lot more and that I couldn't possibly get by on such a small amount.

I packed my things and went to my sister Mercedes' place. That's where I would take refuge when I was in or out of work. But it was only a few days before I had a new position, this time without the aid of the Placement Agency, but on the recommendation of a friend who was in the same line of work.

GEORGINA HERRERA

Questions only she can answer

Taken from **Poetisas cubanas** (Women Poets of Cuba), Letras Cubanas, Havana, 1985, pp.297-8.

Ethiopian eyes, tell me,
resolve, you who can,
this patch of tenderness
in which I flail.
Why do I love you to the limits
of grief?
Why the pity,
if you stretch out to happiness?
Gentle little butterfly and lily,
daughter
of my joining together all
the desires to live, for the first time...
Why do I not cross the sea
if not with you, to my breast, as
my defence?
Why do you hang from me
like a necklace?
Why, if I jump out of bed, without kissing you,
do I return in dread, as if you were
my sacred amulet?

SOLEIDA RÍOS

The true door

Taken from **Poetisas cubanas** (Women Poets of Cuba), Letras Cubanas, Havana, 1985, p. 343.

From now on
whosoever comes alone will have my company
to cross other thresholds.

Nobody is alone.
Nobody sleeps.
The time has come for much-needed dreams
and necessary bloodshed on the mud
and green fields.
The time to chart the definitive course
of these waters
of all earth's fires.

Not a single verse to the solitary lover.
Not a single word to those who are silent.
Let December flowers bloom
and butterflies come now
to love and fight
for where wings once slept
will come the precise time
to reclaim their rightful unanimous condition

SERGIO GIRAL

Images and icons

Based on an interview by Jean Stubbs, Havana, May 1991

JS: Taking up the thread of three films based on three historical moments, starting with **El Otro Francisco** (The Other Francisco). Can you explain how the film came about, and what motivated you in doing it.

SG: I started out in film in 1961, with no technical training. I did have an arts background, in painting, but nothing specifically to do with film. My apprenticeship was years of working on documentaries. I had great ambitions of directing feature films but didn't get the chance until 1974, and thanks to Titón — Tomás Gutiérrez Alea — who was sensitive to not only my aspirations but also those of Sara Gómez. He was the backer of our early projects. It was Titón who had been considering doing a film called **The Other Francisco** based on the novel by Anselmo Suárez y Romero, and suggested I do it. For me, there was a contradiction. The early 19th-century Cuban novel was very much influenced by European romanticism and very tied up in the social realities of Cuba. Suárez y Romero was the son of a slave-owning plantation family on the decline. He became very much aware, in what was perhaps at the time humanitarian, altruistic fashion, of the slave suffering. Politically, he was part of the reform movement of Domingo del Monte that met at Aldama Palace. There were other pro-independence tendencies that Del Monte veered away from, guaranteeing his own life and wealth, but that's a whole other story. Suárez y Romero is, to my mind, the intellectual reflection of a class that is in growing contradiction with elements that have gone to make up that class. He wrote a novel called **Francisco**, that has a highly sophisticated, very paternalistic and romantic vision of the slave. Years later, in an interview with the English traveller Richard Madden, he was to express his own contradictions with his work. When I found those contradictions, it made me look at the author's own contradictions and reread slave history in Cuba, so as to situate the author and deconstruct the novel as a novel. There are various levels of deconstruction: firstly, to deconstruct the literary work with an objective beyond that of an intellectual endeavour, in this case, the reform movement. There is the novel as a means of communication. There is the novel in terms of the socio-economic background of the author, the validity of his vision of a reality in which he is involved intellectually as master. And there is also a whole range of political, ideological and economic factors in play at that moment to produce such a novel. Of course, it was banned and remained unpublished practically until the end of the 19th century.

JS: In the case of **Francisco** and **The Other Francisco**, I wonder if there isn't a certain truth in the two Franciscos, because you set out to combat the romanticism of one...

SG: No. The film's treatment is very respectful of Suárez y Romero's **Francisco**. I don't believe the romantic version but I think it had an authenticity in its time, it might have been authentic. Thinking in terms of the camera, Suárez y Romero points the camera from his angle as master, and focuses on the protagonists of his story, forgetting the extras who in this case would be the rest of his plantation slaves. **The Other Francisco** turns the camera on the extras to look at the same story seen through those who apparently have no identity and yet whose story this really is.

JS: After ten years you went back to the same period with **Plácido**...

SG: Yes, but a lot happened in those ten years. I made **El Rancheador** (Bountyhunter) and **Maluala**. I thought with **Maluala** that I'd dealt with slavery and revindicated that part of black Cuban history that had long been marginalized and falsified. In 1980 I felt there was a historical need to turn to the contemporary period, and I made a film called **Techo de vidrio** (Glass House) dealing with bureaucratic corruption. That film was unfortunate. It was finally considered valid but inopportune and wasn't released until several years later. That was hard to take, because I've always felt a sense of political and social responsibility and wanted what I do to serve the revolutionary process. You exercise a form of self-censorship in not wanting to destroy the cake by sticking your fingers in it too much. Curiously, Plácido was not someone I particularly identified with. I saw the play by Gerardo Fulleda León and was moved on a personal level. I empathised with the story, the psychology of the person and his fate. I didn't know too much about Plácido, and as I researched realized that Plácido has not been rehabilitated historically; he remains an obscure figure of history because he is very contradictory. Some consider him a traitor and an informer, others a martyr. I decided to give my own personal, artistic view of Plácido.

JS: What is your view of Plácido, and the Escalera Conspiracy, because that's another obscure and controversial period of Cuban history?

SG: Plácido is a poet, Gabriel de la Concepción Valdés, born of the "illicit" love of a Spanish woman and a creole mulatto man and left in an orphanage from birth, registered racially as "looks white". And that's very important. It completely conditions your life when you look something you aren't. That's what interested me: Plácido as an outcast. He was later taken from the orphanage by his father and raised befitting his craft, that of poet. He was part of a growing mid-19th-century class of free black and mulatto artisans. He's poor, but intelligent, conscious of his condition but not his nationhood, caught between two worlds, the saccharocracy, as Manuel Moreno Fraginals called it, and the slaves. He doesn't exactly know which of the two worlds he belongs to, but the end-product of his contradictions is that he becomes a passive member of the reform movement. The colonial authorities, in an attempt to deter creole whites — who never backed the great South American Liberator Bolívar, among other things, because they would have had to free their slaves and arm them for battle, that's one of the reasons why the independence struggle in Cuba came much later — raised the specter of a black conspiracy against whites, Haiti-style. There was no such conspiracy, it was apocryphal, it was no more than a current of thinking and perhaps a handful of disparate uprisings, part of a growing desire for freedom and independence in a country without any real national sentiment.

JS: Looking beyond the films as such, how do you see your development as a black filmmaker? What is it you've tried to do?

SG: I think there's a very personal factor involved. I'd have to talk about myself, which I don't particularly like doing. There's the concept of Afro-Caribbean you might find in Jamaica, Martinique or Guadeloupe, but in Cuba the conceptualization has been of white, black and mulatto. In slave times, a distinction was made between the black brought from Africa and the creole or Cuban-born black; and the mulatto was the offspring of slave master and female slave, of power and the oppressed. Mulatto had the special connotation, socially, economically and politically, of being the very child of slavery. In itself highly alienating, this was reconfirmed during the period of bourgeois social democracy with racism U.S.-style. I can make that kind of comparison because I lived part of that reality — I'm the generation of transition — and because I also lived for ten years in the United States. At the time, the U.S. South was segregated, but in the North there was much more racial tolerance than in Cuba. This gave me more of a sense of judgment about racism in Cuba. At that point in my life, I, like so many others, as a product of my culture, had little notion of the whys and wherefores. It's a kind of original sin that's in your subconscious. It was my immediate identification with the revolution as a process of popular revaluation, rather than class revindication, as I personally don't come from a socially or economically dispossessed class. I was going beyond that. I saw the process as rehabilitating elements that had been negated for many years, and one of the first elements to be addressed was race. This was bound to surface since the revolutionary government was inspired in one way or another by the political heritage of Cuban ideologues like José Martí and Antonio Maceo. And this liberated other forces in the work of ethnologists, historians and folklorists, and in the cultural field in general — like myself. Little by little, through a process of knowledge, I overcame the alienation of racial taboo within me. I not only began to understand racial conflict but also to feel a sense of liberation from within, in being able to broach and process that reality.

JS: Where does that situate you in the history of ICAIC, where filmmaking has been mainly white?

SG: One thing's been proven in Cuba, which is that not only blacks are capable of dealing with black themes, not only women can deal with the theme of women, and today the theme of gays is being dealt with by people who are not gay. It's something about our reality that you can have a theme dealt with sensitively by people who are not directly affected. There have only been three black film directors in ICAIC, myself, Sara Gómez and Nicolás Guillén Landrián. In our different ways, we all ended up in ICAIC...

JS: And **María Antonia**?

SG: **María Antonia** is different. I wanted to do contemporary, social cinema that transcended abstract artistic values, to communicate immediate, day-to-day problems of the individual in society. **María Antonia** is a play written by Eugenio Hernández Espinosa in 1965, and when it opened in 1967, it was very innovative in attracting a different kind of audience that was not your usual theatre-going public. What happened then is very complex, in that dogmatism prevailed and the play was shelved for many years, but then the dogmatism passed and the play was rehabilitated.

JS: Why do you think it was shelved? For its *santería,* or marginalism?

SG: That I don't know, but what I do know is that it was rehabilitated and it's now considered a classic of contemporary Cuban theatre.

JS: Was it the character or the story that interested you?

SG: Ever since I saw **María Antonia** open in 1967, I identified with the play and its staging by Roberto Blanco, and I promised myself that one day there would be a film version, and I'd be the one to do it. It took me many years but I did it, and was emotionally and intellectually charged by it. I repeat, I'm not from a socially or economically marginalized sector, though there are such groups here...

JS: The story's set in the 1950s, so it's not really a contemporary film...

SG: No... It's set in the 1950s, but I think the discourse is universal and atemporal. The characters might be conditioned by social, economic and historical conditions but I don't think they are strictly representative of an epoch but of an idiosyncrasy, a way of thinking, a culture of certain existential behavior patterns in life. I interpret **María Antonia** in existential terms.

JS: How do you see the dialogue established between the end-product and the spectator? Your historical films show the ugly side of slavery, with scenes of violence and whiplash, that could be counter-productive... there are people who would deny it, others who accept it, yet other's who don't want to see it...

SG: The intrinsic value of this kind of historical reconstruction is generally recognized among intellectual or educated circles. People are made to think; they are moved to reflect on 19th-century black history, on the fact that blacks were an essential and determining factor in the accumulation of wealth in 19th-century Cuba in the most degrading conditions for a human being. Curiously enough, I do know that part of the black population did not want to see themselves reflected on screen in such a denigrating way. We're not used to it, and they were perhaps ashamed of their own past having such a racist tradition.

JS: There does seem to be a tendency to equate black=slave=poverty=denigration=humiliation. And yet in Cuba's history there has been a strong mulatto class of professionals and artisans. Perhaps there's a need to show that also to restore a dignity.

SG: Yes. There are many things. Without blacks and the negation of the "black fear", without blacks in the Liberation Army, Cuba would not have freed itself from Spain. It seems to me that "fear of the black" as a socio-economic class, displacing Spanish and creole traders, is very important but it pales by comparison with the role of the black ex-slaves in the liberation struggle. Without an army, there'd have been no war, and the army was black. All of that was systematically negated, forgotten, erased from popular memory, especially in the post-colonial period, to keep blacks down.

JS: **María Antonia** was a box-office hit, whereas I imagine your others are more film theatre material. What made you want to open that space?

SG: It's difficult to say. I needed to bring things up to date. The marginal sectors under capitalism were largely black... no longer ex-slaves but ex-fighters, who were slaves and then fighters, and then totally marginalized. Culturally, the marginalism went beyond color or ethnicity to the seemingly white, but I do think it shaped our popular thinking, which is conditioned by the thought structures of marginal, as well as petit-bourgeois, elements.

JS: One last thing. I ask myself, and I ask you, whether now there isn't a new challenge for cinema and culture in general. It seems to me that the attempt to rescue the forgotten runs the risk of creating stereotypes. Since you made a comparison with the United States, to take Hollywood or U.S. independents, there are now films that aren't necessarily black films, about black themes, they might be a love story that just happens to have black or brown or Indian protagonists. Cuban cinema hasn't reached that point and I wonder if it isn't time.

SG: The problem, as I see it, is a trap, because yes, you can put to one side the black element, as a cultural, ethnological or socio-economic element. But my theory is that what defines a black more than anything else is the color of his skin. That's an undeniable fact.

JS: A straightforward story, a couple who fall in love on a street corner, can it be done with protagonists that aren't white?

SG: I'm getting to that, but I can't answer your question without making clear my own position on the race question. I repeat, the black is an ethnic-economic product of a history of discrimination and prejudice in a society into which he was inserted as a slave, and on top of all that, there's the condition of appearance, because he can be seen to be black. Any other kind of segregation or discrimination is much more difficult, except for the case of women, when they are obviously women... Two blocks away, it's hard to tell who's fascist and who's communist; it's hard to tell who's an Aryan and who's a Jew. But two blocks away you can tell who's white and who's black. That conditioning of centuries on our continent I think has to be represented. Why? Because the public has been conditioned. You were talking about the United States, but there, during the 1950s, all their heroes were whites, and the blacks on screen were the servants. After the civil rights movement and all that, then there began to be blacks in film, until the independents of today with black filmmakers making black films on the racism in U.S. society. In our case, there has been a historical filmmaking tradition in which I've not been the only one to deal with black history. There's Tomás Gutiérrez Alea, with **La Ultima Cena** (The Last Supper), Humberto Solás with **Simparelé** on Haiti, Manuel Octavio Gómez with **La Tierra y el Cielo** (The Earth and the Sky) also on Haiti. They're white but I'm referring to the image. I do think, and understand it more now, that non-blacks approach this from their own life experience, which is perhaps one in which blacks have played a small or chance part, and so they make a film with blacks in a similarly small or chance part. I understand why, when Sara Gómez made **De Cierta Manera** (One Way or Another), the male lead is black, or mulatto, because it's part of her life experience. It would be very difficult for me to make a film in which all the characters were white, because it might be part of my life experience but not my conscience. I am conscious of the problem whereas perhaps others aren't. That's where the individual artist comes in, and his way of seeing life... I once threatened to do a remake of Strindberg's **Miss Julie**, with Swedes... talking of which, we're working on a script with Sweden that's the story of a romance between a Cuban mulatto woman, or black, we're not sure yet, and a tourist who in this case is Swedish. Set right now, it could bring together a set of elements, from **Cecilia Valdés** through **María Antonia**, to the present day... Hopefully, we'll pull it off.

surrendered himself to her one more time, just as she stuttered: "Pleeeease, now!"...

Clara Spencer kept her personal diary for many years and although she didn't write in it every day, its entries picked up the stories of her life, her background and states of mind. The diary had the value of narrative and personal introspection. Andrés knew about this practice of his mother, who, moreover, had never hidden from her children problems that might affect them, seeing her life as a mirror image of reality. When she took a decision, she did so with such a sense of responsibility that she wasn't afraid of the risks and always prepared her defence, the most objective possible, even where the children were concerned.

Though kept discreetly by her over the years, Clara Spencer's diary was no mystery in her house. There were times when she would write her notes after the meal, with others present as she listened to the radio or was talking or studying. More than once her children asked her about something of interest that had happened when they were little and Clara Spencer would get out her diary and read to them what she had written about the day that... and if she hadn't written anything she would be angry with herself...

Andrés Rey left San Vicente at nightfall, steeped in memories and convinced of the validity of his oral research after that long conversation about literature, traditional medicine, and the development of science and technology with his step-father, who after lunch also hung his hammock in the patio with the fragrance of basil, jasmine, orange blossom from the nearby orange grove, and the unmistakable smell of *biscochuelo* mango. His mother joined in the conversation seated on her favorite whicker rocking chair, remonstrating with the dogs because they wouldn't leave her be. Those weren't the same chihuahuas he'd seen when he first came to San Vicente as a boy, but their descendants to whom Cassamajour had given the same names.

The surveyor got back to the hotel at nine in the evening with his memories in his head and the diary his mother had given him since she hadn't written in it for several years, because, she said, her life was now too placid with only the pain of Robert's absence and for that she had his letters...

For Clara Spencer to move to San Vicente there had to be no special talk between her and Cassamajour. The doctor simply proposed "taking" Robert to "the house" where it would be better for his recovery and because "he is up on charges of contempt of authority, illegal trade union organization and in the summary he was labeled a Jamaican" and so was subject to forced repatriation, arbitrarily applied, which was the last straw for West Indian laborers in Cuba.

That afternoon, when Clara and Andrés arrived in San Vicente, each one had a room and Robert another that the doctor had furbished. In Clara's room, the bedroom suite was white, with a wardrobe and a dressing table with three mirrors, and a chest with eight drawers. There was an imperial bed, with a thick horsehair mattress covered with blue and white striped satin. The bedlinen was fine cotton and the towels white so they wouldn't lose their color through boiling. The spacious room, the largest in the house, had two high-backed rockers and a small rattan table, a whicker armchair with a foot-rest, a console with an RCA Victor radio and gramaphone player with its cabinet full of records.

There were single rooms for the boys, like Cassamajour's, with the only difference that his had a carved mahogany writing desk and bookcase.

That night Arturo visited Clara in her room to tell her, as if it had been agreed beforehand, that the next day Dr Caballero would arrange for the Notary to register Robert as his son and also register their marriage. Sitting on the bed they talked about many more things concerning the future of their first-born, until he lay back on the pillow and fell soundly asleep. It was the second time Clara Spencer spent a whole night in his company, but now she had seen him wake up in her bed, for the first time. He couldn't forgive himself for having fallen asleep after so many years of separation. But it was early still, and they had always made love in daylight.

For Cassamajour it was a revelation rediscovering the naked body of Clara who didn't have the appearance of a woman who had borne three children. How he would have enjoyed her pregnancy! He would have kissed her large, tense belly to feel the palpitation of a being that had been engendered by him and was coming to life. His lips lightly brushed her black nipples. Cassamajour said only one thing: "Our son blessed your breasts and now so do I, in his name and mine." Their bodies were reproduced as many times as there were looking glasses in the room.

Clara loved the pleasure of the delicate long ritual of Arturo Cassamajour's original openings and his sustained love making. In that he hadn't changed one bit.

When they married, she was 38 and he was 44. Clara wore a short, two-toned, tailored muslin suit, fitted at the waist, in a challenge to femininity, and she wore a hat to one side; the jacket was gray and the skirt black, with a pink crepe chiffon blouse. Her shoes and bag were black. They were married in the Notary of Dr Juan Caballero, as Cassamajour had planned. It was the day before young Robert Cassamajour left for New York, where he would stay. When Arturo and Clara left him in that city, after spending a week in his company, they never supposed he wouldn't return to live in Cuba, nor that their son Robert Cassamajour would take the stage name of Bob Spencer...

Every night for many years the records most listened to in San Vicente, in Clara's room, were the ones Robert had sent them in the forties and fifties, or had brought as a gift when the United States had still not broken relations with the Cuban Revolution. The first of those records was an LP by the famous black singer Lena Horne whose accompanying band Robert had joined as clarinettist. At the time she received the record, Clara Spencer sang **Stormy Weather** with as expressive a voice as Lena Horne. He had also given them records of Sarah Vaughan, who had an exceptional voice. Cassamajour was alive then and wrote to Robert as he would to a friend from his youth. He recommended Cuban music that he could use to incorporate other rhythms into his compositions because the doctor had no doubt that his son would be as successful playing as he would composing and arranging. He aspired to him being great like Miguelito Valdés and there were times when he ended his letters with the words *ae bruca maniguá*, a Cuban musical hit.

Among Cassamajour's favorites were Alejandro García Caturla and Ernesto Lecuona. When Robert traveled with his parents to New York he took a case of the best Cuban music, and afterwards the doctor sent him Caturla's **Berceuse campesina**... a piece that the musicologist Alejo Carpentier described as admirable especially for piano, "a composition with surprising unity of style, in which Caturla achieved a melodic and rhythmic synthesis of peasant and black music..."

Time and its effect whittled away any reserves Robert might still have had with respect to the conduct of his father when he left Clara. Cassamajour lamented many times with her at not having been able to enjoy him together: "Our boy was very fleeting, too fleeting for me", he would say, and then immediately make clear that she should not interpret that as a reproach because she had educated him to overcome any adverse circumstance in life.

On his sick bed, Cassamajour listened with delight to Clara reading Robert's letters. She knew that was his greatest satisfaction in those moments and since correspondence was so delayed in coming, because of the North American blockade of the island, Clara herself wrote some of the letters...

Hours before his death, Arturo Cassamajour kissed the palms of Clara's hands even more tenderly than usual and thanked her for having loved him so. He drew her to him and recommended that she be well prepared for the most natural of life's acts, and told her not to be ashamed of having tricked him; because that little trick of the letters from "our Robert", that sweet lie, had been charming, had made him happy, and she should tell their son when she talked to him on the phone or wrote to him. Referring to those apocryphal letters, he assured her that "his had never been so lovely as those you invented for me. I have enjoyed these days so much; I would wake in the middle of the night laughing for joy at your farce; the beautiful descriptions of the landscape, the tones of the music, Robert's state of mind... and above all I loved listening to you, because it was your voice, the love of your words, your first caress for me on Duán Cay came from your voice, remember that Clarita"...

Her digital watch marked the hour she was waiting for, according to the time difference. It would be the slow dusk in Spain; from that moment she was on the alert for the FAX. Her auxiliary, another student on training at the data base, was with her; they had been talking for a while and the topic had been precisely the importance of conversation... Her students scarcely engaged in it and Juliana criticized them for it... The green light lit up, there was a buzz, and the FAX began to print a message, abruptly cutting into the conversation she was having. It was a letter from Seville...

> My dear wife: A kiss from your only lover. I rewrote the beginning of the novel, or rather, I completed it, and you'll be somewhat surprised when you read it...:
>
> Hidden among the branches of the "miracle" silk-cotton tree, I saw her for a second time; I had watched her before from the same tree and my figure had taken her by surprise at dusk, imagining me to be Christ appeared. She was dressed in yellow; her dress was embroidered organdy and her white sandals were scuffed from the thorns of the scrub. Her dark brown hair looked wet from the excess glycerine put on it to make the ringlets Shirley Temple-style. A big yellow and white taffeta bow adorned her head, contrasting harmoniously with her brown skin. We were more or less the same age. She was my first love. That morning, Juliana slid on a piece of palm bark from the top of Enramada hill toward the bed of the Maná River, which we had never seen swollen...
>
> I'm looking at the volume with its title — **The Swing,** by Rey Spencer — in gold lettering on a dark blue background...
>
> Though they pressured me to dedicate the novel to the Quincentennial festivities, because the theme is Caribbean, I refused and insisted on my irrevocable decision to dedicate this book — the one I love best — to

my deceased mother, because her voice dictated it to me. My adorable Juliana, you more than anyone know that without Clara Spencer — for the double reason that she gave birth to me and she told me almost everything — there wouldn't have been **The Swing**...

Your loving husband,

ANDRES REY SPENCER

Notes on contributors

DOMINGO ALFONSO (b. Jovellanos, 1935). Poet and architect. Author of **Sueños en el papel** (Dreams on Paper, 1959), **Poemas de hombre común** (Poems of an Ordinary Man, 1964), **Historia de una persona** (Story of a Person, 1968), **Libro de buen humor** (Book of Good Humor, 1979) and **Esta aventura de vivir** (This Life's Adventure, 1988). **Reino del tiempo** (The Kingdom of Time) is as yet unpublished.

MARCELINO AROZARENA (b. Havana, 1912). Teacher and journalist. Member of the Society for Afro-Cuban Studies founded in 1937 by Fernando Ortiz, and founder member of the National Union of Journalists and National Union of Writers and Artists. Author of **Canción negra sin color** (Colorless Black Song, 1966) and **Habrá que esperar** (Having to Wait, 1983).

MIGUEL BARNET (b. Havana, 1940). Writer and ethnologist, professor and currently editor at the National Union of Writers and Artists. Author of **La piedrafina y el pavo real** (The Precious Stone and the Peacock, 1963), **Isla de Güijes** (Island of Spirits, 1964), **Biografía de un cimarrón** (Autobiography of a Runaway Slave, 1966), **La sagrada familia** (The Holy Family, 1967), **Canción de Rachel** (Rachel's Song, 1969), ***Akeké* y la jutía** (*Akeké* and the Hutia, 1978), **Gallego** (Gallician, 1983), **La fuente viva** (Living Memory, 1983), **La Vida Real** (Real Life, 1986), **Carta de noche** (Night Letter, 1982), **Viendo mi vida pasar** (Watching My Life go By, 1987), **Mapa del tiempo** (Map of Time, 1989) and **Oficio de angel** (Angel's Craft, 1989).

NATALIA BOLÍVAR AROSTEGUI (b. Havana, 1934). Specialist in museum science, director of the National Museum of Fine Arts, Napoleonic Museum and Numismatic Museum. **Los orishas en**

Cuba (The Orishas in Cuba, 1990) is the first of several volumes of ethnographic material she is preparing for publication: **Opolopo Owó: Los sistemas adivinatorios de Cuba, Ifá, Diloggún, Obbí** (Polopo Owó: Ifá, Diloggún and Obbí Adivination Systems in Cuba), with Carmen González **La muerte en la mitología afrocubana** (Death in Afro-Cuban Mythology), **Mitos y leyendas de la comida afrocubana y criollo** (Myths and Legends of Afro-Cuban and Creole Food), with E. Reyes **Cuba, imagenes y relatos de un mundo mágico** (Cuba, Images and Stories of a Magical World), **Changó y/o Santa Barbara: sincretismo religioso** (The Religious Syncretism of Shango-Santa Barbara).

SALVADOR BUENO (b. Havana, 1917). Critic and literary historian, he was professor of literature at the University of Havana. His publications include **La letra como testigo** (Literature as Witness, 1957), **Historia de la literatura cubana** (History of Cuban Literature, 1963), **Figuras cubanas** (Cuban Figures, 1964), **Temas y personajes de la literatura cubana** (Themes and Figures of Cuban Literature, 1964), **Aproximaciones a la literatura hispanoamericana** (Approximations to Hispanic American Literature, 1967) and **El negro en la novela hispanoamericana** (The Black in the Hispanic American Novel, 1985).

WALTERIO CARBONELL (b. Jiguaní, 1925). Historian at the José Martí National Library. Author of **Cómo surgió la cultura nacional** (Birth of a National Culture, 1961) and several articles on Africa in Cuba, he is currently working on the 1844 Escalera Conspiracy.

JESÚS COS CAUSSE (b. Santiago de Cuba, 1945). Director of International Relations at Casa del Caribe. Author of **Con el mismo violín** (With the Same Violin, 1970), **Las canciones de los héroes** (The Songs of the Heroes, 1974), **El último trovador** (The Last Troubadour, 1975), **Escribo Fidel** (I Write Fidel, 1976), **De antaño** (From Before, 1978), **Las islas y las luciérnagas** (Isles and Fireflies, 1981), **Balada de un tambor y otros poemas** (Drum Ballad and Other Poems, 1987) and **Como una serenata** (Like a

Serenade, 1988). **Concierto de jazz para un angel subitamente humano** (Jazz Concierto for a Suddenly Human Angel) is as yet unpublished.

PEDRO DESCHAMPS CHAPEAUX (b. Havana, 1913). Historian, who has specialized in Afro-Cuban history at the Academy of Sciences of Cuba. Author of **El negro en el periodismo cubano en el siglo XIX** (The Black in 19th-Century Cuban Journalism, 1963), **El negro en la economía habanera del siglo XIX** (The Black in the 19th-Century Havana Economy, 1970), **Rafael Serra y Montalvo: obrero incansable de nuestra independencia** (Rafael Serra y Montalvo: Tireless Worker for Our Independence, 1974), **Contribución a la historia de la gente sin historia** (Contribution to the History of People without a History, 1974), **Batallones de Pardos y Morenos** (Battalions of Free Coloreds and Blacks, 1976) and **La presencia de la mujer en el periodismo cubano del siglo XIX** (Women in 19th-Century Cuban Journalism, 1979).

RAFAEL DUHARTE JIMÉNEZ (b. Baracoa, 1947). Historian and researcher at Casa del Caribe. Author of **La burguesía santiaguera, 1940-1950** (The Santiago Bourgeoisie, 1940-1950, 1983), **Seis ensayos de interpretación histórica** (Six Essays of Historial Interpretation, 1983), **El palenque: economía y sociedad** (Maroon Settlement: Economy and Society, 1986), **Cien capitanes de cimarrones del Caribe** (One Hundred Maroon Leaders of the Caribbean, 1987) and **El negro en la sociedad colonial** (The Black in Colonial Society, 1988).

PABLO ARMANDO FERNÁNDEZ (b. Delicias, 1930). Poet and novelist. Assistant editor of **Lunes de Revolución** (1959-61), editorial chief of Casa de las Américas (1961-1962) and diplomat (1962-65). After many years as editor in the Academy of Sciences of Cuba, became editor of **Unión**. Author of **Salterio y lamentación** (Psalm and Lament, 1953), **Nuevos poemas** (New Poems, 1955), **Toda la poesía** (All the Poetry, 1961), **Himnos** (Hymns, 1962), **Libro de los héroes** (Book of Heroes, 1964), **Los niños se despiden** (The Children say Good-Bye, 1968), **Un sitio permanente** (A Permanent Place, 1970), **Aprendiendo a morir**

(Learning to Die, 1983), **Campo de amor y de batalla** (Love and Battlefield, 1984), **El sueño, la razón** (Dream and Reason, 1988), **El vientre del pez** (The Belly of the Fish, 1989).

TOMÁS FERNÁNDEZ ROBAINA (b. Havana, 1941). Librarian, specialist in Cuban bibliography, at the José Martí National Library in Havana. Author of **Bibliografía de estudios afroamericanos** (Bibliography of Afro-American Studies, 1969), **Indice de revistas folklóricas** (Index of Folklore Journals, 1971), **La prosa de Guillén en defensa del negro cubano** (The Prose of Guillén in Defence of the Black Cuban, 1982), **Recuerdos secretos de dos mujeres públicas** (Secret Recollections of Two Women of the Streets, 1984), **Bibliografía de temas afrocubanos** (Bibliography of Afro-Cuban Themes, 1986), **Carlos M. Trelles y la "Bibliografía de autores de raza de color"** (Carlos M. Trelles and the "Bibliography of Authors of the Colored Race", 1988) and **El negro en Cuba, 1902-1958** (The Black in Cuba, 1902-1958, 1990).

JOSÉ LUCIANO FRANCO (b. Havana, 1891; d. 1990). Cigar maker, journalist and historian. Author of **Folklore criollo y afrocubano** (Afro-Cuban Creole Folklore, 1959), **Afroamérica** (1961), **Historia de la revolución de Haíti** (History of the Haitian Revolution, 1966), **El gobierno colonial de Cuba y la independencia de Venezuela** (The Colonial Government of Cuba and the Independence of Venezuela, 1970), **Folklore criollo y afrocubano** (Creole and Afro-Cuban Folklore, 1971), **Los palenques de los negros cimarrones** (The Maroon Settlements of Runaway Black Slaves, 1973) **Antonio Maceo: apuntes para una historia de su vida** (Antonia Maceo: Notes for the Story of his Life, 3 vols, 1975), **La diaspora africana en el Nuevo Mundo** (The African Diaspora in the New World, 1975), **Contrabanda y trata negrera en el Caribe** (Caribbean Slave Trade and Contraband, 1976), **Las conspiraciones de 1810 y 1812** (The 1810 and 1812 Conspiracies, 1977), **Ensayos sobre el Caribe** (Essays on the Caribbean, 1980), **Comercio clandestino de esclavos** (Clandestine Slave Trade, 1980) and **La reacción española contra la libertad** (The Spanish Reaction to Freedom, 1988). Prior to his death, he contributed to the UNESCO history of Africa.

SERGIO GIRAL (b. Havana, 1937). Documentary and feature filmmaker at the National Film Institute. His filmography includes **Cimarrón** (Runaway, 1967), **Que bueno canta Ud** (You Sing So Well, 1973), **El otro Francisco** (The Other Francisco, 1974), **Rancheador** (Slave Hunter, 1976), **Maluala** (1978), **Techo de vidrio** (Glass Roof, 1982), **Plácido** (1986), **Chicago Blues** (1987) and **María Antonia** (1990).

GLADYS GONZÁLEZ BUENO (b. Santiago de Cuba, 1942). Researcher at Casa del Caribe and cultural adviser at the Ministry of Culture in Santiago de Cuba. She has various articles published on Afro-Cuban religious practices.

REINALDO GONZÁLEZ (b. Havana, 1940). Journalist and writer, currently director of the National Film Archive. His books include **Miel sobre hojuelas** (Honeyflakes, 1964), **Siempre la muerte su paso breve** (Always Death's Short Step, 1968), **Che comandante** (1969), **La fiesta de los tiburones** (Sharks' Feast, 1978), **Contradanzas y latigazos** (Contredanse and Whiplash, 1983), **Lezama Lima: el ingenuo culpable** (Lezama Lima: Guilty Naif, 1989), **Llorar es un placer** (The Joy of Crying, 1990). **El bello habano** (The Fine Havana Cigar) is as yet unpublished.

TOMÁS GONZÁLEZ (b. Santa Clara, 1938). Theater director, actor, singer, poet, painter and adviser to the National Folklore Group. Scriptwriter for the films **De cierta manera** (One Way or Another, Dir. Sara Gómez, 1974) and **La última cena** (The Last Supper, Dir. Tomás Guitérrez Alea, 1976). His published stage plays can be found in **Delirios y visiones de José Jacinto Milanes** (Delirium and Visions of José Jacinto Milanes, 1988) and **Repertorio teatral** (Theater Repertoire, 1991). **Unis persona** and **El bello arte de ser** (The Fine Art of Being) are as yet unpublished. Others include **Escambray 61**, **El monstruo** (The Monster), **El trapo sobre el muro** (The Rag on the Wall), **La otra tarde** (The Other Afternoon) and **La artista desconocida** (The Unknown Artist), **Iago tiene feeling** (Iago's Feeling Blue), **Otelo vino en charter** (Othello Came by Charter) and **Cuarto agamenon de Santa Clara** (Fourth Agamemnon of Santa Clara).

MANUEL GRANADOS (b. Santa Clara, 1931). Has worked as a film archivist and factory time and motion man. Author of **El orden presentido** (The Order Foretold, 1962), **Adire y el tiempo roto** (Adire and Broken Time, 1967), **El viento en la casa-sol** (Wind in the Sun-House, 1970), **País de coral** (Coral Country, 1988) and **Expediente de Hombre** (Man's Record, 1988).

EUGENIO HERNÁNDEZ (b. Havana, 1936). Playwright and director of the Popular Art Theater Group. His plays include **El sacrificio** (The Sacrifice), **María Antonia** (1967), **La Simona** (Simone, 1977), **Obedí el cazador** (Obedí the Hunter, 1984) and **Mi socio Manolo** (My Pal Manolo, 1988). He is also scriptwriter for the film **Patakin** (dir. Manuel Octavio Gómez, 1982). Several of his plays are published in **Teatro**, 1989.

GEORGINA HERRERA (b. Jovellanos, 1936). Has published in many journals and newspapers. Collections of her poetry are **G.H.** (1962), **Gentes y cosas** (People and Things, 1974) and **Granos de sol y luna** (Grains of Sun and Moon, 1978).

JOEL JAMES FIGAROLA (b. Havana, 1941). Director of Casa del Caribe. Author of **Los testigos y otros cuentos** (The Witnesses and Other Stories, 1973), **Cuba 1902-1928, la República dividida contra sí misma** (Cuba 1902-1928, the Republic Divided, 1979) **Aproximaciones al diario de campaña de José Martí** (On the Campaign Diary of José Martí, 1979), **Hacia la tierra del fin del mundo** (To the Land at the End of the World, 1982), **Sobre muertos y dioses** (On the Dead and the Gods, 1989).

ARGELIERS LEÓN (b. Havana, 1918; d. 1991). Musicologist and composer. Author of **Influencias africanas en la música cubana** (African Influences in Cuban Music, 1959), **Música folklórica cubana** (Cuban Folklore Music, 1964), **Del canto y el tiempo** (Of Song and Time, 1984) and **Introducción al estudio del arte africano** (Introduction to the Study of African Art, 1980). His works as a composer include **Akorin** and **Elegía a Jesús Menéndez** (Elegy to Jesús Menéndez).

ELOY MACHADO PÉREZ (b. Havana, 1940). Construction worker-poet, cultural activist in the construction sector. Author of **Caman lloró** (Come and Cry with Me, 1984) and **Poesía VI** (Poetry 6, 1989). **Vagón de Mezcla** (Cement Barrow), **Jacinta Ceiba Frondosa** (Flowering Silk Cotton) and **El callejón del suspiro** (Street of Sighs) are as yet to be published.

ROGELIO MARTÍNEZ FURÉ (b. Matanzas, 1937). Folklorist specializing in the history of African civilizations and their influence in Afro-America. Pioneer of the study of African literature in Cuba and founder adviser to the National Folklore Group. Author of **Poesía Yoruba** (Yoruba Poetry, 1963), **Poesía anónima africana** (Anonymous African Poetry, 1968), **Dialogos imaginarios** (Imaginary Dialogues, 1979) and **Diwán africano: poetas de expresión francesa** (African Diwán: French-Speaking Poets, 1988).

NANCY MOREJON (b. Havana, 1944). Poet and literary critic, currently director of the Center for Caribbean Studies at Casa de las Américas. Author of **Mutismo** (Mutism, 1962), **Amor, ciudad atribuida** (Love, City Attribute, 1964), **Richard trajo su flauta** (Richard Brought his Flute, 1966), **Lengua de pájaro** (Bird's Tongue, 1971), **Recopilación de textos sobre Nicolás Guillén** (Texts on Nicolás Guillén, 1974), **Octubre imprescindible** (Crucial October, 1978), **Parajes de una época** (Places of an Age, 1979), **Where the Island Sleeps Like a Wing** (1985), **Nación y mestizaje en Nicolás Guillén** (Nation and Miscegenation in Nicolás Guillén, 1982), **Piedra pulida** (Polished Stone, 1986) and **Baladas para un sueño** (Dream Ballads, 1989).

GERARDO MOSQUERA (b. Havana, 1945). Art critic, regular columnist, and author of **Exploraciones en la plástica cubana** (Explorations in Cuban Art, 1983).

FERNANDO ORTIZ (b. Havana, 1881, d.1969). Anthropologist, ethnologist, sociologist, linguist, historian, folklorist and archaeologist, also a scholar of law, geography, art and literature. A disillusioned member of the Liberal Party, and Liberal member of the House of Representatives (1917-22), he became active in the nationalist civic revival movement. He was a founding figure of the journals **Revista Bimestre Cubana, Archivos del Folklore Cubano** and **Estudios Afrocubanos.** A prolific writer, his major works include **La hampa afrocubana: Los negros brujos** (The Afro-Cuban Underworld: Black Obeah, 1902), **Las rebeliones de los afro-cubanos** (Afro-Cuban rebellions, 1910), **Entre cubanos: psicología tropical** (Among Cubans: Tropical Psychology, 1913), **Hampa afro-cubana: Los negros esclavos** (Afro-Cuban Underworld: The Black Slaves, 1916), **La fiesta afrocubana del 'Día de Reyes'** (The Afro-Cuban Festival 'Day of the Kings', 1920), **Historia de la arqueología indocubana** (History of Indo-Cuban Archaeology, 1922), **Glosario de afronegrismos** (Glossary of Black Africanisms, 1924), **Glosario de cubanismos** (Glossary of Cubanisms, 1924), **Contrapunteo cubano del tabaco y el azúcar** (Cuban Counterpoint of Sugar and Tobacco, 1940), **Martí y las razas** (Martí and the Races, 1942), **Las cuatro culturas indias de Cuba** (The Four Indian Cultures of Cuba, 1943), **El engaño de las razas** (The Deception of the Races, 1945), **El huracán, su mitología y sus símbolos** (The Hurricane, its Mythology and Symbols, 1950), **Los Bailes y el teatro de los negros en el folklore de Cuba** (Black Dance and Theater in Cuban Folklore, 1951), **La africanía de la música afrocubana** (The African in Afro-Cuban Music, 1955), **Los instrumentos de la música afrocubana** (The Instruments of Afro-Cuban Music, 1955), **Historia de una pelea cubana contra los demonios** (History of a Cuban Fight Against the Demons, 1959). Posthumous publications include **Bio-bibliografía de Fernando Ortiz** (Bio-Bibliography of Fernando Ortiz, 1970) **Orbita de Fernando Ortiz** (Orbit of Fernando Ortiz, 1973) and **Los negros curros** (Black Dandies, 1986).

ALBERTO PEDRO (b. Havana, 1930). Researcher at the Institute of Ethnology of the Academy of Sciences of Cuba. Adviser to the National Council for the Performing Arts, the Fernando Ortíz African Cultural Center, and the Yoruba Cultural Association of Cuba, founded in 1991. He has various articles published on black freedom struggles and Cuban, Haitian and Caribbean cultural identity.

TATO QUIÑONES (b. Havana, 1942). Journalist, scriptwriter and narrator. Author of **Al final del terraplén el sol** (At the End of the Bank the Sun, 1971) and **A pie de obra** (On the Spot, 1990).

SOLEIDA RÍOS (b. Santiago de Cuba, 1950). Primary teacher and education adviser in the Sierra Maestra (1968-72), and subsequently literary adviser on the Isle of Youth. Author of **De la Sierra** (From the Sierra, 1977), **De pronto abril** (Suddenly April, 1979) and **Entre mundo y juguete** (Between World and Toy, 1987).

MARTA ROJAS (b. Santiago de Cuba, 1931). Journalist and writer. Author of **La generación del centenario en el juicio del Moncada** (The Centennial Generation at the Moncada Trial, 1965), **Escenas del Vietnam** (Scenes from Vietnam, 1969), **Tania, la guerrillera inolvidable** (Tania, the Unforgettable Guerrilla, 1971), **El que debe vivir** (He Who Must Live, 1978), **El aula verde** (The Green Classroom, 1982), and **La Cueva del Muerto** (Deadman's Cave, 1983). She is currently preparing **El columpio de Rey Spencer** (Rey Spencer's Swing) and **Se venden papeles en blanco** (Blank Paper on Sale) for publication.

EXCILIA SALDAÑA (b. Havana, 1946). Poet, critic, researcher, publisher, and children's writer. Her publications include **Cine de horror y misterio** (Horror and Mystery Movies, 1976), **Soñando y viajando** (Dreamers and Travellers, 1980), **Cantos para un mayito y una paloma** (Songs for a Blackbird and a Pigeon, 1984), **Kele, Kele** (1987) and **Poemas de la noche** (Poems of the Night, 1989). Poems from the unpublished collections **Para el día de paz** (For Times of Peace), **Enlloró** (Tears), **Ibá Oñí, Poesía y magia en la mítica Yoruba** (Ibá Oñi, Poetry and Magic in Yoruba Mythology) have appeared separately.

RODOLFO SARRACINO (b. Havana, 1934). Department chief at the Ministry of Foreign Affairs and historian at the Center for African Studies. Author of **El Grupo Rockefeller actúa** (The Rockefeller Group in Action, 1982), **La injerencia británica en las rebeliones abolicionistas cubanas** (British Intervention in Cuban

Abolitionist Rebellions, 1986), **La guerra chiquita: una experiencia necesaria** (The Little War: A Necessary Experience, 1982) and **Los que volvieron a Africa** (Those Who Returned to Africa, 1988).

PEDRO SERVIAT (b. Havana, 1914). Graduate of the 1920s José Martí Popular University and worker activist in the communist movement ever since. He was the first director of the Ñico López National School when it was set up by the Communist Party of Cuba in the 1960s, and then became head of the Party Movement of History Activists. Prior to his death, he was director of the Party Institute of History of the Communist Movement and the Socialist Revolution of Cuba. Author of **El problema negro en Cuba y su solución definitiva** (The Black Problem in Cuba and its Definitive Solution, 1986).

ODILIO URFÉ (b. Madruga, 1921; d. 1989). Musicologist, pianist, flutist, conductor and organizer of popular music festivals. Founder of the Research Institute of Folkloric Music (1949) and author of several articles on Cuban music. He contributed to the UNESCO volume **Africa in Latin America**. Prior to his death, he was professor of music history and appreciation at the Higher Institute of Art and director of the National *Charanga*.

AfroCuban glossary

abakuá male secret society founded in Havana in the 19th century by Africans of Calabar; known also as ñañiguismo
aberiñán abakuá dignitary
aberisán/aberisún abakuá dignitary
aché/ashé power or force of the orisha
aggayú /argayú solá orisha son of changó, patron of Havana
aguzá group of the lucumí nation
akpwón solo singer in ceremonies to invoke the orishas
alagguaná/lagguaná see elegguá
alona/alonna/anima sola see elegguá
amalá food dish of cornmeal and lamb
ambia "pal" or friend in abakuá
ardimú offering to the orishas
arere African whitewood used for thatching
arrubó elder in santería
asere "brother", trusted friend; term meaning "I greet you" in abakuá
ashé see aché
ayúa/yúa thorn, cockspur, hedgehog spine
babalao/babaláwo high priest in santería
babalarube see elegguá
babalú-ayé main orisha, for the pox, leprosy, venereal and skin diseases; syncretised with catholic Saint Lazarus
bantu nation of the Congo, West Africa
batá the three drums: okonkolo, itótele, iya
bembé fiesta for the saints in santería, known also as toque and toque de santo
biriyumba see regla de palo
bomba Afro-Cuban rhythm
bongó Afro-Cuban small twin drum
brican nation from Calabar, southern Nigeria

cabildo black chapter or organization
canastillero cupboard or dresser containing the sacred attributes of the orishas
carabalí nation from Calabar, southern Nigeria
casa de santo/casa templo home-shrine for the orishas
changó/shango main orisha of fire, lightning, thunder and war; syncretised with the catholic Saint Barbara
chekeré Afro-Cuban rhythm instrument consisting of a gourd covered in netting and beads
clave Afro-Cuban rhythm instrument consisting of two wooden sticks
columbia Afro-Cuban rhythm
comadre godmother
cordón spiritual medium gathering
conga see regla de palo
congo nation of West Africa, comprising various groups: muriaco, loango, real
corojo species of palm whose seeds give oil
cumbia Afro-Cuban rhythm
danzón Afro-Cuban dance of French influence
dilogún/diloggún shell used in divination
ebbó exorcism
echu/eshu orisha of good and evil, with two faces, devilish brother of elegba, who can take various paths: agroi, afrodí
ediyó grief, crime
ekuelé/okuelé necklace of eight pieces of tortoiseshell, coconut or metal used by the babalao in divination
eleddá orisha guardian angel
elegguá/elegba/legba/elegbara main orisha, opens the path for other orishas, who can take 21 different paths: alagguaná, alona, babalarube, lubaniba, muñunga, nkyuyu; syncretised with catholic Saint Anthony
elegún/eleggún chosen for initiation in santería, also called iyawó
elló group of the lucumí nation
endabio "brother" or friend in abakuá
enkame santería talk
erere sacred wild tree, small and thorny

eri-wole literal meaning "my head is turning"
eshu see echu
espiritista de cordón spiritual medium
ewe-fon nation of Dahomey
fanti nation of the Gold Coast (today Ghana)
firma abakuá signature
fon nation of Dahomey
gandó abakuá sign
gangá group of the bantu nation
guaguancó Afro-Cuban rhythm
guásima sacred wild tree, leafy with medicinal properties
güije river or water spirit, appears naked and black
hijo(a) de santo son (daughter), or initiate of an orisha
iddé wrist amulet
ifá main orisha of fortune
ikú death
iroku/iroko sacred silk cotton tree
isué dignitary in abakuá
itótele see batá
iyá see batá
iyamba dignitary in abakuá
iyalocha/iyalosha see santera
iyawó/iyabó see elegún
ladino creolised, Spanish-speaking, African-born black (in Cuba)
lagguana see alagguana
laroye/ala roye talker, polemicist
lubaniba see elegguá
lucumí nation of Yoruba origin, comprising various groups
madrina godmother
mambi/mambisa 19th-century Cuban independence fighter
mandinga nation of West Africa
mañunga see elegguá
mayombe see regla de palo
mayombero dignitary in regla de palo
mina nation of the Gold Coast, today Ghana
moreno/a black
mulato/a mulatto, born of one black and one white parent
ñañigo practitioner of ñañiguismo

ñañiguismo see abakuá
nbele ceremonial machete
nfumbe the dead of the nganga
nganga receptacle for the attributes of the spirits in regla de palo
nkuyu see elegguá
obatalá/obbatalá main orisha, creator of earth and humankind
obbá king
obedí orisha hunter
obí dried coconut
ocana sign in the diloggún: Okana sode, Okanasorde, number one sign, only one shell speaks, which is a bad omen
ocha see regla de ocha
ochosi orisha hunter, doctor and diviner
ochun/oshun main orisha of sexuality, goddess of rivers and springs, can take various forms as in ochun kolé
oddí sign of seven shells, treason and stomach sickness
odu pot, receptacle or support-object for the aché of the orisha
ogún/oggún principal orisha of iron and war; syncretised with the catholic Saint Peter and Saint John Baptist
ojuani number eleven in the diloggún
okanasorde see ocana
okonkolo see batá
okuboro king of Añagui, father of elegguá
oló batá/olú batá master of the drums
oloddu mare/oluddumare all the elements of the universe, to be reached through olofi
olofi supreme orisha, eternal father
omiero holy water for washing the stones, shells, beads and other attributes of the orishas
orisha god in santería
orisha mayor main god in santería
orula orisha of portent
osaín orisha of medicinal plants
oshinshin food for the orishas and humans
oshun see ochun
osun/ozún main orisha, messenger of obbatalá and olofí
osusu group of the Mandinga nation
otá stone for the orishas

oyá orisha of the cemetery and lightning
padrino godfather
palenque maroon settlement of runaway slaves
palero practitioner of regla de palo
palo see regla de palo
palo monte see regla de palo
pardo mulatto
quirimbaya see regla de palo
rayamiento en palo initiation in regla de palo
regla conga see regla de palo
regla de ifá see santería
regla de ocha see santería
regla de palo Afro-Cuban religion of Congo origin and from Angola, also known as palo, palo monte, regla conga and conga, with its variants: mayombe, biriyumba, quirimbaya
san antonio Saint Anthony, syncretised with elegguá
san cristobal Saint Christopher, syncretised with aggayú
san lázaro Saint Lazarus, syncretised with babalú ayé
santa bárbara Saint Barbara, syncretised with changó
santería Afro-Cuban religion of Yoruba origin from Nigeria, syncretised with catholicism, also known as ocha, regla de ocha and regla de ifá
santero/a priest/practitioner of santería
santo saint, and initiate in santería
shango see changó
siguaraya/ciguaraya wild, gnarled, sacred tree
son Afro-Cuban rhythm
tamborero conga drum player
tata father
tata nganga father priest
toque/toque de santo see bembé
tumba Afro-Cuban drum
tumba francesa rhythm originating from Haiti
vodun/vodú religion originating from the ewe-fon nation and Haiti
yagruma sacred wild tree, with high foliage, green on the upside, grey underneath
yemayá main orisha of the sea, and motherhood, sister of ochún

yemayá oloku orisha of death who lives at the bottom of the sea
yemu orisha mother of elegguá
yúa see ayúa

Bibliographical note

The rationale for this book was to provide a selection of Cuban writing translated from Spanish into English for the non-Spanish reader. There are few aspects of Cuba over the past four centuries that have been unaffected by the Afro-Cuban presence, and race has attracted a voluminous literature. A good introductory guide to that literature can be found in the end bibliographical section, "Race", in Louis Pérez Jr, *Cuba: Between Reform and Revolution*, New York, 1988, and in the chapter on "Race" by Pedro Pérez Sarduy and Jean Stubbs in Joel Edelstein (ed), *Cuba*, Perian Press Resources on Contemporary Issues, forthcoming.

Periodicals in Spanish are: for pre-revolutionary Cuba: *Archivos del Folklore, Bohemia, Cuba Contemporánea, Estudios Afrocubanos, Fundamentos, Revista Bimestre Cubana;* for revolutionary Cuba: *Annales del Caribe, Bohemia, Casa de las Américas, Del Caribe, Etnología y Folklore, Islas, Revista de la Biblioteca Nacional 'José Martí', Revolución, Revolución y Cultura, Santiago, Unión, Universidad de La Habana.* Useful English-language periodicals are: *Afro-Hispanic Review, Calibán, Cimarrón, Cuba Update, Cuban Studies, The Black Scholar* (special issues summer 1977 and winter 1980). Articles can also be found in: *Afrique, Afrocuban Studies Association of the West Indies, Bulletin of Hispanic Studies, Caribbean Quarterly, Caribbean Review, Caribbean Studies, Granma Weekly Review, Hispanic American Historical Review, Jeune Afrique, Latin American Research Review, New Beacon, Présence Africaine, Review Interamericana, Science and Society, Southwestern Journal of Anthropology, Journal of Black Studies, UNESCO Courier.*

The following bibliography includes recent books, and articles in books, in English which are not mentioned elsewhere in this volume:

Barredo, Pedro, *The Black Protagonist in the Cuban Novel*. Amherst, Mass: 1979.

Bergad, Laird, *Cuban Rural Society in the Nineteenth Century*. Princeton: 1990.

Bettelheim, Judith (ed), *Cuban Festivals: An Anthology with Glossaries*. New York: 1993.

Deutschmann, David (ed), *Changing the History of Africa*. Melbourne: 1989.

Entralgo, Armando and David González López, "Cuba and Africa: Thirty Years of Solidarity." In H. Michael Erisman and John M. Kirk, *Cuban Foreign Policy Confronts a New International Order*. Boulder, Colorado: 1991.

----"Cuban Policy for Africa." In Jorge I. Domínguez and Rafael Hernández, *U.S-Cuban Relations in the 1990s*. Boulder, Colorado: 1989.

Foner, Philip S, *Antonio Maceo: The 'Bronze Titan' of Cuba's Struggle for Independence*. New York: 1977.

García Domínguez, Bernardo "Garvey and Cuba". In Rupert Lewis and Patrick Bryan (eds) *Garvey: His Work and Impact*. Kingston: 1988.

Helg, Aline, "Race in Argentina and Cuba, 1880-1930: Theory, Policies and Popular Reaction." In Richard Graham (ed), *The Idea of Race in Latin America. 1870-1940*. Austin: 1990.

Knight, Franklin W, "Jamaican Migrants and the Cuban Sugar Industry, 1900-1934." In Manuel Moreno Fraginals, Frank Moya Pons and Stanley L. Engerman (eds), *Between Slavery and Free Labor: The Spanish-Speaking Caribbean in the Nineteenth Century*. Baltimore: 1985.

Luis, William, *Literary Bondage: Slavery in Cuban Narrative*. Austin: 1990.

Marquez, Roberto (trans), *Patria o Muerte! The Great Zoo and Other Poems by Nicolás Guillén*. New York: 1972.

----& David Arthur McMurray (trans), *Man-Making Words: Selected Poems of Nicolás Guillén*. Amherst: 1972.

Martínez-Alier, Verena, *Marriage, Class and Colour in Nineteenth-Century Cuba*. 2nd ed. Ann Arbor: 1992.

McGarrity, Gayle, "Race, Culture and Social Change in Contemporary Cuba." In Sandor Halebsky and John Kirk,

Cuba in Transition. Boulder, Colorado: 1992.

Mesa Lago, Carmelo and June Belkin (eds), *Cuba in Africa*. Pittsburgh: 1982.

Moreno Fraginals, Manuel, *The Sugarmill*. New York: 1978.

----(ed), *Africa in Latin America: Essays on History, Culture and Socialization*. New York: 1977.

Mullen, Edward J (ed), *The Life and Poems of a Cuban Slave: Juan Francisco Manzano, 1797-1854*. Hamden: 1981.

Paquette, Robert L, *Sugar is Made with Blood: The Conspiracy of La Escalera and the Conflict Between Empires over Slavery in Cuba*. Middletown, Conn: 1988.

Pérez de la Riva, Francisco, "Cuban Palenques." In Richard Price (ed), *Maroon Societies: Rebel Slave Communities in the Americas*. Baltimore: 1979.

Sardinha, Dennis, *The Poetry of Nicolás Guillén*. London: 1976.

Scott, Rebecca, *Slave Emancipation in Cuba*. Princeton: 1985.

Valdés, Nelson P, "Revolutionary Solidarity in Angola." In Cole Blasier and Carmelo Mesa-Lago (eds), *Cuba in the World*. Pittsburgh: 1979.

Index

Acana Revolt, 47
Africa/African influence, 6, 7, 9, 10, 15, 19, 20, 21, 23, 29, 30, 40, 55ff, 67ff, 111ff, 138, 196ff, 218, 222, 230ff, 267
Aldana, Carlos, 4
Almeida, Juan, 9
Andalucia, Andalucians, 116, 230
Angola, 15, 75, 230
Antigua, 243, 248
Aponte, 8, 78, 85, 200
Arango y Parreño, Francisco, 38, 201
Armand, María Rita, 47
Association for the Study of Black Culture and History, 79
Atenas Club, 31, 84
Autonomist Party, 40

Bahamas, 115
Banderas, Quintín, 40
Baraguá, 3, 5, 24, 25, 42, 49
Barbados/Barbadians, 243, 277
beguine, 115
Bella Unión Society, 252
Betancourt, Juan René, 84, 85, 86
Bishop, Maurice, 7
black nationalism, 84ff
Brazil, 9

Cabrales, María, 25, 48
Calabar, 155
calenda, 115
calypso, 115
Camagüey, 23, 78, 227
camboulay, 115

Carlota, 25
Castro, Fidel, 3, 6, 7, 13, 16, 86, 87, 102, 103
Castro, Raúl, 88
Cayman Islands, 115
Cayo Hueso, 19
Cervantes, Ignacio, 66
Cespedes, Carlos Manuel de, 3, 39, 40, 48
Chinese, 13, 81, 113, 202, 231, 232
cocuye, 115
Colombia, 116
Comité de Veteranos y Sociedades de la Raza de Color, 93, 94
Communist Party of Cuba, 3, 10, 11, 16, 80, 82ff, 97, 98, 99
Communist Revolutionary Union, 98
Communist Youth, 4
Confederation of Cuban Workers, 89, 98
Congo, 6, 196, 230
Constituent Assembly, 82, 83, 92
Cuban Revolutionary Party, 94, 99
Cubop, 19
Cuesta, Ramiro, 93

Cuffy, 60

Delicias, 21, 245ff
Demajagua, La, 3, 39, 48
Díaz Albertini, Rafael, 65
Directorate of Colored Societies, 77, 94
Dominican Republic, 95
D'Ou, Lino, 48, 93
Dubois, W.E.B., 79

El Cobre, 47
Escalera Conspiracy, 67, 266
Estenoz, Evaristo, 16, 78, 85, 94ff

Federation of Cuban Women, 89
Fedon, 60
Fermina, 47
Floral Dance, 21, 250ff
Fraternal Union, 84

Ganga Zumba, 60
García Aguero, Salvador, 83, 86, 88
García Caturla, Alejandro, 66
Garvey, Marcus, 63, 79
General Workers' League, 80
Ghana, 10
Gómez, Juan Gualberto, 16, 77ff, 85, 92ff
Gómez, Máximo, 41, 44, 45, 49, 77
Grajales, Mariana, 15, 25, 47ff
Grand Maceo Society, 252
Grenada, 7
Grobart, Fabio, 97
Guadeloupe, 63, 115, 267
Guanabacoa, 29
Guevara, Ernesto "Che", 11, 87, 88
Guarico, 38, 87, 88
Guillén, Nicolás, 13, 88, 96, 219, 225, 227ff
Guinea, 196
Guyana, 7

Haiti/Haitians, 5, 6, 8, 14, 21, 22, 37, 38, 39, 62, 80, 81, 82, 100, 114, 115, 218, 267, 275
Havana, 18, 19, 21, 66, 71ff, 78, 80, 114, 147, 148, 155, 206, 207, 221

Iglesias, Arcelio, 8, 84, 100
Independence, 3, 5, 39
Independent Colored Party, 16, 44, 94ff
Ivonet, Pedro, 16, 78

Jamaica/Jamaicans, 6, 21, 49, 50, 51, 80, 81, 82, 115, 218, 243, 267, 277

King, Martin Luther, 7
Kuban Ku Klux Klan, 16, 96, 97

lagghia, 115
Lagos, 15, 67ff
Lam, Wifredo, 18
Lazo, Esteban, 3
limbo, 115
L'Ouverture, Toussaint, 63
Luyanó, 18, 46

Maceo, Antonio, 3, 5, 13, 14, 15, 24, 25, 40, 41, 47ff, 77, 85, 88, 268
Maceo, José, 14, 40, 42, 48, 49, 147

Mackandal, 60
magical realism, 20, 144ff
Malcolm X, 7
malembe, 115
mangulina, 116
Manzano, Francisco, 22, 222, 264ff
Mandela, Nelson, 6
Mañach, Jorge, 100, 101
Margarita Island, 116
Marley, Bob, 7
maroons/marronage, 4, 55, 60, 224
Martí, José, 8, 12, 13, 15, 16, 24, 40, 41, 43ff, 49, 87, 88, 94, 103, 232, 268
Martinique, 63, 115, 267
Marxism, 11, 12, 20, 90, 199, 200
Masó, General Bartolomé, 11, 92
Matanzas, 15, 65, 66, 71ff, 78
mediatuna, 116
Menéndez, Jésus, 8, 84, 100
Mestre, Armando, 9
merengue, 115
midwives, 58, 59
Mocada, Domingo, 25
Moncada, Guillermón, 40
Monte, domingo del, 201, 264
Montejo, Esteban, 20, 222ff
Morúa Delgado, Martín, 77
Movement of Non-Aligned Countries, 6
Mozambique, 230

Nanny, 60
National Assembly of People's Power, 4, 12
National Association for the Advancement of Colored People, 79
National Association of Small farmers, 89
National Federation of Black Societies, 82
National Federation of Cuban Societies, 82, 99
National Organization for Economic Rehabilitation, 84
negrismo, 20, 84
Netherlands Antilles, 115
Niagara Movement, 79
Nigeria, 15, 67ff, 155, 196

Ooni, 10
Oriente, 42, 45, 80
Oriente Black Strip, 16, 97

Panama, 115, 116
Pedroso, Paulina, 25
Pedroso, Regino, 15
Peña, Lazaro, 8, 84, 86, 88
Pinto, Angel, 101
Plácido, 22, 266
Platt Amendment, 16, 92ff
plena, 115
Popular Socialist Party, 100
porro, 115
Puerto Rico, 115
punto guajiro, 116
puntillano, 116

Regla, 29, 148
Roca, Blas, 100
Rosa La Bayamesa, 25
Roumain, Jacques, 63
runaway slaves, 55ff

Saco, José Antonio, 39, 201
Saint Domingue, see Haiti
Saint Kitts, 243
Saint Lucia, 243
Salas, Justo, 83

Sánchez, Maria de la Luz, 47
Sánchez Figueroa, Silverio, 93
Sandoval, Pablo, 84
sangueo, 115
sanjuanero, 116
Santa Clara, 21, 250ff
Santa María del Rosario, 18, 152
Santiago de Cuba, 3, 9, 83, 97, 204, 206
Saumell, Manuel, 66
Serra, Rafael, 78
Sierra Maestra, 19, 187ff, 230
slavery, 3, 5, 6, 8, 9, 15, 31, 37ff, 55ff, 67, 68, 224, 230, 231
Socialist Workers Party, 80
Socialist Party of Cuba, 99
Spain/Spanish influence, 3, 5, 7, 21, 30, 39, 40, 51, 81, 82, 111, 112, 113, 144, 196ff, 283
Suarez y Romero, Anselmo, 264
Suriname, 7

tahona, 115
tamborito, 115
Taquechel, Juan, 84
Torres, Mariano, 40
Torriente, Eduardo, 84
Tortola, 243
transculturation, 228ff
Trinidad, 114, 115, 243

Universal Negro Improvement Association, 79
United States of America/US influence, 3, 4, 5, 7, 9, 10, 16, 21, 23, 51, 78, 80, 190, 202, 222

Valdés, Inocencia, 25
Venezuela, 115, 116
vidée, 115

Washington, Booker T., 78, 79
White, José, 65, 66

zapateo, 116

Also published by Ocean Press

Island in the storm —
The Cuban Communist Party's fourth congress
by Gail Reed
Island in the storm describes Cuba's strategy for survival, as it emerged from the most critical meeting in the revolution's history. This volume contains the unedited texts of all Congress resolutions, Fidel Castro's first detailed disclosure of the state of the Cuban economy and biographies of the new Cuban leadership.
200 pages plus 16 pages photos
ISBN paper 1-875284-48-6

The Cuban Revolution and the United States —
A chronological history
by Jane Franklin
An invaluable resource for scholars, teachers, journalists, legislators, and anyone interested in international relations, this volume offers an unpredented vision of Cuban-U.S. relations. Cuba watchers will wonder how they got along without it.

Based on exceptionally wide research, this history provides a day-by-day, year-by-year report of developments involving Cuba and the United States from January 1, 1959, through 1990. An introductory section, starting with the arrival of Christopher Columbus in the Caribbean, chronicles the events that led to the triumph of the revolution in Cuba in 1959.

Indispensable as a reference guide, *The Cuban Revolution and the United States* is also an eye-opening narrative, interrelating major crises with seemingly minor or secret episodes.

Published in association with the Center for Cuban Studies.
276 pages plus 8 pages photos
ISBN paper 1-875284-26-5

Also published by Ocean Press

Fidel and Malcolm X — Memories of a meeting
by Rosemari Mealy
The first extensive account of the 1960 encounter between Fidel Castro and Malcolm X in Harlem's Hotel Theresa. With testimonies from contemporaries of both figures, the story is told of the stay in Harlem of Castro and the Cuban delegation after they were forced from a downtown Manhattan hotel. Previously unpublished photos are included, along with Amiri Baraka's (LeRoi Jones) award-winning 1959 essay "Cuba Libre".
80 pages plus 16 pages photos, chronology
ISBN paper 1-875284-67-2

Tomorrow is too late — Development and the environmental crisis in the Third World
by Fidel Castro
During the most controversial and widely discussed speech to the 1992 World Earth Summit in Rio, Cuban President Fidel Castro caught the imagination of the summit's delegates when he cast blame for the world's environmental crisis on Western consumer societies and called for the use of science to sustain development without pollution. Comprising Castro's speech and the full text of the document he prepared for the delegates — both printed in English for the first time — this book presents the international environmental crisis in a new and important perspective.
56 pages
ISBN paper 1-875284-73-7

Changing the history of Africa: Angola and Namibia
Edited by David Deutschmann
The most detailed account ever published of Cuba's participation in Africa, particularly its military support for Angola's independence. It includes contributions by Gabriel García Márquez, Fidel Castro, Jorge Risquet and Raúl Castro.
175 pages plus 32 pages photos, chronology
ISBN 1-875284-00-1

Caribbean titles from the Latin America Bureau

The Dominican Republic: Beyond the lighthouse
by James Ferguson
'An essential book for anyone interested in this singular country and its role in the Caribbean.' Isabel Hilton, *The Independent*
118 pages £6.75/US$11.50 ISBN 0-906156-64-5 1992

Far From Paradise: An Introduction to Caribbean Development
by James Ferguson
Traces Caribbean history from Columbus to the present day, looking at slavery, the colonial period, the struggle for independence and the rise of US regional influence. Large format, highly illustrated.
64 pages £5.75/US$9.50 ISBN 0-906156-54-8 1990

Cuba: The Test of Time
by Jean Stubbs
'A lively and searching analysis of Cuba by a writer who knows the country intimately.' Hugh O'Shaughnessy, *Observer* Latin America correspondent
142 pages £5.75/US$9.50 ISBN 0-906156-42-4 1989

The Poor and the Powerless: Economic Policy and Change in the Caribbean
by Clive Y Thomas
'A historical and contemporary survey of Caribbean economic development armed with a degree of detail which makes it, at the most fundamental level, a useful reference work as well as a good introduction to the region.' *Caribbean Insight*
396 pages £11.00/US$13.50 ISBN 0-906156-35-1 1988

Prices are paperback editions and include post and packing. For a complete list of books write to the Latin America Bureau, 1 Amwell Street, London EC1R 1UL. LAB books are distributed in North America by Monthly Review Press, 122 West 27th Street, New York NY 10001